The Gardener's Peony
Herbaceous and Tree Peonies

'Fen Mian Tao Hua' (Peach Blossom Complexion)

The Gardener's Peony
Herbaceous and Tree Peonies

Martin Page

Timber Press
Portland · Cambridge

Published in 2005 by

Timber Press, Inc.

The Haseltine Building

133 s.w. Second Avenue, Suite 450

Portland, Oregon 97204-3527, U.S.A.

Timber Press

2 Station Road

Swavesey

Cambridge CB4 5QJ, U.K.

Designed by Dick Malt

Printed through Colorcraft Ltd., Hong Kong

Library of Congress Cataloging-in-Publication Data

Page, Martin, 1953-.

  The gardener's peony : herbaceous and tree peonies / Martin Page.

      p. cm.

Includes bibliographical references and index.

  ISBN 0-88192-694-9

  1. Peonies. 2. Peonies--Varieties. I. Title.

SB413.P4P342 2005

635.9'3362–dc22

                          2004066099

A catalogue record for this book is also available from the British Library.

Contents

For Melissa

Foreword

Peonies have always fascinated me. Since the days, now many years ago, when I helped my grandfather in his Devon garden, I have nurtured a great interest in them. Whether it was their relative ease of cultivation, their voluptuousness, or their intoxicating fragrance that first attracted me I cannot say, and I cannot even remember exactly which ones my grandfather grew, but by then it was too late, I was hooked. Later as a botanist at the Royal Botanic Gardens, Kew, I was responsible for the lower families of flowering plants, in those days referred to as the "primitive families"; these fortunately included several genera of prime interest to me including *Clematis*, *Pulsatilla*, *Meconopsis* and *Paeonia*.

To the botanist, the genus *Paeonia* poses a complex pattern of variability that is difficult to interpret, and the species delineation is by no means clear-cut. Indeed, despite the fact that various authors have written on the subject in recent years, there has been no consistency of approach.

I have known Martin Page over a number of years and we have often discussed peonies. His breadth of knowledge on the subject and his consistent and unbiased approach has always impressed me, whether he was discussing the species or the equally challenging subject of hybrids and cultivars. It therefore gave me great delight to learn that he was writing a book on peonies, not a botanical monograph (that we hope may come later!) but a book for gardeners. Despite the fact that several books have appeared on the subject in recent years I am confident that this new work fills a gap, after all peonies are one of the most popular groups of garden plants. Few come in such a wide range of colours and have such large blooms. It has been a joy reading through the proofs of this book to realize that here at last is a definitive work for gardeners and horticulturists. It is not only a book about species, hybrids and cultivars in cultivation but also covers the history, cultivation and morphology of the genus, all aspects of cultivation and hybridization, pests and diseases and much much more besides.

Tree peonies are becoming far more widely cultivated, especially as gardeners come to realise that they are not that difficult to grow. The stand of these riveting plants put on by Kelways Nursery at the Chelsea Flower Show in recent years has attracted huge attention. Wonderful as these are, it is the chapter on the so-called Itoh hybrids (hybrids at one time thought to be impossible between herbaceous peonies and tree peonies) that are catching the imagination today, particularly in North America. These hybrids have hugely extended the range of peonies available to gardeners with a breathtaking range of colours as well as flowers with eye-catching flares on the petals. They also greatly extend the flowering season.

The debate on the classification of *Paeonia* is certain to continue well into the future, indeed the more popular a genus becomes the more conversation and controversy it engenders. In the meantime Martin Page has provided us with an extremely valuable reference work which I am certain will be come a standard work on many a gardener's bookshelf, a work for which I am extremely grateful.

Christopher Grey-Wilson

Acknowledgements

Through my passion for peonies I have been fortunate to meet many wonderful people. Many of them have become good friends.

I would particularly like to thank Claire Austin and her husband Ric Kenwood of Claire Austin Hardy Plants, and David Root, the Manager of Kelways Ltd., who have helped me during the preparation of this book. Chris and Liz Johnson, the owners of Kelways, for allowing me to photograph their peonies; Hugh Bennison; Stephen Haw; Will McLewin; and Mike Sinnott; The Kenneth Allsop Memorial Trust, which owns Steep Holm Island; and Chris Beardsley, the Manager of Highdown Garden in West Sussex.

In the United States I thank Roger and Sandra Anderson; Anne, Bill and Chris Countryman; David and Kasha Furman of Cricket Hill Garden; Don and Lavon Hollingsworth; and Roy and Sarah Klehm, the owners of Song Sparrow Perennial Farm. The original botanical research was carried out at the Royal Botanic Gardens, Kew, and the Royal Botanic Garden Edinburgh. I would like to thank Professor Sir Peter Crane, Director of the Royal Botanic Gardens Kew for permission to use its facilities. Further research was carried out in the Royal Horticultural Society's Lindley Library, in London and the library at the Royal Botanic Gardens Kew.

I would also like to thank Mike Grant, the Senior Botanist at the Royal Horticultural Society's Garden at Wisley; Dr. Brent Elliott, RHS Librarian and Archivist; the staff of the Lindley Library; and Kuri Suematsu, Editor of RHSJ, for providing details of Japanese peony collections.

Photographs

I am very grateful to Roy Klehm for allowing me to reproduce his superb photographs of peonies. Roy's photographs were a great inspiration to me when I read his revision of Alice Harding's *The Book of the Peony* and *Peonies in the Little Garden* (Harding, 1993). The majority of the photographs in this book are by the author, using a Nikon F90X or F4 and Fuji Sensia or Provia 100F film and a 60mm f4 Micro-Nikkor lens.

Peonies present a particular challenge for photographers and need to be photographed in diffuse sunlight. The best results are usually obtained on a slightly overcast day, with soft natural light.

My thanks also to Gail Harland for taking the picture of the *RHS Colour Chart*.

Abbreviations

I have used the following abbreviations in the book:

AGM   RHS Award of Garden Merit.

APS   American Peony Society.

GM   American Peony Society Gold Medal.

ISH   Intersectional Hybrid.

NCCPG The National Council for the Conservation of Plants and Gardens (U.K.).

RHS   Royal Horticultural Society.

Chapter 1
Introduction: history of peonies

Plants have adopted many different strategies to allow them to survive difficult growing conditions. The world's deserts may look barren and devoid of life, but occasionally, after rare periods of rain, they are transformed from a barren wilderness into a multi-coloured tapestry. The majority of these desert flowers are annuals, whose seeds only germinate after rare periods of rain. When this happens the plants grow very quickly, produce flowers, set seed and then die again, the whole life of the plant being compressed into a few weeks. Peonies are, by contrast, very long-lived plants and have adopted a very different strategy for survival. Many of the species are found in mountainous regions and their large rounded seeds get washed down the hillsides when it rains. The seeds do not travel far and usually germinate close to the parent plant, eventually forming a large colony.

These beautiful plants can live for an extraordinary period of time and it is not uncommon to find cultivated specimens that are more than a hundred years old. In poor growing conditions herbaceous peonies are able to survive by exploiting the food reserves stored in their tuberous roots. If conditions fail to improve the plant gradually shrinks in size, until only a small piece of root and a single shoot survive. If the environment continues to deteriorate the plant may eventually give up the ghost and die, but in many cases it hangs on until conditions improve. This has been an extremely important adaptation, which has allowed peonies to survive for millions of years.

Paeonia officinalis, *P. mascula* and other tetraploid species are thought to have arisen in Europe during the Pleistocene, when the world was affected by a series of glaciations, and were probably found in forest clearings and among scrub. The period immediately after the last ice age (the Holocene) must have provided a great opportunity for plants that were adaptable enough to exploit the vast expanses of bare soil, but in the short term the climate would have been too cold for peonies. In Western Europe the most critical time was during the Boreal-Atlantic transition (approximately 8000 years ago), when the climate became warmer and oak trees spread north, eventually forming extensive deciduous forests. People had little impact upon these forests until the Mesolithic, when they started to fell trees and began to grow domestic crops.

It has been widely accepted that the natural woodland of post-glacial Europe had a closed canopy and gaps only arose when senescent trees fell or fire destroyed parts of the forest. While these factors were no doubt important they do not explain the spread of peonies into Northern Europe, because peonies need several years to develop from seed. However, Frans Vera (2000), a Dutch ecologist, has proposed that Europe's ancient forests were far more open than was previously thought, and that large herbivores such as the auroch (the ancestor of domestic cattle) and European bison maintained the forest clearings as pasture and prevented the trees from re-colonizing the land. This forest pasture would have provided an ideal habitat for peonies and, if the scenario were correct, we would have expected the plants to be far more widespread, indeed common, before human beings started to exploit them for medicinal purposes. Vera's work is controversial, but it is already having an impact on conservation policy in Europe, where people are suggesting the introduction of grazing animals into woodland nature reserves would increase their biodiversity and may be a more natural form of management.

Peonies can also be found in steppe grassland, where the climatic conditions have prevented the development of woodland. The majority of peonies are very hardy and well adapted to the rigors of a continental climate, with its very cold winters and hot summers. A few species, such as *Paeonia clusii* and *P. rhodia*, are adapted to a Mediterranean climate where summers are very hot. These plants start to grow very early in the spring, flower and then become dormant before the worst of the summer heat. Tree peonies have a reputation for being delicate plants, but in China, where their very existence is threatened by over collection, they survive on inaccessible cliffs, where they are subject to drought and extremes of temperature.

Paeonia mascula subsp. *mascula*.

Peonies have suffered an inexorable decline during the past hundred years because their very beauty makes them vulnerable to collection by people. In Victorian times many highly respected nurseries included a wide range of species peonies in their catalogues, the great majority of which were obtained by digging up wild plants. While this is now considered unacceptable, there is no doubt that small numbers of rare peonies are still collected from the wild for specialist collectors, who find it necessary to grow every species in the genus.

In medieval Europe the male peony (*P. mascula* subsp. *mascula*) was highly regarded as a medicinal plant and was considered to be more efficacious than the female (*P. officinalis* subsp. *officinalis*). Large quantities were collected from the wild and this seems to have contributed to the local extinction of the species. However, the population of medieval Europe was much lower than it is now and it is likely that this harvesting was sustainable until the middle of the sixteenth century. However, by the middle of the seventeenth century the famous herbalist Nicolas Culpeper (1653) is reporting that "The female is often used for the purpose aforesaid, by reason the male is so scarce a plant, that it is possessed by few, and those great lovers of rarities in this kind".

Large quantities of peony seed were collected during the Middle Ages and this, coupled with the harvesting of mature plants for roots, must have had a dramatic effect upon the wild populations. The paucity of information from this time makes it very difficult for us to assess the distribution of the male peony in medieval Europe, but it was clearly more widespread than it is now. There are a couple of tantalizing records of peonies being found in Southwest England during the seventeenth century, but it is uncertain whether these were naturalized or wild plants.

While peonies are protected by legislation in most European countries there is still a considerable demand for the roots of *Paeonia mascula*, which continues to be used in modern herbal medicine. This has meant that collecting is now concentrated in those countries where legislation is less strictly enforced. Most of these roots are harvested from Turkey and countries in the Balkans. According to Özhatay *et al.* (2000) 500–1000 kg (1102–2205 lb.) of peonies are exported to Western Europe every year from Turkey. *Paeonia peregrina* is widely collected by Turkish street florists, who sell the flowers on the streets of Istanbul. While this is not so damaging as the trade in roots, it is unsustainable and is already having a detrimental effect on the wild populations of this species.

The trade in endangered species of plants and animals is monitored by an organization called TRAFFIC, a joint programme between the Worldwide Fund for Nature and IUCN (The International Union for the Conservation of Nature). TRAFFIC has shown that there is a large trade in medicinal plants throughout the Balkans and this is affecting the wild populations of many plants, including peonies. While most of these countries have introduced legislation to protect their wild flowers it is only really effective in Bulgaria. In Romania *Paeonia mascula* is classed as endangered, while *P. officinalis* and *P. peregrina* are considered to be vulnerable. In Albania the national law protects all species of peony, while in Hungary a license must be obtained before they can be collected. While plants cannot be dug up in Western Europe they are still at risk from urban development and the construction of hotels for tourists. On the island of Majorca the local goats have developed an appetite for the carpels of *P. cambessedesii*.

In other parts of the world peonies are still widely used by native peoples in traditional medicine. *Paeonia emodi* was once widespread in northern India, but the growing trade in medicinal plants has meant that in IUCN parlance it should be treated as a vulnerable species, one step from being endangered (BCPP, 1998).

The Chinese have used tree peonies in their medicine for at least 2000 years and large quantities are cultivated for this purpose. While tree peonies still grow wild in China they receive little statutory protection from the Chinese government and wild plants are widely exploited by the local people. The Chinese scientific community has done much to raise the profile of wild tree peonies, but on one occasion the discovery of a wild population of tree peonies was published in a local newspaper, whereupon the local residents descended upon the site and dug up all of the plants. The growing international interest in Chinese tree peonies may mean that the People's Republic of China will introduce legislation to protect them, but in the meantime these beautiful plants remain at risk.

The great majority of countries now have legislation to prevent the digging up of their wild flowers, but it still continues to a varying degree. Peonies are among the most valuable of all ornamental plants and there is a growing demand for wild species. While the great majority of suppliers are completely legitimate and grow their plants from wild collected seed, purchasers should be on the look out for peonies that could have been taken from the wild. In the long term the systematic collection of seed from wild plants could threaten their survival and it is incumbent upon the collector to ensure that they leave enough seed to allow the survival of the colony. The problem is compounded by the time it takes peonies to grow from seed into flowering plants. The demand for species peonies is likely to increase and the only way of ensuring the supply of pure, un-hybridized plants is to persuade national governments to encourage the establishment of nurseries that specialize in producing stock of endemic plants.

Chapter 2
Morphology

One of the most frustrating things about peonies is that while it is possible to distinguish the different species by eye, it is often far more difficult to quantify the difference and put it into a formal description. This is the main reason why there are so many disputes about how many species of peony exist.

The polymorphic nature of peonies, the fact that they show variation in their morphological features, has made the taxonomy of the genus quite complex. Specimens from one population can appear very different from those of another and the observer is then faced with the problem of deciding whether they both belong to the same species or should be treated as separate ones. *Paeonia caucasica* and *P. kavachensis* are a good example of this; they appear quite distinct to the human eye, but it is sometimes difficult to quantify the difference and both species could just be regional variants of *P. mascula*. The situation is not helped by the fact that species concepts are applied differently in Eastern Europe than in Western Europe. In the former U.S.S.R. three species of fern-leaved peony are recognized—*P. biebersteiniana*, *P. lithophila* and *P. tenuifolia*—while western botanists only accept *P. tenuifolia*. This is the main reason why there are so many synonyms for peonies. (See also chapter 3, Plant Names.)

The woody members of the genus have been given the grand title of tree peony, which is inaccurate because in reality they are shrubs. However, they are well adapted to living in exposed situations and can tolerate extremely low temperatures when they are dormant. Herbaceous peonies are long-lived perennials whose aerial shoots grow from a well-developed crown.

Roots and crown

Young peony roots are quite slender and may extend some distance from the crown, however as they age they become more tuberous and serve as the plant's storage organs. These storage roots are covered with varying quantities of fibrous feeding roots, which penetrate the soil and extract nutrients and water. The development of the storage roots has clearly given peonies a major evolutionary advantage because they enable the plant to survive in conditions that are less than ideal.

If the surrounding vegetation becomes too rank or the surrounding trees grow too tall, the peony will usually survive until circumstances improve. During this time the plant becomes smaller, but the peony is able to recover quickly when conditions improve. The tuberous roots have also allowed peonies to succeed in habitats where there is very little water in the summer months. Several of the species that are found around the Mediterranean Sea, such as *Paeonia rhodia* and *P. clusii*, start to grow very early in the year and their foliage dies in the summer after the plant has flowered. Another species, *P. californica*, can survive in the arid landscape of central and southern California. The current concerns about global warming may mean that peonies will become increasingly popular as garden plants, able to cope with periods of extended drought during the summer months as occurs in Mediterranean and Continental climates.

In some species the roots are swollen and connected to the crown by a narrow piece of root, while in others they taper gradually towards the apex. This characteristic has been known for a long time, but it is only recently that botanists have realized that the roots can help to characterize the different species of peony. Some botanists have used the shape of the roots in the dichotomous keys that are used to identify species. This is not a very useful character for field botanists because it involves digging the plant up, which is often illegal and will probably result in the death of the peony.

In herbaceous species the crown has a number of buds, which vary in size according to their state of development. The largest buds will develop during the next growing season, but if they are damaged for any reason the smaller buds will grow to take their place. The young buds are covered by a number of scale-like leaves that protect the shoot as it pushes through the soil in the spring. The young shoots are white below ground but quickly turn reddish purple when they are exposed to sunlight. Some species, such as *Paeonia officinalis* and *P. peregrina*, produce adventitious buds at the tips of the roots which can be separated from the crown and will eventually grow into an independent plant. The shoots grow extremely quickly during the spring and turn green as the leaves unfurl.

Leaves

Peony leaves are very variable and a specimen from one location can appear very different from another, even though they are the same species. This causes serious problems for botanists and explains why plants from different locations have been given various names, later to be regarded as a single species. Lower leaves tend to be the largest and most divided, while those at the top of the stem and immediately beneath the flower may only have three to six lobes.

Most peonies have biternate leaves which are composed of a terminal primary leaflet and two lateral primary leaflets. These primary leaflets are divided again into secondary leaflets. In the case of *Paeonia tenuifolia*, the leaves are tripinnate and so divided that they produce delicate ferny foliage. The leaf stalk is referred to as the petiole, while stalks of the leaflets are called petiolules.

The majority of herbaceous peonies are placed in the section *Paeon*, which is divided again into two subsections, dependent upon whether the secondary leaflets are simple or further subdivided into lobes. The subsection *Foliolatae* includes species such as *Paeonia mascula* in its widest sense and *P. wittmanniana*, with simple leaflets, while the subsection *Dissectifoliae* is composed of species such as *P. officinalis* and *P. veitchii*, whose leaflets are further divided into as many as 80 leaflets and lobes (in *P. clusii*). While this system works fairly well, some peonies have an intermediate number of leaflet segments and consequently fall between both categories. These terms may seem excessively complex, but they are necessary if you wish to describe the species and distinguish them from one another.

Flowers

Peony flowers are pentamerous, which means that the various parts of the flower are in groups of five, or multiples of five. Wild peonies have between 5 and 13 petals, 5 sepals and 5 carpels, but in some species such as *P. emodi* and *P. ludlowii*, there may only be a single carpel. Bracts are inconspicuous in most species, but in *P. delavayi* they form a conspicuous whorl, or involucre, beneath the flower. Cultivated peonies with single flowers normally have between 50 and 150 stamens, but in some cultivars these are converted into petal-like structures called staminodes. These may be completely infertile or can retain a small amount of functional pollen grains. They often have a yellow base, which imparts a yellow glow to the centre of white peony flowers. In some flowers the outer petals are much larger than the others and are called guard petals.

 The stamens sit on an organ called the staminoidal disc. In hybrid herbaceous peonies this may be enlarged and brightly coloured, while in tree peonies the disc is extended to envelop the carpels. It has become a convention in gardening books to refer to this simply as the sheath, while in scientific papers it is usually called the disc. In this book I have used the term staminoidal disc to describe the fleshy tissue beneath the stamens and sheath to refer to the leathery tissue that covers the carpels.

 The ovules develop in large dehiscent carpels or follicles, which are useful for distinguishing the species. The carpels may be glabrous, pilose (with short hairs) or more frequently tomentose (with long, rather matted hairs). At the top of the carpel is an elongated structure called the

The fern-leaf peony, *Paeonia tenuifolia*.

Anemone-form peony 'Gay Paree'.

Tree peonies can be distinguished from their herbaceous cousins by the presence of a leathery sheath, which encloses the carpels.

Unfertilized ovules are bright red.

Tree peony seeds are enclosed by a tough, rather woody carpel.

Single peonies, such as 'Honor', have functional carpels and stamens.

Japanese-flowered 'Bowl of Beauty'.

style, which is topped by the stigma, the receptive surface that accepts pollen from visiting insects. The stigma is actually a narrow band at the apex of the style, but many books refer to the whole structure (style and stigma) as the stigma. The style is often brightly coloured and may be straight or curved like a sickle or more rarely like a bishop's crosier.

The carpels of fully double flowers are often developed into petal-like structures called carpelodes. These are frequently the same colour as the other petals but are often wavy and distorted; in some flowers only the styles are petal-like. When the ovules have been fertilized they develop into large ovoid seeds with a fleshy dark blue-black or brownish black outer coat. In some peonies and particularly species, the unfertilized ovules become vivid red.

Flower Form and Colour

Flower development is temperature dependent and growth may cease on cold days. The flowers of species peonies may not open on dark overcast days, when there is a high risk of rain. In cultivated forms the doubling up of petals results in several flower types, but cultivars with double flowers may not develop their characteristic blooms until the plants are two or three years old. It is quite common for semi-double peonies to have single flowers developing from the side buds. Intermediates between these flower types often occur.

Single
All peony species and some hybrids have single flowers. They have 5–13 petals and normal functional stamens.

Japanese
Sometimes these are referred to as imperial peonies, the flowers have normal outer petals, but the majority of the stamens are converted into narrow petal-like staminodes. The carpels are usually functional and the outer petals are referred to as guard petals. 'Bowl of Beauty' is one of the best-known Japanese peonies.

Anemone

These flowers have all of the stamens converted into petal-like staminodes. *Paeonia lactiflora* 'Gay Paree' is a particularly well-known cultivar with vivid pink guard petals and contrasting staminodes. The term is infrequently used.

Semi-double

Stamens are scattered throughout the flower, or more rarely in concentric circles, alternating with the petals. This is often referred to as a flower within a flower. The carpels are usually functional and fully developed. The hybrid peony 'Buckeye Belle' is a good example of a semi-double flower.

Semi-double 'Kelway's Fairy Queen'

Crown

The flowers are very double with a raised dome of small petals, surrounded by larger guard petals. *Paeonia lactiflora* 'Monsieur Jules Elie' is one of the best-known examples.

Bomb

Large, double flowers with a raised centre of erect petals. The flowers have a large number of petals, which makes them quite heavy and they may need to be supported with canes. *Paeonia lactiflora* 'Raspberry Sundae' is one of the best-known cultivars with pink guard petals, surmounted by a band of yellow petaloids and topped by a mass of pink petals.

Crown-shaped peony 'Monsieur Jules Elie'

Colour

In the following chapters I have always tried to be objective in the way that I describe peonies and have used the third edition of the *Royal Horticultural Society's Colour Chart*, giving the code number to define the colour of the flowers. However these colour charts were designed to be used for a wide range of flowers and they do not always have sufficient options to enable the correct determination of some peonies. This is particularly the case with crimson-red hues, which are under represented. The *RHS Colour Chart* is extremely useful, but unfortunately it does not provide any names for the colours, only codes.

Bomb-shaped peonies, such as 'Raspberry Sundae', are named after their resemblance to an ice cream bombe.
(Credit: Roy Klehm).

The *RHS Colour Chart* provides an objective
way of judging flower colour.
(Credit: Gail Harland).

Therefore I have taken the names from the *Horticultural Colour Chart*, which was published in 1939 and 1941 by the British Colour Council. These names are widely used in older gardening books and while the charts have long been out of print, the American Rhododendron Society published a table of equivalents in 1984.

There will be occasions when my choice of colour may seem inaccurate or arbitrary when judged without the RHS chart, but you should bear in mind that the colour of a peony's flower can depend also upon its age, the quality of light at the time of viewing and the soil conditions. Wherever possible I have tried to judge colour on the first day that the flower is fully open and before the stamens have started to dehisce (to shed pollen). Peonies are often described as having crimson flowers, but this is misleading. The majority of the cultivars of *Paeonia lactiflora* have magenta flowers, but this colour can be dramatically modified by the quality of daylight at particular times of the day. This is particularly apparent in the early evening when the warm sunshine can alter the colour of the flowers so that they appear pink or lavender.

The flowers of some hybrid tree peonies and intersectional hybrids have mixed pigments which age at different rates and this makes it very difficult to describe the overall colour. When peony flowers are subjected to bright sunlight the outer petals can become bleached, while the inner petals remain the original colour because they are shaded. This is called silvering.

Many semi-double and double flowers possess staminodes or carpelodes, which are petal-like structures derived respectively from stamens and carpels. When these are converted into petals, they often retain the yellow or green pigment that would have been in the unconverted structures. These additional pigments are very important in white flowers because the petals reflect their colour. This adds character to the depths of the flower and greatly increases its beauty.

A table showing the RHS swatch numbers and their equivalent names can be found on the Peony Society web site (www.peonysociety.org). In the instructions that accompany the *RHS Colour Chart* it is recommended that the colour group, for example red-purple, be cited along with the swatch number and hue. However, I believe that this is superfluous because the numbers are unique and cannot be confused with any other.

Flowering time

The majority of gardening books give some indication of when the different peony cultivars flower. This works well with herbaceous peonies, but in the case of *Moutan* tree peonies (in Chinese Mudan; in Japanese Botan) the flowering time appears to be more dependent upon the weather and how much shade the plant receives, than the time of year. However, it is possible to generalize. In the United Kingdom *Moutan* tree peonies flower from late April to early May, while hybrid herbaceous peonies flower in May and lactifloras in June. In the American Midwest the *Moutan* tree peonies flower from the middle to end of April, while in New England they flower from the middle of May. Hybrid tree peonies flower ten days or so later.

Flowering time is very dependent upon the ambient temperature and extended periods of cold weather can delay flowering by a week or more.

Chapter 3
Taxonomy and Classification of the Genus *Paeonia*

The Evolution of the Genus *Paeonia*

In evolutionary terms peonies have always been considered to be representative of primitive plants and both Worsdell (1908) and Kumazawa (1935) placed the genus *Paeonia* in the order Magnoliales. However recent phylogenetic research suggests that peonies are far more advanced than was previously thought and Soltis *et al.* (1997) have included the Paeoniaceae in the Saxifragales, which includes the witch hazels (Hamamelidaceae), stonecrops (Crassulaceae), currants and gooseberries (Grossulariaceae) and saxifrages (Saxifragaceae). Fishbein *et al.* (2001) have tried to determine the inter-relationships of the families within the Saxifragales, by analyzing the gene sequences within cell chloroplasts and nuclei. Their work suggests that the Paeoniaceae is closest to the succulent plants of the Crassulaceae (*Sedum*, *Crassula* and *Aeonium*) and the water-milfoil family, the Haloragaceae (*Myriophyllum* and *Haloragis*). According to the fossil record the Saxifragales is at least 89.5 million years old (Magallón-Puebla *et al.*, 1999) and several lineages appeared in quick succession 80–100 million years ago. It is likely that this is when the Paeoniaceae arose, but in the absence of peony fossils this is impossible to prove. From our perspective the distribution of *Paeonia mascula* and *P. officinalis* appears disjointed *senso lato*.

During the Pleistocene the herbaceous species in the section *Paeon* are thought to have undergone rapid evolution, which resulted in several new species. The diploid species were the least adaptable and became confined to limited geographical areas, but the tetraploid were well adapted to the post-glacial environment and spread throughout southern and central Europe, where they gave rise to a number of subspecies. Tao Sang *et al.* (1997) believe that the ancestral species, *Paeonia mairei*, *P. veitchii* and *P. lactiflora*, were originally widespread in Eurasia but became confined to Asia during the coldest periods of the Pleistocene. From our perspective the distribution of *P. mascula* and *P. officinalis* appears disjointed, but this could be because they have been over collected by people and have become extinct in some of their former locations. The tetraploid species are very variable and populations in different localities can appear quite distinct. Given enough time they would almost certainly become sufficiently different for botanists to recognize them as separate species, but in the meantime there is considerable debate as to whether these differences are sufficient to justify treating them as more than subspecies. While the results of DNA analysis have to be treated with care it seems likely that it will be invaluable in determining the inter-relationships of the different species.

The Study of the Genus *Paeonia*

The earliest known written record of a peony can be found in the famous *De Materia Medica*, which was written in the first century AD by the Greek physician and botanist Pedanios Dioscorides (AD 40–90). Dioscorides recognized two types of peony; the male, which had leaves like those of a walnut, and the female, whose leaves were more divided and similar to those of alexanders (*Smyrnium olusatrum*). This distinction was recognized throughout the Middle Ages, partly because the *De Materia Medica* formed the basis for many medieval herbals. One of the most famous medieval illustrations of the male and female peony can be found in Pierandrea Mattioli's *Commentarii in sex Libros Pedacii Dioscoridis* (1565), which clearly shows the distinction between the two species.

Carl Linnaeus (1707–1778) placed all peonies in one species, which he called *Paeonia officinalis* (*officinalis* refers to the peony's reputation as a medicinal herb). He famously said: "I have not discovered limits between species, hence I have united them." However, he still recognized the distinction between the male and female peonies by treating them as botanical varieties and called them α *femina* and ß *mascula*. Linnaeus's classification was based strictly upon the structure of the flower.

Phillip Miller (1691–1771), curator of the Chelsea Physic Garden, in London, adopted Linnaeus's binomial system (with a Latin name for the genus and species), but recognized six species of peony in the eighth edition of his *Gardener's Dictionary*, which he called *mascula, foemina, peregrina, hirsuta, tatarica* and *lusitanica*.

The first thorough study of the genus was a monograph by George Anderson (1818), which describes a total of thirteen species. Anderson was killed in a coach accident shortly before the paper was due to be delivered to a meeting of the Linnaean Society of London. His friend Joseph Sabine, who subsequently wrote an important study of tree peonies, completed his work. The next important work is by Richard Lynch (1850–1924), who was Curator of Cambridge University Botanic Garden. Lynch gives a detailed description of the known species of peony in his "A new classification of the genus *Paeonia*", published in *The Journal of the Royal Horticultural Society* in 1890.

One of the most important milestones in the study of the genus is Frederick Stern's monograph, *A Study of the Genus Paeonia*, which was published by the RHS in 1946. This beautifully illustrated volume was published by subscription at a time of financial constraint after the Second World War and it is now a valuable collector's item. The monograph describes thirty-three species and is still one of the most important single publications on the genus. A considerable proportion of the taxonomic work in Stern's monograph was actually carried out by his assistant, William T. Stearn. Stearn subsequently became one of Britain's leading botanists and a considerable amount of information about the genus can also be found in *Peonies of Greece*, published in 1984 with Peter Davies.

Perhaps the greatest change that has occurred since the publication of Stern's monograph is the realization that tree peonies have a far more complex ancestry than was originally thought. Stern only includes a single species (*P. suffruticosa*), which was described at the beginning of the nineteenth century from a number of cultivated Chinese tree peonies. Recent work by Chinese scientists, particularly by Professor Hong Tao, has shown that the situation is far more complex than was previously thought and that there may be as many as seven species of tree peony.

The name *Paeonia suffruticosa* is still widely used in gardening books, as it is a convenient pigeonhole for cultivated hybrid tree peonies. In my previous book I proposed that *P. suffruticosa* should be treated as a hybrid species, signified by a multiplication sign between the genus and specific epithet (Page, 1997) and this was accepted by Haw (2001). Chinese scientists have demonstrated that tree peonies are far more widespread than was previously thought and Hong Tao *et al.* (1992) have gone a long way to elucidating their taxonomy. Haw (2001) has reviewed the plethora of Chinese tree peony species and has reduced them to five.

Classification

The majority of early botanists included peonies in the buttercup family (Ranunculaceae) and many modern floras still do this. However, in 1830 Rudolphi decided peonies were sufficiently different to be given their own family, together with the genus *Glaucidium*.

Stern (1946) split the genus *Paeonia* into three botanical sections, the section *Moutan*, which contains the tree peonies and the sections *Paeon* and *Onaepia*, which include the herbaceous peonies. The section *Paeon* includes those peonies where the petals are longer than the sepals, while the section *Onaepia* is composed of two very unusual North American species where the petals are approximately the same length as the sepals. The name may appear rather unusual, but it is actually an anagram of *Paeonia*.

The great majority of herbaceous peonies were placed in the section *Paeon*, which was then split into two subsections, depending upon whether the leaflets were entire (subsection *Foliolatae*) or undivided (subsection *Dissectifoliae*). While this is a convenient way of dividing the species, Tao Sang (1995) has shown that it is completely artificial and results in some species that are closely related being placed in separate subsections.

In 1961 Kemularia-Nathadze created the section *Flavonia* to include those peonies with yellow flowers, such as *Paeonia wittmanniana*, *P. macrophylla* and *P. mlokosewitschii*.

Traditional plant taxonomy uses differences in morphology to determine the inter-relationships of different species. This works well with most plants, but in some genera, including the peonies, the differences can be quite slight and it is more difficult to justify splitting or creating a species. Tao Sang has analyzed the sequence of genes in peony DNA and determined the inter-relationships of the different species. His research suggests that the majority of peonies are allotetraploids and have arisen by hybridization between the different species of peony (as opposed to being autotetraploid, where polyploidy arises from the doubling up of the number of chromosomes during mitotic cell division).

He has split the section *Paeon* into three subsections:

Subsection *Paeonia*
  P. anomala
  P. emodi
  P. lactiflora
  P. sinjiangenis
  P. veitchii
Subsection *Foliolatae*
  P. banatica
  P. japonica
  P. mairei
  P. obovata
Subsection *Intermedia*
  P. arietina
  P. broteroi
  P. cambessedesii
  P. clusii
  P. coriacea
  P. humilis
  P. mascula
  P. mlokosewitschii
  P. officinalis
  P. parnassica
  P. peregrina
  P. rhodia
  P. russoi
  P. sterniana
  P. tenuifolia
  P. wittmanniana

Phylogenetic analysis has revolutionized the study of plant systematics and may indicate inter-relationships between species that were hitherto unrecognized. This is particularly useful with peonies, where the differences between species are sometimes difficult to describe. Among the most important conclusions in Sang's analysis is that *Paeonia emodi* appears to be a natural hybrid between *P. veitchii* and *P. lactiflora,* while *P. sterniana* is a hybrid between *P. emodi* and *P. mairei.* The analysis also suggests that *P. peregrina* arose when *P. anomala* was crossed with the ancestor of a group of plants that includes *P. officinalis, P. parnassica* and *P. arietina.*

Sang *et al.* (1997) found nucleotide substitutions at a total of fifty-three nucleotide sites among all of the peony species that they studied. (The smaller the number of nucleotide substitutions between two species, the more closely related they are to one another.) They determined that *Paeonia mascula* subsp. *mascula* is a hybrid between *P. lactiflora* and *P. japonica* or *P. obovata*, while *P. mascula* subsp. *russoi* is a hybrid between *P. lactiflora* and *P. mairei* (if this is the case then subsp. *russoi* cannot be a subspecies of *P. mascula*).

There is no doubt that their work is very interesting and it goes a long way towards explaining the inter-relationships between the different species. Sang *et al.* analyzed their data using several software packages, including the widely used PHYLIP suite of programs. However, the final results have to be interpreted by human beings and a different piece of software or different samples of the same species may have given slightly different results.

In 1997 Josef Halda produced a new classification for the genus *Paeonia*, which created new sections and subsections and absorbed several perfectly good species into others. In Halda's classification *Paeonia sterniana* becomes a subspecies of *P. emodi*, *P. japonica* is reduced to a subspecies of *P. obovata* and *P. macrophylla* becomes a subspecies of *P. wittmanniana*. His most surprising decision was to subsume *P. ostii* and *P. rockii* within a resurrected *P. suffruticosa*. This flies in the face of Hong Tao's treatment of Chinese tree peonies, which has been widely accepted by most botanists. The main weakness of Halda's paper is that he does not provide a reasoned argument for his changes and as a result most people still adhere to the earlier classification.

Halda has retained his classification in a recent monograph with James Waddick (Halda and Waddick, 2004). This includes a so-called phylogenetic tree of the genus *Paeonia*, but there is no indication of its source and it does not tally with the work of Sang (1995) or Sang *et al.* (1997). Halda and Waddick have also created several higher taxa, which suggests that there are greater differences between the species than actually exist.

It may be some years before anyone produces a definitive monograph about the genus that adequately explains the variation that can be seen among the species. The debate about the taxonomy of the genus will leave most gardeners cold and for the purposes of this book I have decided on a conservative treatment.

The following classification is a synthesis of my own personal experience of the genus and takes into account the work of Frederick Stern (1946), Davis and Stearn (1984), Hong Tao *et al.* (1992 and 1994), Stephen Haw (2001) and several other workers. Frederick Stern divided the Section *Paeon* into two subsections, depending upon whether the leaflets were divided or entire. However, recent phylogenetic research by Tao Sang (1995) has shown that *Paeonia rhodia* is closely related to *P. clusii* and *P. arietina* to *P. officinalis* and on this basis I have moved *P. rhodia* and *P. arietina* to the subsection *Dissectifoliae*. Sang has proposed a more radical classification, but for the purposes of this book I have retained the traditional scheme.

Family Paeoniaceae (Augustin Pyramus de Candolle) F. Rudolphi
  Genus *Paeonia* Carl Linnaeus
  Section *Moutan* Augustin Pyramus de Candolle
   Subsection *Vaginatae* Frederick C. Stern
    P. decomposita Heinrich Handel-Mazzetti

subsp. *decomposita*
subsp. *rotundiloba* Hong De-Yuan
P. ostii Hong Tao & J. X. Zhang
P. qiui Y. L. Pei & Hong De-Yuan
P. rockii (Haw & Lauener) Hong Tao & J. J. Li
subsp. *linyanshanii* Hong Tao & G. L. Osti
subsp. *taibaishanica* Hong De-Yuan
P. spontanea (Rehder) Hong Tao & W. Z. Zhao
P. ×suffruticosa (Andrews) Stephen Haw
P. ×yananensis Hong Tao & M. R. Li
Subsection *Delavayanae* Frederick C. Stern
P. delavayi Adrien Franchet
P. ludlowii (Frederick C. Stern & George Taylor) Hong De Yuan
P. lutea Jean Marie Delavay ex A. Franchet
P. potaninii Vladimir Leontovich Komarov
var. *trollioides* (Otto Stapf ex Frederick C. Stern) Frederick C. Stern
Intersectional hybrid
P. ×lemoinei Alfred Rehder
Section *Onaepia* John Lindley
P. brownii David Douglas ex Thomas Nuttall ex John Torrey and Asa Gray
P. californica Thomas Nuttall ex John Torrey and Asa Gray
Section *Paeon* Augustin Pyramus de Candolle
Subsection *Foliolatae* Frederick C. Stern
P. bakeri Robert Irwin Lynch
P. broteroi Pierre Edmond Boissier & George Francis Reuter
P. cambessedesii Heinrich Moritz Willkomm
P. caucasica Nicola Schipczinsky
P. ×chamaeleon Troitsky ex A. A. Grossheim
P. coriacea Pierre Edmond Boissier
var. *atlantica* (Ernest St. Charles Cosson) Frederick C. Stern
P. emodi Nathaniel Wallich ex John Royle
var. *glabrata* Joseph Hooker & Thomas Thomson
P. japonica (Tomitaro Makino) Kingo Miyabe & Hisayoshi Takeda
P. kavachensis G. V. Aznavour
P. kesrouanensis Joseph Marie Thiébaut
P. lactiflora Peter Simon Pallas
var. *trichocarpa* (Alexander Bunge) Frederick C. Stern
P. macrophylla (Nicholas Albow) Aleksandr Aleksandrovich Lomakin
P. mairei Augustin Abel Hector Léveillé
P. mascula (Carl Linnaeus) Philip Miller
subsp. *mascula*
subsp. *bodurii* Neriman Özhatay

subsp. *hellenica* Dimitrios Tzanoudakis

subsp. *russoi* (Antonio Bivona) Peter H. Davis & William T. Stearn ex James Cullen
    & Vernon Heywood

    var. *leiocarpa* (Ernest Cosson) Frederick C. Stern

    var. *reverchoni* Antoine Le Grand

subsp. *triternata* (Edmond Boissier) Peter H. Davis & William T. Stearn

P. mlokosewitschii Aleksandr Aleksandrovich Lomakin

P. obovata Carl Johann Maximowicz

subsp. *willmottiae* (Otto Stapf) D. Y. Hong & K. Y. Pan

P. sterniana Fletcher

P. turcica Peter H. Davis & James Cullen

P. wittmanniana Hartwiss ex John Lindley

    var. *nudicarpa* N. V. Schipczinsky

Subsection *Dissectifoliae* Frederick C. Stern

P. anomala Carl Linnaeus

    var. *intermedia* (Carl Anton Meyer) Boris Aleksevich Fedtschenko

P. arietina Anderson

    var. *orientalis* (J. Thiébaut) Frederick C. Stern

P. clusii Frederick C. Stern & William T. Stearn

P. mollis George Anderson

P. officinalis Carl Linnaeus

subsp. *officinalis*

subsp. *banatica* (Anton Rochel) Soó

subsp. *humilis* (Andres Retzius) James Cullen & Vernon Heywood

subsp. *villosa* (Ernest Huth) James Cullen & Vernon Heywood

P. parnassica Dimitrios Tzanoudakis

P. peregrina Philip Miller

P. rhodia William T. Stearn

P. sinjiangensis K. Y. Pan

P. ×smouthii Van Houtte

P. tenuifolia Carl Linnaeus

P. veitchii Robert Irwin Lynch

    var. *beresowskii* (Vladimir Leontovich Komarov) N. V. Schipczinsky

    var. *woodwardii* (Otto Stapf & Evan Cox) Frederick C. Stern

Plant Names

For many years there has been a dispute about the correct spelling of a number of peony species names. This was finally resolved by the adoption of a new version of *The International Code of Botanical Nomenclature* (*The St Louis Code*) in 1999. As a result *Paeonia mlokosewitschii* has gained an extra "i"; *P. broteroi* has gained the letter "o"; and *P. mascula* subsp. *russi* has become *russoi*.

The term hybrid is widely used in the peony world. However, in this book the term hybrid peony refers to interspecific hybrids between two or more species, while intersectional hybrids (Itoh) are between two botanical sections, for example the section *Moutan* (tree peonies) and section *Paeon* (herbaceous peonies). Hybrids between two cultivars of the same species, for example white and red cultivars of *P. lactiflora*, are called intraspecific hybrids.

Wherever possible I have tried to use the original name for a plant, whether this is in English, Japanese, Chinese or any other language. In some cases it is impossible to know whether a peony was bred in Europe or the Far East. This is certainly the case with tree peonies, because a large of number of plants with well-known European names, such as 'Reine Elizabeth', could have been raised in China and renamed when they reached the West.

Chapter 4
The Species

Subsection *Vaginatae*

Tree peonies caused a sensation when they first arrived in Western Europe at the end of the eighteenth century. At that time there were no known species of wild tree peony and all of the cultivars were placed in *Paeonia suffruticosa*, which had been described by Henry Andrews in 1804. The new plants were first described in detail by Joseph Sabine (1826), whose work was subsequently plagiarized by other writers for the remainder of the nineteenth century.

When *Paeonia rockii* was found in 1926 it was assumed to be the wild form of *P. suffruticosa* and Frederick Stern used a specimen from his own garden to describe the latter species in his monograph (Stern, 1946). It was only later that *P. rockii* was recognized as a distinct species.

In 1992 the Chinese sprang a surprise on the botanical world when Hong Tao *et al.* described three new species of tree peony, namely *Paeonia ostii*, *P. jishanensis* and *P. yananensis*, and raised *P. suffruticosa* subsp. *rockii* to the status of an independent species. It soon became clear that cultivated tree peonies were actually hybrids between several wild species, which had been bred by the Chinese over several centuries.

Paeonia decomposita

Until recently this tree peony was known as *Paeonia szechuanica*, having been described as a new species by Wen Pei Fan in 1958. However, it is now believed to be identical to a tree peony collected in 1939 by Handel-Mazzetti, and the earlier name of *P. decomposita* must therefore take precedence. It can be distinguished from other tree peonies by the leathery cup-shaped sheath, which surrounds the lower part of the carpels.

It has alternate biternate leaves measuring 9–12 CM (3.5–4.7 IN.) long with ovate, obovate or oblong-ovate leaflets with three lobes, which are further divided into three smaller lobes. The leaflets have an acuminate tip and cuneate base. They are dark green above and pale green below, glabrous on both sides. Each stem has one single flower up to 13 CM (5 IN.) across, with rose pink or purple petals, yellow anthers and white filaments. There are 4–6 cone-shaped, glabrous carpels with a short style and flat recurved stigma, enclosed by a white sheath. It is endemic to Northwest Sichuan, where it grows in thickets on the slopes of hills and on riverbanks, at altitudes of approximately 2700–3100 M (8700–10,200 FT.).

D. Y. Hong (1997) has divided it into two subspecies. The typical subspecies has narrow lanceolate to ovate-lanceolate leaflets, while subsp. *rotundiloba* has broader, ovate to suborbicular leaflets. The former usually has 5 carpels, while the latter has 2–5. The two subspecies occupy adjacent river valleys and are separated by the 4000 M (13,100 FT.) high Qionlai Range.

Paeonia ostii

According to Hong Tao *et al.* (1992), who first described this species, *Paeonia ostii* occurs in the Chinese provinces of Henan, Hunan, Gansu and Shaanxi, where it grows at altitudes of 1100–1400 M (3600–4600 FT.). However Haw (2001) says that over collection has now resulted in it being restricted to western Henan. It was named after Gian Lupo Osti, the Italian dendrologist, and is thought to be an ancestor of many cultivated tree peonies.

Paeonia ostii grows to a height of approximately 1.5 M (5 FT.) with greyish brown bark and yellowish green annual branches (those that have grown during the current year). The leaves are biternate, with 9–15 greyish green, ovate-lanceolate or narrowly long ovate leaflets with acute tips; the terminal leaflets are 1–3 lobed. The upper surface is slightly hairy along the midrib, but glabrous below. The flowers are extremely beautiful, 13–15 CM (5–6 IN.) across, solitary and either pure white or with a hint of reddish purple at the base of the petals. There are no flares, but the petals can be marked with pink or magenta veins. There are five sericeous carpels with dark purple styles and a similarly coloured sheath. The stamens have pale yellow anthers with purple filaments.

The majority of the plants offered for sale as *Paeonia ostii* are actually 'Feng Dan Bai' (White Phoenix), a cultivated plant that is extensively grown as a medicinal plant in China. 'Feng Dan Bai' is usually more vigorous than the true species and is probably a hybrid with another species of tree peony. While some people may prefer the true species, 'Feng Dan Bai' is an acceptable substitute and makes a good garden plant. The plant is extremely variable and I would advise you to see the plants flowering before you purchase one.

Paeonia qiui

Paeonia qiui was first described in 1995 by Pei and Hong (1995) and grows in the Hubei and Henan Provinces of China.

It forms a small deciduous shrub, which grows to a height of between 60–80 CM (24–32 IN.) with brownish grey bark. The flowers are pink or rose with red flares, yellow anthers and pink filaments. Its leaves are biternate with 9 ovate to almost circular leaflets measuring 6.5–8.2 × 5–6.5 CM (2.75–3.2 × 2–2.75 IN.); its lateral leaflets are entire and the terminal one is divided into 3 lobes. The sheath is dark reddish purple and surrounds 5 tomentose carpels.

To the best of my knowledge this species has not been introduced into cultivation.

Paeonia rockii

Widely sought, but rarely available, this beautiful tree peony has achieved almost mythical status among gardeners. Reginald Farrer (1880–1930), the famous plant hunter, was probably the first westerner to find it when he visited Gansu Province in Western China in 1914. He describes the discovery of a white tree peony with "deepest maroon" flares in his book *On the Eaves of the World* (1917):

> Through the foaming shallows of the copse I plunged, and soon was holding my breath with growing excitement as I neared my goal, and it became more and more certain that I was setting eyes on *Paeonia Moutan* as a wild plant. The event itself justified enthusiasm, but all considerations of botanical geography vanish from one's mind in the first contemplation of that amazing flower, the most overpoweringly superb of hardy shrubs. Here in the brushwood it grew up tall and slender and straight, in two or three unbranching shoots, each one of which carried at the top, elegantly balancing, that single enormous blossom, waved and crimped into the boldest grace of line, of absolute pure white, with featherings of deepest maroon radiating at the base of the petals from the boss of golden fluff at the flower's heart.

Paeonia rockii 'Rock's Variety' is one of the world's most beautiful shrubs.

Farrer was a dedicated plant collector, but for many years it was believed that he hadn't collected a specimen of this remarkable species (see Stern, 1946). However, Haw and Lauener (1990) have since identified one of Farrer's specimens in the Herbarium at the Royal Botanic Garden Edinburgh, Scotland, which they believe is the first specimen of *P. rockii* to be collected.

Nothing further was heard about the plant until 1926, when Dr. Joseph Franz Rock (1884–1962) discovered it growing in a garden within the central courtyard of a lamasery, in Gansu Province. Rock's expedition was an amazing achievement, during which his team collected approximately 20,000 herbarium specimens for the Arnold Arboretum. The latter distributed seed of *Paeonia rockii* to botanic gardens in Canada, the United Kingdom, United States and Sweden where they all flowered in 1938.

One recipient of the seed, the famous English horticulturalist Sir Frederick Stern, wrote to Rock and received the following response, which was subsequently published in the *Journal of the Royal Horticultural Society* (Stern, 1939):

> The seeds of the *Paeonia* about which you enquire I collected from plants which grew in the Yamen of the Choni Lamasery (elevation 8,500 FT.), in S.W. Gansu. I occupied the Yamen in that Lamasery for about a year. In the court of the Yamen grew a very beautiful single-flowered *Paeonia*. There were no double-flowered ones, all were

single. I remarked at the time that it looked to me like a wild species. The Lamas told me it came from Kansu [sic] but from which exact locality they did not know. I never came across it in a wild state. It had been kept for years in the Lamasery. I took a photo of it growing in the court and I enclose a copy with my compliments. The Lamasery has been entirely destroyed and the Lamas all killed in 1928 by the Mohammedans, so the plant, in all probability, does not exist any more, as the entire Lamasery was burnt to the ground.

Stern believed that *Paeonia rockii* was the ancestor of all cultivated tree peonies and when he wrote his monograph (Stern, 1946) he based his description of *P. suffruticosa* on the plant of *P. rockii* in his garden. This important specimen still survives, but it is now a substantial shrub, almost a small tree, with branches the thickness of a human arm. It is a spectacular sight in the spring and bears as many as 100 beautiful white flowers.

Haw and Lauener (1990) subsequently determined that Rock's peony was a subspecies of *Paeonia suffruticosa*. In 1994 the Chinese botanist Professor Hong Tao and his colleagues reported on the presence of wild specimens of this tree peony in China and raised it to the status of an independent species: *P. rockii*.

The plants that grew from Rock's original seed collection are known collectively as 'Rock's Variety' and are among the most famous of all shrubs. Individual plants vary slightly, but they can be distinguished from other forms of *Paeonia rockii* by having particularly large flowers and distinctive blush pink buds. It seems likely that the original specimen was collected from the wild by the monks because of its incomparable beauty, and if this is the case 'Rock's Variety' should be considered as a cultivar group, rather than a cultivar. European specimens have rather frilly, more flamboyant flowers than those that were raised in the United States, but both forms are extremely beautiful. Until recently all of the specimens of *P. rockii* in the western world were descended from Rock's original collection at the Choni Monastery.

'Rock's Variety' grows to form a very large shrub, with glabrous, slightly pendent branches up to 30 CM (12 IN.) in circumference and up to 2 M (6.5 FT.) long. The leaves are bipinnate, with toothed or lobed, ovate lateral leaflets, measuring 4.5–9 × 3.2–5.0 CM (1.8–3.5 × 1.3–2 IN.), with rather short stalks. The lateral leaflets are deeply incised into three lobes, while the lateral lobes are entire, measuring approximately 6 × 2 CM (2.5 × 0.8 IN.) wide, the terminal leaflet coarsely three toothed, measuring 8 × 3.2 CM (3.1 × 1.2 IN.) and with sharply acute teeth. The leaves are bright green above and glaucous below, with a few long hairs along the veins. The fusiform roots are yellow-brown and penetrate deep into the ground.

The distinctive flowers are pure white, with large purple flares that fade at the base into a red margin. The flowers of 'Rock's Variety' can measure as much as 16 CM (6.3 IN.) across and have 10 concave, triangular-ovate or ovate-rounded petals measuring 6.5–9.0 × 4.0–8.5 CM (2.75–3.5 × 1.6–3.3 IN.), with a narrow notch at the tip. The stamens have attractive filaments, which are white at the top and purple at the base and have yellow anthers. The carpels are pale green with creamy white styles and are enclosed by an ivory white sheath, supported by a white staminoidal disc. The sheath splits as the flower matures and the carpels expand. *Paeonia rockii* is a diploid species (2N=10).

The wild species differs slightly from 'Rock's Variety'. Its stems are more erect, the leaves are greyish green and, while the flowers have the distinctive maroon flares of 'Rock's Variety', the petals are usually pure white without the pale blush colouration. It readily hybridizes with other tree peonies and there are many cultivars with double flowers and variously coloured petals. These are collectively referred to as "Gansu Mudan".

In recent years specimens of *Paeonia rockii* have started to become available from China, most of which have been grown from seed and, in consequence, prices have fallen as supply has improved. These plants are usually grown on their own roots and are considerably more vigorous than those that have been grafted. However, many of them are of hybrid origin and while they may look superficially like *P. rockii* they may have different foliage or less attractive flowers. Most reputable nurseries will allow the plants to flower before they offer them for sale and the price that you pay will depend upon the quality of the tree peony. 'Rock's Variety' has proved difficult to propagate and the only practical method has been to graft it onto a *P. lactiflora* rootstock.

Two subspecies of *Paeonia rockii* have been described. Subspecies *linyanshanii* differs from the type in having lanceolate or narrowly ovate leaflets with entire margins or occasionally 2–3 lobes (Hong Tao and Osti, 1994). It was first described from the Gansu and Hubei Provinces of China, where it occurs at altitudes in the region of 1600 M (5250 FT.). It is not currently in cultivation. Subspecies *taibaishanica* occurs on the northern slopes of the Qinling Mountains in southern Shaanxi and Gansu Provinces, in China. It differs from the type in having ovate to sub-orbicular leaflets with 2–5 lobes (Hong de Yuan, 1998).

Paeonia spontanea

In 1910 William Purdom found a pink-flowered tree peony in Shaanxi Province, which Rehder (1920) subsequently described as *Paeonia suffruticosa* var. *spontanea*. Rehder describes the plant as being sterile, with petaloid stamens and suckers.

In 1990 Haw and Lauener described a new species from Shaanxi, which included plants with white flowers. They considered that Purdom's plant was identical to their own and decided to call it *Paeonia suffruticosa* subsp. *spontanea*, raising Rehder's plant to the status of a subspecies. In 1992 Hong Tao *et al.* concluded that the white peony was in fact a new species, which they called *P. jishanensis*. The Chinese botanists considered that Purdom's specimen was a cultivated plant, because the stamens were converted into staminodes, and wrongly thought that his original name was illegitimate. However, Haw (2001) has pointed out that it is possible for a botanical name to be based upon a cultivated plant and Hong Tao and Zhao have subsequently raised it to species level, as *P. spontanea*.

Paeonia spontanea is a small shrub measuring approximately 1.2 M (4 FT.) high, with single, pink, purple or white flowers. There are no flares, but the petals are often flushed with reddish purple at the base. It has 9–15 bipinnate leaves with subsessile or sessile, ovate or broadly ovate leaflets, measuring 2.8–5.5 × 1.3–4.9 CM (1.1–2.25 × 0.5–1.9 IN.). They are dark green and glabrous above, glaucous and slightly sericeous beneath, becoming glabrous. The flowers have 5 carpels, which are covered by soft pale yellow hairs and enclosed by a reddish purple sheath. The stamens have yellow anthers and purple filaments, which become white towards the top (Hong, T. *et al.*, 1992). It is diploid (2N=10). It flowers in the spring, but is not currently in cultivation.

Paeonia ×suffruticosa

A large number of people still describe tree peonies as belonging to the species *Paeonia suffruticosa*, even though it is clearly heterogeneous. Hong (Hong, T. *et al.*, 1992) suggested that *P. suffruticosa* was probably a group of cultivars and I regard it as an interspecific hybrid (Page, 1997).

Paeonia ×yananensis

Originally treated as an independent species, *Paeonia ×yananensis* is now considered to be a hybrid between *P. rockii* and *P. spontanea* (Haw, 2001). It is recorded from Shaanxi Province, in China. Haw also believes that *P. yunnanensis*, which was described by Fang in 1958, is a hybrid tree peony and has treated it as a synonym of *P. ×suffruticosa*.

It is a small shrub, which grows to a height of 40 CM (16 IN.) and has biternate leaves with up to 11 ovate-rounded or ovate leaflets. The leaflets have blunt tips and a cuneate base, measuring 2.5–7.5 × 1.9–8.3 CM (1–3 × 0.75–3.2 IN.). The lateral leaflets are almost stalkless and have patches of long silky hairs, which lie flat against the surface of the leaflet. It has solitary pale purple or white flowers with purplish black flares. The anthers are yellow with purple and white filaments. It has a deep purple sheath with hirsute carpels and deep purple styles. It is diploid (2N=10).

Subsection *Delavayanae*

This group of vigorous clump-forming tree peonies has long been thought to include three species, namely *Paeonia delavayi*, *P. lutea* and *P. potaninii*. The plants appeared to be good species, which could be distinguished by clear morphological differences. *Paeonia delavayi* and *P. lutea* have proved extremely useful for plant breeders, producing a range of hybrids with the *Moutan* tree peonies (*P. ×suffruticosa*). The French nurserymen Victor and Emile Lemoine produced the first, followed by the American breeders Arthur Saunders, William Gratwick and Nassos Daphnis (see chapter 12). In 1948 the Japanese nurseryman Toichi Itoh used the Lemoines' 'Alice Harding' to raise the first intersectional hybrids.

However, in the last decade a number of Chinese scientists have studied the *Paeonia delavayi* complex and have come to a completely different conclusion. Pan (1993) only recognized a single species (*P. delavayi*) with two varieties (var. *lutea* and var. *angustiloba*), while Hong (1997) raised *P. lutea* var. *ludlowii* to the status of an independent species (*P. ludlowii*). To remove any uncertainty Hong *et al.* (1998) visited eighteen populations of the *P. delavayi* complex in Southwest China and the type locations of all the taxa involved.

Their research suggests that the differences between the different taxa are artificial and only represent extreme variants within the different populations. They only recognized two species, *P. delavayi* and *P. ludlowii*. Haw (2001) has accepted these changes and treated the differently coloured plants as botanical formas (forms); namely f. *delavayi* (red flowers) and f. *lutea* (yellow flowers). Tao Sang (1995) discovered that there was only one nucleotide substitution between *P. delavayi* and *P. lutea*, which proves they are very closely related, but it remains to be seen whether this is sufficient justification to reduce them to one species. However, from a horticultural perspective the plants appear quite different and I have described these plants as separate species in the current treatment.

Paeonia delavayi forms a multi-stemmed, spreading bush with deeply dissected leaves.

The flowers of *Paeonia delavayi* are very variable, which is why it is best to see a plant in flower before you purchase it.

Paeonia delavayi

The red-flowered *Paeonia delavayi* is endemic to the northern Yunnan and Southwest Sichuan Provinces of China and the Southeast of Tibet. *Paeonia delavayi* was named after Jean Marie Delavay, a French missionary and botanist, who discovered *P. delavayi* and *P. lutea* in 1884.

In the wild *Paeonia delavayi* usually spreads by vegetative means (Hong De-Yuan, 1997), but it readily self-seeds in cultivation. It is an attractive, spreading, deciduous, clump-forming shrub, which can grow to a height of 1.8 M (6 FT.) and measures the same across. It has deeply dissected, biternate leaves with acuminate tips, which are bronzy purple when they are young, but become green as they mature. The leaves are glabrous and bluish green beneath, with entire or slightly toothed margins. The most desirable plants have deep blood red, cup-shaped flowers, up to 8 CM (3.1 IN.) across, with 12–16 petals. *Paeonia delavayi* is unique among peonies in having a distinctive involucre of bracts beneath the flower. The flowers have 5–10 glabrous, cone-shaped carpels which taper quickly into a short, coiled style and are surrounded by a large number of stamens with red filaments and yellow, orange or red anthers. It flowers in late spring.

The majority of plants that are available for sale are grown from seed and the flowers can be very variable; cultivated specimens tend to have semi-double flowers with more petals than wild plants. If you want to have a good specimen it is a good idea to select a plant that is in flower. It is diploid (2N=10).

Paeonia ludlowii has bright yellow flowers, with only one, or rarely two, sausage-shaped carpels.

Paeonia ludlowii develops into a substantial bush, with wide-spreading branches.

Paeonia ludlowii

For many years *Paeonia ludlowii* was considered to be a variety of *P. lutea*, but in 1997 Hong De-Yuan raised it to the status of a species (Hong, D. Y. 1997). The famous plant hunters Ludlow and Sheriff originally discovered it, while they were exploring Tibet in 1936. It is endemic to Southeast Tibet (Xizang) and the Chinese provinces of Gansu and Qinghai, where it occurs in woods, forests and thickets. In China large numbers of *P. ludlowii* are collected by the local people, which represents a threat to the long-term survival of the species in the wild.

Paeonia ludlowii is easy to grow from seed and forms a large elegant deciduous shrub with arching branches and bright green foliage. A mature plant, approximately thirty to forty years old, can measure up to 2.5 M (8 FT.) high and may spread as much as 4 M (13 FT.). The leaves are broader and less divided than those of *P. lutea*, bright green above and paler below, with nine triangular leaflets. The terminal set of leaflets has a longer petiolule measuring 5–9 CM (2–3.5 IN.), compared to the laterals, which are 2–3 CM (0.8–1.2 IN.) long. The leaflets are trilobed with acuminate tips. It spreads by seed, but is widely collected for its root bark, which is used in traditional Chinese medicine.

Each stem can have up to 4 bright yellow flowers, up to 10 CM (4 IN.) across, with a single, or occasionally 2, carpels. There are 4–5 bracts and 3–4 sepals, which merge into one another, and it has yellow stamen filaments. The large glabrous, cylindrical carpels are green flushed with pink and have yellow styles. The carpels can grow up to 7.5 CM (3 IN.) long and enclose very large blackish brown seeds, measuring up to 1.5 CM (0.6 IN.)

across. It is very fertile and the seeds germinate easily in cultivation. The plant is very vigorous, but can be kept within bounds by pruning and flowers in late spring. It is diploid (2N=10).

Paeonia lutea

Paeonia lutea can be distinguished from *P. delavayi* by its more upright habit, bright yellow flowers, narrow, sword-shaped bracts and the absence of an involucre. It grows in spruce forest and among scrub in upland pastures at altitudes of 3300–4000 M (11,000–13,000 FT.), in the Chinese provinces of Sichuan and Yunnan and in southeastern Tibet.

It forms a deciduous shrub up to 1.8 M (6 FT.) high with glabrous, rigid, greyish brown stems. The leaves are biternate, glabrous, dark green above and glaucous below, deeply dissected with ovate-lanceolate segments up to 12–17 × 0.6–1.1 CM (4.7–6.7 × 0.24–0.43 IN.). The yellow flowers, up to 7 CM (2.75 IN.) across, have yellow stamens measuring up to 1.5 CM (0.6 IN.) long and cone-shaped glabrous carpels with a very short, flattened style approximately 1 CM (0.4 IN.) long. The carpels sit on a fleshy staminoidal disc, but there is no sheath as in the section *Moutan*.

Paeonia lutea will readily hybridize with *P. delavayi*, creating a swarm of seedlings whose flowers can range in colour from yellow, through shades of orange and eventually deep red. *P. lutea* forms a more compact bush than *P. delavayi* and has been crossed with Japanese tree peonies (*P. ×suffruticosa*) to produce hybrid tree peonies with yellow flowers (*P. ×lemoinei*). Although rarely grown, *P. lutea* is more suitable for a small garden than *P. ludlowii*. It is a diploid (2N=10).

Paeonia potaninii

This dwarf shrub was first recognized as a new species by Grigori Potanin and named after him by Komarov in 1921. It was subsequently discovered that Ernest Wilson had collected specimens of the plant in 1904, but believed that they were a dwarf form of *Paeonia delavayi*. It is endemic to the Chinese provinces of Sichuan and Yunnan.

Paeonia potaninii is a short clump-forming shrub with creeping stolons, which grows to 1 M (3.3 FT.) and can have a spread of 1.8 M (6 FT.). The leaves are deeply divided into many oblong leaf segments, measuring 0.5–1.0 CM (0.25–0.4 IN.) wide, with acuminate tips. It has nodding, maroon or reddish brown, cup-shaped flowers, up to 5–6 CM (2–2.5 IN.) across with 5–7 sepals and bracts. The two most attractive forms are 'Alba' which has white flowers and the pretty variety *trollioides*, which has yellow flowers. It flowers in late spring. All forms of *P. potaninii* are diploid (2N=10).

Paeonia potaninii var. *trollioides* is a low-growing shrub with primrose yellow flowers.

Section *Onaepia*

North America is home to two unusual species of peony, which, because they are so different from the other members of the genus, are placed in a separate botanical section, the *Onaepia*. They are distinguished from the old world peonies by having small, rather insignificant fleshy petals, cylindrical rather than rounded seeds and a very conspicuous staminoidal disc.

Sang *et al.* (1997) determined that the section *Onaepia* (containing *Paeonia californica* and *P. brownii*) split off from the remainder of the genus approximately 16.6 million years ago in the middle of the Miocene and that the tree peonies (section *Moutan*) and herbaceous peonies (section *Paeon*) diverged at a later date.

Paeonia brownii

There has been a lot of debate about whether *Paeonia brownii* and *P. californica* should be treated as two separate species. *Paeonia brownii* was the first to be described, in 1829, but nine years later Nuttall (in Torrey and Grey, 1838) described the southern populations as *P. californica*, on the basis that it could be distinguished from the other species by having smaller, less divided leaves, which were deep green on both sides. However, as more plants were collected the distinction between the two appeared less obvious and many later authors did not recognize *P. californica*.

Stebbins (1938) made several collections of the two species and found that they could be distinguished morphologically. He placed a lot of emphasis on the fact the two occupy very different habitats and that there were no known hybrids between the two species. By using the modern technique of gene sequencing Sang *et al.* (1997) have shown that while the two species may not appear very different on the surface, they are genetically quite distinct.

Paeonia brownii is smaller than its southern cousin and grows on the mountains of northern California, Oregon, Nevada and Washington State, at altitudes of 900–1800 M (3000–6000 FT.). It grows to a height of 45 CM (17 IN.) and is glabrous throughout with 5–8 biternate leaves, divided into fleshy, elliptic leaflets with long drawn-out petiolules. The leaves are dark green and glaucous beneath, with rounded or toothed tips, drawn out into a very short point.

The flowers are small and rather inconspicuous, with dark maroon or bronze-coloured petals with a yellow or greenish margin and measure up to 1.3 CM (0.5 IN.) in length. It flowers from June to July in its native habitat and has 2–5 carpels. *Paeonia brownii* is one of the most difficult species peonies to grow because it needs extremely well-drained soil and full sunshine throughout the day. If you want to try your hand at growing it you should build a raised bed and fill it with a mixture of soil, compost, sand and grit.

Paeonia californica

The Californian peony is unique, because it is the only species in the genus that has become adapted to growing in an arid climate. It achieves this by commencing growth in autumn, when there is plenty of water available and dies back in the spring when it has finished flowering. It grows in the deserts of central and southern California, from sea level to 1220 M (4000 FT.).

Paeonia californica is a larger and more luxuriant plant than its northern cousin and can reach as much as 90 CM (3 FT.) in height. The leaves are less divided than in *P. brownii* and it flowers in the early spring, rather than the summer. It has a maximum of 3 carpels, rather than *P. brownii*'s 5.

Paeonia californica is completely glabrous with 7–12 biternate leaves, which are dark green above and slightly paler beneath. The leaflets are almost sessile with short petiolules and divided into many very narrow, oblong segments, each with two to three lobes. The lobes have acute tips or are occasionally blunt. The flowers measure 2–3 CM (0.8–1.2 IN.) across and have deep black-red petals with a pink margin. *Paeonia californica* has 2–3 yellowish green, glabrous carpels, yellow anthers and reddish yellow filaments. It flowers from February to April.

Because it is so well adapted to its native habitat, the Californian peony is quite difficult to grow in a temperate climate. It must be kept completely dry during the summer when it enters dormancy. The flowers are small and inconspicuous.

Subsection *Foliolatae*

This subsection includes a group of species with undivided leaflets. Frederick Stern split the herbaceous peonies in the section *Paeon* into two subsections, depending upon whether the leaflets were further divided into segments and lobes. Sang (1995) believes that this is completely artificial and separates species that are closely related. However his system, which divides the section *Paeon* into three subsections, also has its weaknesses. I have therefore decided to adhere to Stern's original classification until the situation is resolved.

Paeonia bakeri

Paeonia bakeri was discovered growing in the Cambridge University Botanic Garden, in England, and has never been found in the wild. The plant was named after a British botanist, J. G. Baker, who wrote an early monograph about peonies.

It grows to a height of 60 CM (24 IN.) and has dark green, oval or ovate leaves, which are glabrous above and densely hairy beneath. The leaflets are cuneate or truncated at the base and taper to an acute tip. The brightly coloured, roseine purple (68A) flowers have yellow anthers with red filaments and three densely tomentose carpels. It is rarely available and is probably a hybrid between two other species. It flowers in the late spring. *Paeonia bakeri* is diploid (2N=10).

Paeonia broteroi

This distinctive peony is endemic to Portugal and Spain, where it grows on rocky calcareous soil at altitudes of 900–1800 M (3000–6000 FT.).

Paeonia broteroi grows to a height of approximately 40 CM (16 IN.) and is entirely glabrous. It has bright red stems and glossy, biternate leaves, which are dark green above and glaucous beneath, with 19–23 leaflets. The upper leaves have entire leaflets, but the lateral leaflets of the lower leaves are often divided into 2–3 segments. The leaflets are more or less sessile, elliptic to broadly elliptic in shape with an acute tip and cuneate base.

The striking, crimson-red flowers measure 8–10 CM (3.1–4 IN.) across and have yellow anthers with similarly coloured filaments, the stamens measure 2.0–2.5 CM (0.8–1.0 IN.) long. It has 2–4 densely tomentose carpels. *Paeonia broteroi* is diploid (2N=10).

Plants grow best in well-drained soil and an open situation. It is not entirely hardy and may need some protection during cold winters. It flowers from late spring to early summer.

Paeonia cambessedesii flowers extremely early in the year and is best planted at the foot of a west or south-facing wall. The true species has wavy edged leaves.

Paeonia cambessedesii

The Majorcan peony is a particularly beautiful species endemic to the Balearic Islands. It grows on limestone cliffs and rocky ground, but is threatened by hotel development on the islands and by the local goats, which eat its carpels.

Paeonia cambessedesii is easy to distinguish from other peonies because the leaves are deep greenish purple beneath and have a wavy edge. Mature plants may produce dozens of seedlings, which can be dug up and transplanted.

It grows to a height of 60 CM (24 IN.) and has glabrous, reddish purple stems. The leaves are greyish green above and dark greenish purple below, with entire, lanceolate to ovate leaflets. The veins of the leaflets are transparent, which can be seen clearly if the leaves are held up to the light. *Paeonia cambessedesii* is one of the first peonies to flower in the spring and has beautiful pale magenta or pink petals, with darker veins and a wavy outer margin. The stamens have yellow anthers and deep reddish purple filaments, surrounding 5–8, glabrous, deep reddish purple carpels. It is diploid (2N=10).

While *Paeonia cambessedesii* is easily grown from seed, it can hybridize with other early flowering species, such as *P. mascula* subsp. *russoi*. Hybrids may be hardier than the true species, but the flowers are not as attractive and the leaves may not have the typical characteristics. It is best grown from wild-collected seed or as a division of an established plant.

It appears to be quite hardy, but needs to be grown in well-drained soil and may need some protection during the winter months. Plant it in a sunny position, against a south or western facing wall, and add plenty of grit to the soil at planting time to ensure good drainage. In the Northern Hemisphere it flowers from late March to early April.

Paeonia caucasica

Paeonia caucasica is endemic to the Caucasus in Eastern Europe, where it occurs in forests, woodland clearings, meadows and scrub (Komarov, 1937). Botanists in Eastern Europe consider it to be an independent species, but both Busch (1901) and Stern (1946) considered it to be a synonym of *P. mascula* subsp. *triternata*.

The live specimens of *Paeonia caucasica* that I have seen are quite different from those of *P. mascula* subsp. *triternata* and I feel that there is some justification in considering *P. caucasica* to be an independent species. However it is very similar to *P. kavachensis* and I suspect that it is best regarded as a synonym of that species, which was described twenty years earlier. The edge of the leaves is flat, rather than undulating and upturned as in *P. mascula* subsp. *triternata*. Certain characteristics, such as the glaucous nature of the leaves, are reminiscent of another Caucasian peony, *P. mlokosewitschii*.

Paeonia caucasica is a vigorous peony that can grow to 1 M (3.3 FT.) high in ideal conditions and has a more erect habit than *P. mascula*, with strong upright stems. The stems are glabrous, glaucous and suffused with red pigment, with large biternate leaves and 9 entire leaflets. The leaves are dark green above and paler beneath, glaucous on both sides, occasionally pubescent beneath and glabrous above. The leaflets are oblong-obovate, oval or oval-elliptic, 2.5–11 × 1.8–8.5 CM (1.0–4.3 × 0.7–3.3 IN.), with a cuneate base and acute or obtuse tips. The petioles and main veins are usually red.

It is a very decorative plant with large purplish red flowers up to 5 CM (2 IN.) across. It has yellow anthers, red or violet filaments and 5 white tomentose carpels.

It is easily grown from seed and readily available from specialist nurseries. Plants flower between May and June (late spring to early summer) and is very hardy.

Paeonia ×chamaeleon

Paeonia ×chamaeleon is an interesting plant, for while it is said to be a natural hybrid between *P. mlokosewitschii* and *P. caucasica* it is not very vigorous. It grows to a height of 50 CM (20 IN.) and has glaucous dark green leaves. The flowers are rather variable; some are pink when they open, fading to creamy white with pink veins, while others are ivory white with only a hint of pink. It has golden yellow anthers and reddish pink filaments. It can be grown from seed, but the results are rather unpredictable. Divisions are preferable, but you should see the parent in flower before you part with your money.

It originates from Georgia, where it grows on rocky slopes and among open woodland (Halda and Waddick, 2004).

Paeonia ×chamaeleon

Paeonia coriacea

This distinctive species grows on rocky slopes, in upland meadows and among deciduous trees in Spain and Morocco, at altitudes of 1220–1800 M (4000–6000 FT.). The name is derived from the leathery nature of its leaves (*coriaceous* means leathery).

It grows to a height of 60 CM (24 IN.) and has glabrous stems. The leaves are also glabrous and divided into as many as 16 leaflets, some of which are entire, while the others are divided into two. The leaves are rather dull, bluish green above and glaucous below, broadly elliptic, lanceolate or ovate in shape with an acute tip and cuneate base. The flowers measure 7.0–15.0 CM (3–6 IN.) across and are pinkish magenta, with yellow anthers, red filaments and two glabrous carpels. It is tetraploid (2N=20).

Paeonia coriacea is a challenge to grow because it not very hardy and the shoots appear early in the spring. It needs protection from frost and should be kept dry in summer, when it is dormant. It flowers from early to late spring. A slightly different form of the species, var. *atlantica*, can be found growing in Algeria. It has larger leaflets, with a slightly pubescent under surface and pubescent petioles.

This species was used by Arthur Saunders to produce Lavender Strain, the closest that anyone has ever come to producing a peony with blue flowers.

The elegant *Paeonia emodi* originates from the Himalayan mountains and is a great deal tougher than many gardening books suggest.

Paeonia emodi will eventually form a large clump. It can be grown in dappled shade or in full sun.

Paeonia emodi

The Himalayan peony, *Paeonia emodi*, is an aristocratic perennial with large, pure white flowers. It grows naturally in Northwest India, Kashmir, western Nepal, North Pakistan and Tibet (Xizang) (Hong de Yuan *et al.*, 2001a).

There is a lot of confusion about the plant in the nursery trade and many of the plants that are sold as *Paeonia emodi* are actually hybrids with *P. veitchii* ('Early Windflower' or 'Late Windflower'). The true *P. emodi* is a much bigger plant, which can be distinguished by having larger flowers and broader leaflets, but the difference is sometimes difficult to appreciate until you have seen the Himalayan peony "in the flesh".

It grows to a height of 80 CM (32 IN.) and has a similar spread, with glabrous stems and leaves. The foliage is bronze coloured when it appears in the spring, turning dark green as the season progresses. The leaves have up to 15 oblong-elliptic or oblong-lanceolate leaflets with acuminate tips and decurrent leaf blades. *Paeonia emodi* has 2–4 flowers, which are held elegantly on the tall stems and measure 8–12 CM (3.1–4.7 IN.). They have 3 rounded sepals, two of which have a leafy appendage. Young flowers are cone-shaped when they open, but become cup-shaped as they mature, with pure white, obovate petals. The flowers are unusual because they have a single (rarely 2) greenish yellow carpel, which is covered with stiff yellow hairs and has an erect, greenish white style. The anthers are approximately 1 CM (0.4 IN.) long and supported by yellow filaments. It flowers from April to May (mid to late spring) and produces black seeds. It is diploid (2N=10).

The buds are more elongated than those of most other species and start to develop early in the season. The majority of early authors suggested that *Paeonia emodi* is rather delicate and should be planted beneath deciduous trees. However this is at variance with how it grows in nature and plants at the Cambridge University Botanic Garden and Royal Botanic Gardens at Kew, in England, grow happily in exposed situations. It needs well-drained soil and will suffer from crown rot if it becomes waterlogged.

Paeonia japonica

Widely distributed in Japan, where it occurs in mountainous areas in deciduous and coniferous woodland. For many years it was confused with *Paeonia obovata*, but the latter species is more robust with obovate leaflets: that is they are broader towards the tip than at the base. It was first described in 1898 by the Japanese botanist Tomitaro Makino, who considered it to be a variety of *P. obovata*, but in 1910 Miyabe and Takeda raised it to the status of an independent species.

Paeonia japonica is often included in *P. obovata*, but it is a distinct species with elliptic or narrowly ovate leaflets. *Paeonia obovata*, by contrast, has obovate leaves. which are broader at the tip than at the base.

Paeonia japonica has rather delicate light green, glaucous stems up to 35 CM (14 IN.) in height, which are marked on the surface by five shallow channels. The leaves are divided into 9–11 elliptic to narrowly ovate leaflets, with acute or shortly acuminate tips. The plant is almost completely glabrous, but some plants have scattered, simple hairs on the lower surface of the leaves. The stems have solitary white flowers, measuring 5.0–7.0 CM (2in–2.8 IN.) across, with 6–7 petals and 3 sepals. The flowers have 3–5, slightly glaucous, erect carpels, with recurved, crosier-shaped styles, yellow anthers and red filaments. *Paeonia japonica* is a diploid (2N=10).

This species is fully hardy but it can be damaged by high winds and is therefore best planted beneath deciduous trees or close to shrubs. It should be planted so that the dormant buds are at ground level, but protected with a small amount of mulch. *Paeonia japonica* is not very vigorous but it makes a good addition to the woodland garden. A detailed discussion of this species can be found in Page and Sinnott (2001).

Although the flowers and leaves are different, some botanists consider that *Paeonia kavachensis* should not be a separate species but included in *P. mascula.*

Paeonia kavachensis

Many botanists treat this species as a synonym of *Paeonia mascula* subsp. *triternata*, but it is quite different. If anything it is closer to *P. caucasica.*

Riedl (1969) says that it occurs in Azerbaijan, the Caucasus, Iraq, Lebanon and Turkey. It grows to a height of 70 CM (28 IN.) and has biternate leaves, which are dark green and glaucous above and beneath, pale green. The leaves have obovate-lanceolate to broadly lanceolate leaflets, measuring 5–12 × 3–7 CM (2–4.7 × 1.2–2.8 IN.). The flowers are bright reddish magenta with a reddish tinge (somewhere between 64B and 66A on the *RHS Colour Chart*) and the leaves are glabrous on both sides. It is very vigorous and has 2–3 tomentose carpels. *Paeonia kavachensis* flowers from late April to early May. It is tetraploid (2N=20).

Paeonia kesrouanensis

This species grows to a height of 60 CM (24 IN.) and has up to 14 broadly elliptic, oblong-ovate or ovate-oval leaflets. Its leaves are dark green above and slightly glaucous beneath, with a purplish midrib and veins. The rose pink flowers have yellow anthers and red filaments. It is similar to *Paeonia mascula* subsp. *mascula*, but has glabrous carpels and a 7 MM (0.3 IN.) long style, which is coiled at its apex. *Paeonia kesrouanensis* was originally discovered by Joseph Marie Thiébaut and named after the Lebanese county of Kesrouan, where it was found. Halda and Waddick (2003) have reduced it to the status of a subspecies within *P. mascula* and consider that it is a synonym of *P. turcica.* The plant grows in maquis and *Abies cilicica* forest and is a tetraploid with (2N=20). It is rarely found in cultivation.

Paeonia lactiflora

This is the Chinese peony, the most widely cultivated of all peony species and many thousands of cultivars have been produced. The main reasons for its success have been its ability to produce side buds, double flowers and the fact that many cultivars have a sweet fragrance. These desirable traits have resulted in it being crossed with many other species of peony, creating a range of highly attractive garden plants. *Paeonia lactiflora* is also widely cultivated as a cut flower.

The first plants to be introduced into Western Europe were 'Fragrans' in 1805, 'Whitleyi' in 1808 and 'Humei' in 1810. These three Chinese cultivars were widely distributed around Europe and it seems likely that they are the main ancestors of our modern cultivars. Until recently it was thought that 'Whitleyi' was a single peony with white flowers, but I recently discovered that the original plant had double flowers. 'Whitleyi' was renamed 'Queen Victoria' towards the end of the nineteenth century and was widely distributed in the U.S.A. The plant that is sold commercially as 'Whitleyi Major' may be of more recent origin.

The Chinese have been cultivating this species for almost 2000 years, both for medicinal purposes and as an ornamental flower. It occurs naturally in Japan, Korea, Siberia, Mongolia, China and Tibet, where it grows among scrub and in steppe grassland. Wild plants have white or pink flowers.

Paeonia lactiflora is a robust herbaceous perennial, which grows to a height of 1 M (3.3 FT.) or more. In the early spring the sharply pointed buds give rise to erect, reddish purple, glabrous stems. The leaves are biternate with elliptic to lanceolate leaflets, dark green and glabrous above, light green with small hairs along the veins beneath. The leaves have distinctive papillose margins, which feel rough to the touch. The stems have two or more flowers with glabrous carpels and pink styles.

It has large single, pure white or pink flowers with 5 green glabrous carpels, surrounded by a ring of yellow stamens. The carpels turn purple as the flowers mature and have pink styles. A few cultivated specimens have hairy carpels and have been called var. *trichocarpa*. *Paeonia lactiflora* is a diploid species ($2N=10$).

Cultivars are described as being early, mid or late flowering, because the different forms of this species flower over a period of approximately six weeks, from late spring to early summer. *Paeonia lactiflora* and its cultivars should be grown in full sunshine and in well-drained fertile soil. It should not be planted in situations that are prone to waterlogging in winter.

Paeonia macrophylla

Nicholas Albow first described this interesting plant in 1895, but like many subsequent people, considered it to be a form of *Paeonia wittmanniana*. It is quite distinctive, with very large, orbicular leaves, and has an acrid smell, which some have likened to that of boxwood—it is unclear whether this is a reference to the plant or its wood. No other peony has such a fragrance, which suggests it is a distinct species.

I have not seen mature specimens of this species, but there is no doubting that it is closely related to *Paeonia wittmanniana* and it is therefore fair to assume that it will grow to form a large clump, measuring approximately 1 M (3.3 FT.) high, with a similar spread. The leaves are biternate, with elliptic-lanceolate, oval, oval-rounded or sub-orbicular leaflets, measuring up to 25 × 15 CM (10 × 6 IN.). The leaves are shiny on the upper surface and have deeply depressed veins, which gives them a distinctive blistered appearance. The upper surface is mid green and glabrous, while below they are slightly lighter in colour with a few long hairs along the main veins. The petioles and stems of the plant are completely glabrous and a rich reddish brown in colour.

The flowers of *Paeonia macrophylla* appear pale yellow in bud, opening to ivory white with the slightest hint of yellow. There is a slight tinge of magenta pigmentation at the base of the petals, which fades after a couple of days. The petals are matt on the inside surface and slightly glossy on the outside, elliptic and slightly concave in shape. The solitary flowers measure up to 7.5 CM (3 IN.) across, with 2–4 glabrous or minutely pubescent carpels (some published descriptions say that they are hirsute). The carpels are green with purple, recurved, crosier-shaped styles, while the stamens have yellow anthers measuring 2 × 5 MM (0.07 × 0.2 IN.)with purple filaments, becoming white towards the top and measuring 5–8 MM (0.2–0.32 IN.) in length. The flowers are subtended by tomentose bracts, which are lanceolate to ovate in shape, green and suffused with purple at the edges, with acute tips. *Paeonia macrophylla* flowers during April. Its fertile seeds are blue-black and its infertile ovules vivid rose red. The flowers of my own specimen were cup-shaped, but some writers state that the petals open more widely than those of *P. wittmanniana*.

Paeonia macrophylla is extremely rare in cultivation, although it is a striking plant and flowers early in the season. The leaves have a pungent, acrid smell, which is particularly conspicuous when the plant is flowering. The smell alone is enough to distinguish it from other species of peony and is most apparent on sunny days. It can be distinguished from *P. wittmanniana* by the distinctive blistered appearance of its leaves.

Paeonia macrophylla is a very rare species and is only known from the western Caucasus, in Georgia, where it occurs at altitudes of 800–1000 M (2625–3280 FT.). Kemularia-Nathadze (1961) says that it grows in woodland and on forest margins in Georgia and Abkhazia. The Caucasus has been a very dangerous area since the Soviet Union broke up and few western botanists have managed to visit the habitat of this fascinating peony. The number of chromosomes is unknown.

Arthur Saunders claimed to have used *Paeonia macrophylla* in his breeding work to produce beautiful hybrid peonies, such as 'Nova' and 'Silver Dawn'. The species is highly regarded by breeders because of the opacity of its flowers, which enables the breeding of plants with pastel colours, such as buff and creamy yellow. However, the true identity of this plant is uncertain. According to Saunders (Stebbins and Saunders, 1938) his specimen of *P. macrophylla* came from C. G. Van Tubergen in Haarlem, Holland, but his description includes the following qualification "*P. tomentosa* Stapf. (= *P. macrophylla* of auth. not Lomak., cf. Stapf 1931)". The implication of this is that Saunders' "*Paeonia macrophylla*" is in reality *P. wittmanniana*. Unfortunately the name has been repeated in hundreds of publications and this has confused people about the true identity of this interesting plant. There is no doubt that *P. macrophylla* is closely related to *P. wittmanniana*, but steps should be taken to conserve this species.

Paeonia mairei

This Chinese endemic was first discovered in 1913 by René Maire in Yunnan and described by Léveillé in 1915. It grows in deciduous broadleaved forests in Gansu, Guizhou, Hubei, Shaanxi, Yunnan and Sichuan Provinces, at altitudes of 1500–2700 M (5000—8700 FT.) (Hong de Yuan *et al.*, 2001a).

Paeonia mairei grows to a height of 1 M (3.3 FT.), with glabrous stems, and has up to 19 glabrous, elliptic, oblong-ovate or oblong-lanceolate leaflets, measuring 6.0–16.5 cm (2.5–6.5 in.) × 1.8–7 cm (0.7–2.8 in.) with caudate or acuminate tips. It has single, solitary pink or red flowers with yellow anthers, supported by purplish red filaments and 2–3 glabrous or tomentose carpels with short golden brown hairs and red styles. It is diploid (2N=10). Plants flower from late April to late May (late spring).

Phylogenetic research suggests that *Paeonia mairei* was originally far more widespread and may be the ancestor of several European species. However its descendants were far more adaptable and it became extinct in many parts of its range, eventually becoming restricted to Asia, where the climate was less extreme (Tao Sang, 1995). It appears to be closely related to *P. obovata* and *P. japonica*.

This Chinese peony is starting to become available in the western hemisphere and appears to be a good garden plant. It grows best when protected from hot sunshine and needs well-drained, humus-rich soil.

Paeonia mascula

The male peony is an extremely interesting species, which seems to be going through the process of speciation. Phylogenetic studies suggest that *Paeonia mascula* subsp. *mascula* and subsp. *hellenica* are descended from *P. lactiflora* and *P. japonica* or *P. obovata*, while subsp. *russoi* is derived from *P. lactiflora* and *P. mairei* (Tao Sang *et al.*, 1997).

Paeonia mascula is a native of Europe and has been used as a medicinal plant for at least 2000 years. The plant was widely collected by apothecaries in medieval times, so that by the early seventeenth century it had become quite rare and they were forced to substitute the less efficacious female peony (*Paeonia officinalis*). The first detailed description of the plant appears in John Parkinson's *Paradisi in Sole Paradisus Terrestris*, which was published in 1629:

Paeonia mascula subsp. *mascula*.

> The Male Peonie riseth up with many brownish stalkes, wheron doe grow winged leaves, that is, many faire greene, and sometimes reddish leaves, one set against another upon a stalke, without any particular division in the leafe at all: the flowers stand at the toppes of the stalkes, consisting of five or six broade leaves, of a faire purplish red colour, with many yellow threads in the middle, standing about the head, which after riseth to be the seede vessels, divided into two, three or foure rough crooked pods like hornes, which when they are ful ripe, open and turn themselves down one edge to another backeward, shewing within them divers round black shining seede, which are the true seede, being full and good, and having also many red or crimson graines, which are lancke and idle, intermixed among the blacke, as if they were good seede, whereby it maketh a very pretty shew: the roots are great, thick and long, spreading in the ground, and running downe reasonable deepe.

The great majority of the plants appear to have been taken from the wild and there is a report of large quantities being collected from Stancombe Wood in Gloucestershire, England, during the seventeenth century. This record cannot be substantiated as the original manuscript appears to have been lost. However if it were true then *Paeonia mascula* may be a native of England, rather than having been introduced in the twelfth century, as is currently thought. The other possible source of the plant is the Romans, who introduced many edible and medicinal plants to the British Isles during the first millennium AD (the remains of several Romano-British villas have been found in the vicinity of Stancombe Wood). It is surprising that no one seems to have taken the trouble to cultivate such a valuable plant during the Middle Ages.

Nicholas Culpeper (1653), the celebrated herbalist, says that "The roots are held to be of more virtue than the seed; next the flowers; and last of all, the leaves."

Paeonia mascula subsp. *mascula*

The following botanical description was made on the 19 July 2000, from the plants growing on the island of Steep Holm, in the Bristol Channel, United Kingdom. The plants on this island are considered to be naturalized and are thought to have been introduced in the twelfth century AD.

The male peony is an herbaceous perennial, which grows to a height of approximately 75 CM (30 IN.) and has glabrous, slightly glaucous stems. The leaves are biternate with 9–12 leaflets, the upper surface green and glabrous, the lower greyish green and slightly glaucous, with a few scattered simple hairs on the veins.

The leaflets are elliptic to ovate with an acute apex and measure between 5.0–8.5 CM (2–7.3 IN.) wide by 10.0–11.5 CM (4–4.5 IN.) long, with a short petiolule 1–5 MM (0.04–0.2 IN.) in length. The terminal leaflets are often much larger, measuring 7.2–9.5 CM (2.9–3.7 IN.) across by 11.0–13.0 CM (4.3–5 IN.) long, broadly elliptic to obovate-elliptic with a short, acuminate apex and a cuneate base, tapering into a 1.0–3.0 CM (0.4–1.2 IN.) long petiolule. The base of the terminal leaflet of the terminal leaflet set is often unequal. The uppermost parts of the stem, petiole and petiolules are tinged reddish brown, this colour extends into the midrib and larger veins on the upper surface of the leaflets. The leaves diminish in size at the extreme top of the stem.

The flowers are solitary and deep magenta in colour, with 5 sepals, 1 foliaceous. The carpels are extremely large, 3–5 in number, 5.5–7.5 CM (2.25–3.00 IN.) in length with a

It is unlikely that the person who painted this antique print of *Paeonia mascula* subsp. *mascula* (syn. *Paeonia corallina*) had ever seen the plant, which in life has bright magenta flowers, rather than dark purple.

The carpels of *Paeonia mascula* subsp. *mascula* are tomentose and strongly recurved.

The foliage of *Paeonia mascula* subsp. *mascula* has superb autumn colour.

diameter of up to 2.0 CM (0.8 IN.). They are strongly re-curved and covered with a brown tomentum. The weight of the mature carpels may be sufficient to cause the stems to bend downwards. It flowers from mid to late spring, depending upon the location.

Paeonia mascula is a very vigorous peony, which can form a clump measuring as much as 1 M (3.3 FT.) across when it is mature. It does best in slightly alkaline conditions, but will thrive in most well-drained soils. It will tolerate a degree of shade, whereas *P. officinalis* needs full sunshine if it is to do well. The leaves turn a wonderful shade of apricot-yellow in autumn.

Paeonia mascula subsp. *mascula* is widely distributed in Europe and has been recorded from Armenia, Bulgaria, Cyprus, England, France, Germany, Greece, Italy, northern Iran, Iraq, Sicily, Syria and Turkey. The foliage of this subspecies varies from population to population; those on Steep Holm are broadly elliptic, while in other plants they may be narrowly elliptic. It is tetraploid (2N=20).

Paeonia mascula subsp. bodurii

This white-flowered peony is similar to subsp. *hellenica*, but according to Özhatay and Özhatay (1995) it differs by having less divided leaflets. It has glabrous, purplish stems and white flowers, which are purple at the base. It grows to 80 CM (32 IN.) and has obovate, broadly elliptic or orbicular leaflets. The leaves are glabrous above, greyish green and glaucous below, while the carpels are covered with a short white tomentum and surrounded by pink or yellow anthers with purple filaments. It is endemic to Turkey and grows among *Quercus pubescens* coppice, at altitudes of between 400 and 700 M (1300–2300 FT.). It is tetraploid (2N=20).

Paeonia mascula subsp. hellenica

An endemic of Sicily, the Southern Peloponnese, Attica and the Greek islands of Evvoia and Andros, this beautiful peony grows to a height of 60 CM (24 IN.), with glabrous stems and glabrous or pilose biternate leaves, which are greyish green above and glaucous beneath. The leaves have 9–21 leaflets, which are obovate or elliptic in shape, with a shortly acuminate tip. The leaf blade of the terminal leaflet extends down the petiolule.

The flowers are pure white with 5–7 crinkled petals, golden yellow anthers and purplish red filaments. It can have 1–5 densely tomentose carpels. The plant grows in slightly shaded, moist situations among *Abies* forest, in scrub or on rocky slopes, at altitudes of 400–850 m (1300–2800 ft.). Molecular studies by Musacchio *et al.* (2000) have suggested that subsp. *hellenica* is not genetically distinct from normal *P. mascula* with magenta-coloured flowers. They have also pointed out that in Sicily single populations of *P. mascula* subsp. *mascula* include plants with red, pink and white flowers. It is tetraploid (2N=20).

While genetic studies suggest that this white subspecies of *Paeonia mascula* is identical to the type it is very difficult to grow successfully.

Recent research suggests that the European peony *Paeonia mascula* subsp. *russoi* is actually descended from *P. lactiflora* and *P. mairei*, both of which are now restricted to Asia.

The flowers of *Paeonia mascula* subsp. *russoi* may be pink or have a lavender cast.

Paeonia mascula subsp. *russoi*

The foliage of this subspecies differs from that of the type, because it has ovate or elliptic leaflets with tapering acuminate tips. The leaves are dark green above and purplish green below, with purple petiolules and veins. The surface of the leaves is glossy and dark green above and purplish green with a sparse covering of hairs beneath. The leaflets vary from 2.5–5.3 × 5.0–8.5 cm (1.0–2.1 × 2.0–3.3 in.). The flowers are magenta or pinkish mauve in colour with white filaments and yellow anthers. It has white tomentose carpels with purplish styles. Plants usually come true from seed and this subspecies is easy to grow. It is tetraploid (2N=20).

Some botanists have considered var. *leiocarpa* to be a synonym of *Paeonia cambessedesii*, but the former flowers approximately two months later and is a tetraploid. According to Stern (1946) it can be distinguished from the typical form of *P. mascula* subsp. *russoi*

The leaves of *Paeonia mascula* subsp. *triternata* have a distinctive upturned and undulating margin.

by the presence of three glabrous, purple flushed carpels. Var. *reverchoni* can be distinguished from the typical form by having glabrous carpels and the undersurface of its leaves is tomentose, rather than pilose.

Paeonia mascula subsp. *triternata*

This peony occurs naturally in Greece, Romania, the Crimea (Krym), Ukraine and Turkey. It grows to 60 CM (24 IN.) and has distinctive leaves with upturned and undulating margins. The lower leaves are biternate with 9–11 broadly elliptic to oblong-oval leaflets with an emarginate or shortly apiculate tip. The leaves are glabrous and deep green above, glaucous and sparsely white hairy beneath. It has relatively large flowers measuring up to 10 CM (4 IN.) across and magenta or pink in colour, with yellow anthers and filaments. There are 2–3 carpels, which are covered with a dense brown tomentum and have pink styles. It is easily grown, with attractive autumn foliage and flowers in mid spring. It is tetraploid (2N=20).

Paeonia mlokosewitschii

Commonly known as Molly-the-witch, this is one of the most beautiful of all herbaceous perennials. It is confined to a small area of the Caucasus, where it grows in oak and beech forest. The plant was named after G. Mlokosiewicz, who discovered the plant in 1900.

Paeonia mlokosewitschii originates from the Caucasus and is one of the most desirable of all herbaceous perennials.

Many plants sold as *Paeonia mlokosewitschii* are actually hybrids with another species and have magenta-tinted flowers. Those of the true species are primrose yellow, without any trace of pink.

Paeonia mlokosewitschii has reddish brown stems and can grow to a height of 1 M (3.3 FT.) with a similar spread. The young shoots are reddish purple, quickly developing into dark green or bluish green foliage, which is glaucous on both surfaces. The biternate leaves have oval, oblong or obovate leaflets and an acute or sub-acute apex. A free-flowering species, in the late spring it produces masses of bright primrose yellow flowers, 8–12 CM (3.1–4.7 IN.) across, with pinkish yellow styles and yellow stamens. The tomentose carpels mature to reveal dark blue seeds and neon pink unfertilized ovules. The leaves turn a wonderful shade of orange-brown in the autumn.

Paeonia mlokosewitschii is best grown in an open sunny position, in well drained soil, where it will eventually form a large clump measuring as much as 1 M (3.3 FT.) across. It can also be grown successfully under the shade of deciduous trees and shrubs, but will not flower so freely. Demand for this peony always exceeds supply and the plants are consequently expensive. If you want a plant with pure yellow flowers it is best to purchase a division, rather than a seedling; the latter are usually hybrid in nature and have varying amounts of magenta in the petals.

This is considered to be an easily grown plant in Europe, but for reasons that are unclear it rarely succeeds in the hotter parts of the United States. To add insult to injury it will often hybridize with other species in Europe, but fails to set fertile seed in the U.S.A. It flowers from late April to early May and is diploid (2N=10).

Paeonia obovata

This is one of the most widespread species of peony, which occurs in China, Japan, North and South Korea and the island of Sakhalin. It obtained its name from the unusual shape of its terminal leaflets, which are broader towards the tip than at the base, in other words obovate.

It is a robust plant with glabrous stems and grows to a height of approximately 60 CM (24 IN.), with solitary pink, white or red flowers. The biternate leaves have 7–9 leaflets, which are dark green and glabrous above and slightly glaucous beneath, with a scattering of simple hairs. The lower leaves are unequal with oval or oblong lateral leaflets and larger terminal leaflets; both are cuneate at the base and acuminate at the tips. The white var. *alba* is the most readily available. Plants can be diploid or tetraploid (2N=10 or 20).

Subspecies *willmottiae* was originally described as an independent species by Otto Stapf (1916), who had found it growing in Ellen Willmott's garden at Warley Place in England. It was originally collected by the famous plant hunter E. H. Wilson and is restricted to a small area of Western China. Frederick Stern (1946) reduced it to the status of a botanical variety, but more recently Hong *et al.* (2001b) have discovered that whereas the type is usually diploid, subsp. *willmottiae* is tetraploid and this justified raising it to the status of a subspecies. It starts to grow earlier in the year than the type and has pure white, cup-shaped flowers, with yellow anthers and red filaments. (2N=20).

Paeonia obovata can be grown under deciduous trees as long as it gets full sunshine for at least part of the day. It will also grow in the open, but needs to be provided with some shade from hot afternoon sun. Both of the white-flowered forms come true from seed.

Paeonia turcica

Paeonia turcica was first described in 1965 by Cullen and Davis and is endemic to the Caria and Lycia regions of southwestern Turkey. It grows to 60 CM (24 IN.) and has glabrous, slightly glaucous stems. The biternate leaves are composed of 9–11 elliptic or ovate-elliptic leaflets with an acuminate tip and measure 9–14 × 5–7 CM (3.5–5.5 × 2–2.8 IN.). The leaves are deep green and glabrous above,

Looking at the carpels is a good way of distinguishing between the different species of peony; those of *Paeonia turcica* are glabrous.

glaucous and white-pilose below. It has saucer-shaped, deep magenta-rose flowers, measuring 10 CM (4 IN.) across, and 2–5 glabrous carpels. Halda and Waddick (2004) treat *P. turcica* as a synonym of *P. kesrouanensis*, but Davis and Cullen say that it differs from the latter species by having a "shorter style and stigma, the stigmatic portion curved from near the base, instead of circinate only at the apex."

Paeonia turcica is a rare Turkish endemic, but it has shown itself to be a good garden plant and is one of the first peonies to flower in the spring. It is hardy and has been proved to tolerate temperatures as low as -7°C (19.5°F), Özhatay *et al.* (2000).

Paeonia wittmanniana

This is one of the largest of the herbaceous peonies and it needs plenty of space when established. It was first found growing in the Caucasus Mountains in Georgia, but also occurs in Azerbaijan, northern Iran and Turkey.

In the same way that *Paeonia officinalis* and *P. mascula* appear to be in the process of speciation, *P. wittmanniana* also seems to be splitting into several new species. It is difficult to know what has caused this, but it is likely to have happened during the Pleistocene, when *P. wittmanniana* started to colonize areas of land that were previously covered with ice. Frederick Stern (1946) divided the species into two, depending upon whether the carpels were tomentose or glabrous. However Kemularia-Nathadze (1961) felt that the form with glabrous carpels (var. *nudicarpa*) was sufficiently different to justify raising

Paeonia wittmanniana is a substantial plant that requires plenty of space when it is established.

The typical form of *Paeonia wittmanniana*
has tomentose carpels and hairy leaves.
Some botanists believe that it should be
treated as a separate species, *P. tomentosa*.

The glabrous form of *Paeonia wittmanniana* (var.
nudicarpa) is quite distinctive, with the flowers
held above the foliage. It is sometimes sold under
the synonym of *P. steveniana*.

it to the status of an independent species, *Paeonia steveniana*. There is no doubt that var. *nudicarpa* is different from the typical *P. wittmanniana*, but it remains to be seen whether this is sufficient to accept it as a new species, particularly when other botanists seem intent on lumping species together.

Paeonia wittmanniana is a substantial plant, which can grow to a height of 1 M (3.3 FT.) and may have a spread of as much as 1.2 M (4 FT.) across. It has glabrous stems measuring up to 2 CM (0.8 IN.) in diameter and large broad ovate or broad elliptic leaves, which are glabrous and dark green above and paler beneath with long white hairs. The leaves can measure as much as 17 × 11 CM (6.7 × 4.3 IN.) and have acute or acuminate tips. The large, bowl-shaped flowers are pale yellow or creamy white, up to 12 CM (4.7 IN.) across. The typical form of the plant (synonym *P. tomentosa*), has large creamy yellow flowers that are somewhat hidden by the foliage and large hirsute carpels. The glabrous form, var. *nudicarpa* (synonym *P. steveniana*), is rather more decorative and carries its flowers well above the foliage; it has hairless carpels and leaves. Both forms are tetraploid (2N=20) and hardy to -15°C (5°F).

Subsection *Dissectifoliae*

The plants in this subsection have the leaflets further divided into lobes and segments. Stern (1946) placed *Paeonia rhodia* in the subsection *Foliolatae*, but the majority of herbarium specimens that I have seen have divided leaflets, which would place them in the *Dissectifoliae*, together with the closely related *P. clusii*.

Paeonia anomala

Paeonia anomala is one of the most widespread of all peonies, occupying a broad swathe from the Ural Mountains in the west to the Kola Peninsula in northern Russia, east to the Gobi Desert and then south to the Tien Shan Mountains in Kazakhstan. *Paeonia anomala* is very similar to the eastern species *P. veitchii*, but it has a solitary flower and no side buds. It grows on rocky hillsides, on steppe grassland and in coniferous woodland.

First described by Carl Linnaeus in 1771, it grows to a height of 50 CM (20 IN.) and has biternate leaves with deeply divided narrowly oblong leaflets, which are drawn out into a narrow tip. The leaves are dark green above and glaucous below with small hairs running down the main veins on the upper side of the leaves. The leaf segments measure up to 10 CM (4 IN.) long and 0.4–1.5 CM (0.16–0.6 IN.) in width. The flowers are larger than those of *P. veitchii*, 7–9 CM (2.8–3.5 IN.) across, deep red or pink in colour with slightly wavy petals and 3–5 glabrous carpels. *Paeonia anomala* can be distinguished from *P. veitchii* by having only one flower to a stem. The leaves have good autumn colour, turning a bright shade of orange-yellow in autumn. It is diploid (2N=10).

The botanical variety *intermedia* has a wide distribution from the Altai Mountains in Siberia to the Kola Peninsula and south to Turkestan. Stern (1946) distinguished it from the typical form because it has tomentose carpels. Hong De-Yuan and Pan Kai-Yu (2004) have raised var. *intermedia* to the level of a separate species, which they have called *Paeonia intermedia*. This can be distinguished by having fusiform (tapering at the top and bottom) or tuberous roots, rather than carrot-shaped as in *P. anomala*. They believe that the hairiness of the carpels is a bad diagnostic feature because plants can be found with hairy and glabrous carpels in the same population of *P. anomala*.

Paeonia anomala is easy to grow but it needs full sunshine and a well-drained position. It does best on acid or neutral soils, but will also tolerate slightly alkaline conditions.

Most botanists consider that *Paeonia hybrida* is a natural hybrid between *P. anomala* and *P. tenuifolia*, although Lynch had long ago (1890) reported that he had seen it growing in the Caucasus. Halda (1997) considers

Subsection *Dissectifoliae* includes species such as *Paeonia officinalis*, whose leaves are divided into twenty or more leaflets.

Contrary to general belief there are pink forms of *Paeonia anomala*, although most wild specimens have single red flowers.

Paeonia hybrida may be a natural hybrid between *P. anomala* and *P. tenuifolia*.

The leaves of *Paeonia officinalis* are deeply divided ...

... as are those of *Paeonia arietina*. (This plant is 'Mother of Pearl'.)

that it is a synonym of var. *intermedia*, but it is much taller than *P. anomala* and has narrower leaf segments. It has bright crimson-red flowers and tomentose carpels.

Paeonia arietina

This beautiful peony was originally described as an independent species, but in 1964 Cullen and Heywood reduced it to the status of a subspecies within *Paeonia mascula*.

To my mind, *Paeonia arietina* is very different from *P. mascula*, with a greater number of leaf segments, hairy stems, petioles and leaves. The carpels are also quite distinctive, pubescent and strongly recurved. From a morphological perspective *P. arietina* appears closer to *P. officinalis* subsp. *villosa* than *P. mascula* and I have therefore decided to opt for specific status. I also regard it as belonging to subsection *Dissectifoliae*, rather than the *Foliolatae* on the basis of the number of leaf segments in *P. arietina*. My decision is supported by the work of Sang *et al.* (1997) whose ITS phylogeny suggests that *P. arietina*, *P. officinalis* and *P. parnassica* are hybrid species with the same parent. They also found that *P. arietina*, *P. officinalis* subsp. *humilis*, *P. officinalis* and *P. parnassica* have identical ITS and matK sequences. If this is the case *P. arietina* cannot be a subspecies of *P. mascula*.

Paeonia arietina grows to a height of 75 CM (30 IN.) and has sparsely villous stems and petioles. The leaves are biternate and divided into 12–15 narrow or broadly elliptic or oblong leaflets, which measure 7.7–13.5 × 2.5–6.5 CM (3.03–5.3 × 1.0–2.75 IN.). The leaves are dark green and glabrous above, but glaucous and obviously villous below. It has beautiful flowers, which can vary in colour from white or pink to dark red, with yellow anthers and red filaments. The carpels have a dark brown tomentum and are strongly recurved, like a ram's horn. The leaves turn a wonderful shade of pinkish brown in autumn.

Stern (1946) and his team mainly worked with herbarium specimens and this led them to believe that *Paeonia arietina* was native to Greece. However, subsequent study of live specimens by Tzanoudakis (1977) revealed that the Greek specimens were actually a new species, which he called *P. parnassica*, after the place where it was first collected. Davis and

Stearn (1984) have determined that *P. arietina* does not occur in Greece, but it is clearly closely related to *P. parnassica*. Further research is clearly needed to determine the distribution of *P. arietina*, but if the existing data can be believed it occurs in Armenia, Crete, Italy, Syria, Turkey and the former Yugoslavia.

At one time there were many different clones of this species, but most of these seem to have disappeared from cultivation. Of the few that survive, 'Mother of Pearl' has pale pink flowers, while those of the vigorous 'Northern Glory' are magenta-pink. A particularly attractive form of *P. arietina* can be found growing at the Royal Botanic Gardens Kew, in London. Originally labelled as *P. orientalis*, this magnificent peony has wavy pink petals. It is tetraploid (2N=20).

Paeonia clusii comes from the island of Crete. It cannot tolerate being wet during the summer, when it is dormant, so is difficult to grow unless you have an alpine house.

Paeonia clusii

Paeonia clusii is a particularly lovely species that occurs naturally on the Greek islands of Crete and Karpathos in the Mediterranean Sea. Most specimens are diploid with 10 chromosomes, but according to Davis and Stearn (1984) those in Eastern Crete are tetraploid with 20 chromosomes, which suggests that they may be allotetraploid (a hybrid between two different species). It grows among dry riverbeds, scrub and on rocky ground, at altitudes of 200–1900 M (656–6200 FT.). As far as we know the French naturalist Pierre Belon first recorded *P. clusii* in 1553, but it was not until 1817 that Franz Sieber collected specimens. It was originally called *P. cretica*, but this had to be changed when it was discovered that the name had already been used to describe another species. In 1940 Frederick Stern and William Stearn named it after Charles de L'Escluse (1526–1609), one of Europe's first naturalists.

Paeonia clusii has glabrous, pink or purplish tinged stems and relatively large pure white or pink-tinged flowers, which can measure as much as 10 CM (4 IN.) across. The plant has a rather spreading habit and may reach a height of 35 CM (14 IN.). The biternate, greyish green leaves have 30 or more narrowly oblong or elliptic leaflets, which taper to an acute or acuminate tip. The carpels are covered with a thick white tomentum and surrounded by orange-yellow anthers with pink filaments. The majority of the plants on Crete have white flowers, but at the east end of the island there are populations with white and pink flowers (J. Fielding, *personal communication*). This may be due to natural variation, but it is more likely the result of out-breeding with another species that has now disappeared from the island. White flowers occur because the gene for manufacturing magenta pigment is absent in these plants, while the yellow colour in *P. mlokosewitschii* and the *P. wittmanniana* complex is caused by the presence of flavonoid pigments. It is diploid and tetraploid (2N=10+20).

In the last few years *Paeonia clusii* has started to become more readily available, but many of these plants are probably hybrids with *P. officinalis*. They are more vigorous than the true species, but are superficially similar and more suited to normal growing conditions in a temperate climate. I used to think that this species could only be grown in an alpine house, but experience has proved otherwise. *Paeonia clusii* will tolerate a few degrees of frost, but the plant must be kept dry during the summer when it is dormant and needs very well-drained soil. Dig a hole and fill it with a mixture of equal proportions of sand, topsoil and grit or fine gravel. It starts to grow in January and the young foliage will need some protection from frosts.

The single red form of *Paeonia officinalis* was grown in medieval gardens. The sticky liquid on the petals is nectar, which attracts pollinating insects.

Paeonia mollis

Paeonia mollis is a very vigorous, free-flowering species, which can grow to a height of approximately 45 cm (18 in.). It has glabrous or softly hairy stems, with bluish green, biternate leaves, divided into many sessile leaflets with decurrent edges. The leaves are glabrous and often glaucous above, paler beneath with a covering of long white hairs.

In late spring it produces masses of bright magenta or more rarely white flowers, borne on short stems. There are 2–3 densely white tomentose carpels, surrounded by numerous yellow anthers with yellow or red filaments. It is very easy to grow and may be a hybrid between *P. officinalis* and *P. arietina*. It appears to be self-fertile and, contrary to most published descriptions, produces plenty of seed. It is tetraploid (2N=20).

Paeonia officinalis

Peonies have been widely cultivated in Europe since medieval times. Male peonies (*P. mascula* subsp. *mascula*) were mainly grown in physic gardens for use as medicinal herbs, but the female peony—*Paeonia officinalis* subsp. *officinalis*—was more popular as a decorative plant.

The female peony is often illustrated in medieval paintings, but the form shown always has single red flowers, rather than the magenta-pink that can be found in modern botanic gardens. One of the earliest representations of a peony in European art can be seen in a painting known as *The Garden of Paradise* by an unknown Rhenish artist and dated to 1410–1420 (see Hobhouse, 1992). This shows the single red form of the female peony growing in a meadow (a "flowery mead") with cowslips (*Primula veris*), bearded iris (*Iris germanica*), lily-of-the-valley (*Convallaria majalis*), spring snowflake (*Leucojum vernum*) and wild strawberries (*Fragaria vesca*). The plant also appears in an oil painting called *The Virgin of the Rosegarden*, by Martin Schongauer, which is dated to 1473. It seems likely that medieval gardeners collected these red-flowered forms in preference to those with magenta flowers, which are now more widespread in nature. Most European floras mention that there are white-flowered forms of *Paeonia officinalis* subsp. *officinalis*, but these are now extremely rare because of over collection.

Many different forms of *Paeonia officinalis* seem to have appeared in European gardens and they were avidly collected until they fell from favour when the fragrant Chinese peony (*P. lactiflora*) became readily available in the nineteenth century. Many of the forms had already disappeared by the time that George Anderson's monograph about peonies was published in 1817. However he says that "Mr Sabine had the good fortune to discover one in the corner of an old garden at Great Berkhampstead in Hertfordshire, where it possibly had remained undisturbed many years." Anderson also says that "an abundant supply, of the plants of this variety, had been imported from Holland since the Peace" (this presumably refers to the end of the Napoleonic wars).

The majority of modern gardeners are familiar with the extremely vigorous 'Rubra Plena', but the medieval plant was far more delicate. The single red form, which I have called 'Rubra', appears to be the form that is illustrated in medieval paintings and makes an ideal plant for small gardens. It is far less vigorous than 'Rubra Plena' and occupies less space when it is fully grown. It has single cardinal red flowers and more delicate mid green foliage.

'Rubra Plena' AGM is one of the most widespread of all peonies and survives both neglect and abuse. It is widely grown in Europe and the United States of America, where it is known as the Memorial Day peony. Its origins are unknown, but it was certainly in existence in the latter part of the sixteenth century and is illustrated in a seventeenth century painting by Johann Walter (1604–1677), which now resides in the Bibliothéque Nationale de France.

John Parkinson (1629) says that

This double Peonie as well as the former single, is so frequent in everie Garden of note, through every Countrey, that it is almost labour in vaine to describe it: but yet because I use not to passe over any plant so slightly, I will set down the description briefly, in regard it is so common. It is very like unto the former single female Peony, both in stalkes and leaves, but that it groweth somewhat higher, and the leaves are of a fresher green colour: the flowers at the tops of the stalkes are very large, thicke and double (no flower that I know so faire, great, and a double; but not abiding blowne above eight or ten daies) of a more reddish purple colour then the former female kinde, and of a sweeter sent: after these flowers are past, sometimes come good seed, which being sowne, bring forth some single flowers, and some double: the roots are tuberous, like unto the former female.

This old peony is a remarkable plant and one that we take so much for granted. It is one of the few plants that will survive in a neglected or abandoned garden and will tolerate drought and almost anything else that is thrown at it. If it was rare I am sure that it would command a high price and would be highly sought after.

Several people have suggested that 'Rubra Plena' exhibits a phenomenon called "hybrid vigour" and it has been proposed that 'Rubra Plena' is actually a hybrid between *Paeonia peregrina* and the single red form of *P. officinalis* subsp. *officinalis*. While it is difficult to prove this hypothesis, there is no doubt that 'Rubra Plena' does have some characteristics of *P. peregrina*, such as occasionally having emarginate (notched), glossy leaflets. It flowers approximately two weeks after the single form of *P. officinalis* and shortly before *P. peregrina*. It has large double flowers with deep cardinal red petals and will grow happily in most soils.

'Rubra Plena' has massive crown-shaped flowers with large, rounded guard petals. The shape of the flower depends upon its position on the stem, the leading bud producing a very large, fully double flower with whorls of large outward-pointing petals, which sit on a ring of very narrow reddish purple staminodes. Staminodes are usually absent from the smaller flowers produced by the side buds. Functional stamens are normally absent, but the tomentose carpels are very large with red sickle-shaped styles. The flowers open a rich cardinal red, but become purple-red after a few days, the petals are often streaked with darker stripes. As Parkinson says, the flowers last for just over a week, whereupon the petals fall like so much purple confetti. One of the biggest problems with the plant is its annoying habit of collapsing when the flowers are fully developed, particularly after heavy rain. This can be prevented if you support the stems with wire stakes.

Paeonia officinalis subsp. *officinalis*

The wild form of *P. officinalis* is an herbaceous perennial, which grows to a height of 70 CM (28 IN.) and has slightly villous stems, which become glabrous as the season progresses. It has biternate leaves, which are mid green and glabrous above and slightly paler beneath, villous or occasionally glabrous. The leaves are divided into 14–35 narrow-elliptic or narrow-oblong segments with acute tips and measure 7–12.5 × 1.2–3.3 CM (2.75–4.9 × 0.47–1.25 IN.). The petioles and petiolules are glabrous or slightly villous. The flowers measure 9–13 CM (3.5–5 IN.) across, bright red, magenta-pink or occasionally white, with broad spreading obovate petals, yellow anthers and red filaments. Each flower has 2–3 tomentose carpels. It flowers from the end of April to the beginning of May (late spring). Like all the subspecies it is tetraploid (2N=20).

While the majority of the old forms of *Paeonia officinalis* have been lost, those that survive are still very good garden plants. 'Alba Plena' is similar to 'Rubra Plena', but is less vigorous and has pure white flowers. 'Rosea Plena' AGM is more robust than 'Alba Plena' and has deep pink flowers, with enlarged, nicely rounded guard petals. 'Anemoniflora Rosea' is a dwarf plant with bright Tyrian purple petals and a mass of yellow-edged Tyrian purple staminodes. Perhaps the best cultivar of all is 'Lize van Veen', which has very large deep pink flowers, which quickly fade to blush pink and finally become pure white with hints of blush where the petals are protected from the full power of the sun.

Paeonia officinalis subsp. banatica

This rare subspecies is named after the Banat region of Eastern Europe where it was first recorded in 1828. It occurs in Hungary, Serbia and Romania and is distinguished from the rest of the species by having a terminal leaflet that is divided into two or three lobes.

It grows to a height of 60 CM (24 IN.). The leaflets are elliptic or ovate and it has bright red flowers and tomentose carpels. Phylogenetic analysis suggests that *Paeonia officinalis* subsp. *banatica* could be a hybrid between *P. mairei* and a group that includes *P. arietina* and *P. officinalis* (Sang, 1995). One weakness of this argument is that *P. mairei* is endemic to China, while its supposed offspring is confined to a small area of Eastern Europe. It is a tetraploid (2N=20).

Paeonia officinalis subsp. humilis

As the name suggests, subsp. *humilis* (syn. subsp. *microcarpa*) is smaller than the type with less deeply divided leaves and broader leaflets with a blunt apex. The young foliage is greyish green in colour and flushed with purplish red. The stems and petioles are hairy and the underside of the leaves varies from being villous to densely tomentose. It has bright magenta flowers and glabrous carpels. It makes a superb rock garden plant and, given the correct conditions, will self seed. It is tetraploid (2N=20).

Paeonia officinalis subsp. villosa

Subspecies *villosa* is similar to subsp. *humilis*, but has bright magenta flowers with hairy carpels. A good plant for rock gardens, as it is very decorative and in the right conditions will self seed. It is tetraploid (2N=20).

Paeonia officinalis subsp. *humilis* has vivid magenta flowers. It makes a good specimen for the rock garden and will self seed if given the opportunity.

Paeonia parnassica

This rare Greek peony was first collected in 1854 on Mount Parnassos, in southern Greece; but because the flowers had lost their colour, the dried herbarium specimens at the Royal Botanic Gardens Kew were thought to be of *Paeonia arietina*. Tzanoudakis (1977) realized it was a new species after he collected some fresh specimens.

Paeonia parnassica is endemic to the mountains of southern Greece, where it grows in *Abies cephalonica* forest, in damp meadows and among limestone rocks, at altitudes of 800–1300 M (2625–4265 FT.). It grows to a height of 65 CM (26 IN.), has hirsute stems and biternate leaves. These are green above, greyish green and pilose beneath, divided into 9–13 leaflets. The leaves are purplish green when they appear in the spring. The leaflets range in shape from obovate to narrowly elliptic or lanceolate and have acute or shortly acuminate tips. The flowers are unusual because, uniquely among herbaceous peonies, they are dark blackish red, and measure 8–12 CM (3.1–4.7 IN.) across. It has 2–3 tomentose carpels, yellow anthers and purple filaments. It is a tetraploid (2N=20).

This peony starts to grow early in the year and flowers from April to May (mid to late spring). It is a very difficult plant to grow and needs a warm position with very well-drained soil. The plant will die if the soil is too wet in the spring or summer.

Paeonia peregrina is also known as the red peony of Constantinople. It has bright red flowers and was introduced into Europe in the late sixteenth century.

Paeonia peregrina produces adventitious buds at the ends of the roots and will eventually form a diffuse clump of erect stems.

Paeonia peregrina

The "red peony of Constantinople" has been a popular garden plant in Europe since it was introduced from Istanbul in 1583. It was introduced into Austria in the late-sixteenth century and then spread across the rest of Western Europe. It was first illustrated in Charles l'Escluse's *Rariorum Plantarum Historia* (1601) and there is a superb illustration in Besler's *Hortus Eystettensis* (1613).

The plant is quite widespread and occurs in Albania, Bulgaria, Greece, Italy, Romania, Serbia and Turkey. It was the first foreign species of peony to enter cultivation and its name means "exotic or foreign". The most widely cultivated clone is 'Sunbeam', which was grown from seed collected near Smyrna (now Izmir), in western Turkey. The English nurseryman Peter Barr (1826–1909) collected a lot of different forms of the plant in Turkey, but very few of these have survived to the present day. Older books often refer to it by the obsolete names of *Paeonia decora* and *P. lobata*.

Paeonia peregrina grows to a height of 50 CM (20 IN.) and has glabrous stems. The lower leaves are biternate and divided into 15–17 segments, which are deeply emarginate at the tips. The leaves are glossy and bright green above, glaucous and glabrous beneath, or slightly pilose. The flowers measure up to 12 CM (4.7 IN.) across and have strongly concave, deep ruby red petals. It has 3–4 densely tomentose carpels with white hairs, golden yellow anthers and red filaments. It is tetraploid (2N=20). It flowers slightly later than *P. officinalis* and looks wonderful when planted in light shade.

There are several named cultivars such as 'Sunbeam', and 'Otto Froebel'. *Paeonia peregrina* has the ability to produce very long roots, which may extend 40–50 CM (16–20 IN.) beyond the crown of the plant. These are capable of producing adventitious buds and will often grow into an independent plant if they are separated from their parent. This makes propagation significantly easier, but it does mean plants make a less compact clump than most peonies. This species used to be widespread in Turkey, but excessive harvesting of wild populations for cut flowers has meant that it is starting to become rarer. In Bulgaria 7500 kg. (7.4 long tons) of cut flowers were exported in 1996 and 1000 kg. (1 long ton) of roots were dug up for home consumption. This type of exploitation is not sustainable and threatens the long-term survival of this species in the wild.

'Otto Froebel' AGM is very different to the other forms of *Paeonia peregrina* and is sometimes referred to as *P. lobata* in older books. The plant has cup-shaped, coral pink flowers with long stamens and tomentose carpels; the colour of the flowers cannot be adequately described from the *RHS Colour Chart*. The anthers are golden yellow and the filaments orange-red. The inner petals are slightly smaller than the outer ones. The colour of the flowers is unique among the species and has been used to produce

'Otto Froebel' is a striking form of *Paeonia peregrina* and has been widely used to produce hybrid peonies with coral red flowers.

many hybrids, such as 'Cytherea', 'Coral Charm' and 'Lovely Rose'. It makes a good garden plant and looks absolutely stunning when backlit by low sunlight. It has glossy mid-green leaves with deeply notched lobes. It seems likely that 'Otto Froebel' was collected in Turkey at the end of the nineteenth century and is listed as "new" in Barr and Sons' 1899 catalogue.

Paeonia rhodia

Paeonia rhodia is a rare endemic peony from the Greek island of Rhodes. Some botanists treat it as a subspecies of *P. clusii*, but it is quite distinct and I believe that it should remain an independent species.

The plant grows to a height of 38 cm (15 in.) and has hairless, brownish red stems. The leaves are dark green and glabrous above, pale green below and divided into 12–30 ovate to oblong-elliptic or lanceolate leaflets, with acute or acuminate tips. The leaflets are sessile or have a short petiole. The flowers are pure white and measure up to 7.5 cm (3 in.) across, with yellow anthers and red filaments, and 2–5 tomentose carpels with reddish purple styles. It is diploid (2N=10).

Paeonia rhodia is hardy when dormant, but it starts to grow very early in the year and the foliage is consequently vulnerable to frost damage. It flowers from late February to the end of April and has one flower per stem. *Paeonia rhodia* is very difficult to grow because it needs dry conditions during the summer months. It will grow best in a raised bed, because if the soil gets too wet the roots will rot and the plant will die.

Paeonia sinjiangensis

Paeonia sinjiangensis was first described by Pan (in Wang, 1979), who says that it is related to *P. anomala* and *P. veitchii*, but differs from the former in having straight roots and from the latter in possessing single flowers. Its branches are terete and the carpels are glabrous. These differences seem insufficient to justify describing it as a distinct species and Hong de Yuan *et al.* (2001a) have treated it as a synonym of *P. anomala*.

Paeonia ×smouthii

This peony has never been found growing in the wild and is thought to be a hybrid between *Paeonia lactiflora* and *P. tenuifolia*. It was probably named after Monsieur Smout, a chemist from Malines. It makes a good garden plant, growing to a height of 45 cm

Paeonia ×smouthii has never been found in the wild, but it makes a colourful subject for the garden.

Paeonia sterniana is rare in cultivation, but makes a good plant for the rock garden. It is smaller than the closely related *P. emodi*.

(18 IN.) with deeply divided, dark green leaves. Its flowers are crimson-red measuring up to 8 CM (3.1 IN.) across. The plant is diploid (2N=10).

Paeonia sterniana

This interesting peony was discovered in 1938, growing in the Tsangpo Valley in southeastern Tibet (Xizang). Until recently the only known plant in cultivation was growing at the Royal Botanic Garden Edinburgh, but the garden distributed seed to several people in the late 1990s and it should become more readily available in the future.

Ludlow and Taylor (1938), who discovered *Paeonia sterniana*, said that it grew to a height of 90 CM (3 FT.) in the wild, but the plant at Edinburgh is much smaller at 45 CM (18 IN.). The entire plant is glabrous with deeply divided leaves, which are dark green above and glaucous beneath. Each stem produces a single white flower, approximately 5–8 CM (2–3.1 IN.) across, with four lanceolate sepals and white stamen filaments. The carpels are green and glabrous with creamy white styles. *P. sterniana* is easy to grow, but needs well-drained soil and makes an ideal plant for the rock garden. It grows in woods at altitudes of 2800–3500 M (9200–11,500 FT.).

Phylogenetic analysis suggests that *Paeonia sterniana* may be a hybrid between *P. emodi* and *P. mairei* (Sang, 1995).

Paeonia tenuifolia

Variously known as the fern-leaf, fringed or the Adonis peony, *Paeonia tenuifolia* grows on the steppes of Hungary, the Ukraine and Romania. The species is unique in having tripinnately lobed foliage, divided three times to form very narrow linear segments, measuring 0.75–2.00 MM (0.03–0.08 IN.) in width with a sub-acute or obtuse tip. The leaves are grass green when they emerge in the spring, becoming dark green, glabrous above and somewhat glaucous beneath. Wild plants have single, deep red flowers with yellow anthers and similarly coloured filaments. 'Plena' used to be the most common

Paeonia tenuifolia makes a good plant for the front of an herbaceous border.

cultivar in cultivation, with double deep red flowers, but the increased supply of wild-collected seed may mean that the majority of plants available for purchase from nurseries will now be single. 'Rosea' has pink and 'Alba' white flowers. It is diploid (2N=10).

Botanists in Eastern Europe and Russia recognize three additional species, but their colleagues in the West have not generally accepted them. The latter claim that they are synonyms of *Paeonia tenuifolia*, while botanists such as Kemularia-Nathadze (1961) make the valid point that their colleagues have not studied enough specimens and that there are very few Caucasian peonies in western herbaria.

Paeonia carthalinica grows in the oak-hornbeam forests of Georgia and ranges in height from 30–100 CM (1–3.3 FT.). It has broader leaf segments than *P. tenuifolia*, measuring from 0.5–1.0 CM (0.2–0.4 IN.) across and larger, dark purple flowers.

Paeonia biebersteiniana is endemic to the montane steppes of the North Caucasus. Most western botanists consider that it is a synonym of *P. tenuifolia*, but Kemularia-Nathadze describes it as having broader leaf segments, 0.3–1.0 CM (0.1–0.4 IN.) in width. The leaves are greyish green and either glabrous or have short hairs growing along the veins on the upper surface of the leaf. It grows to a height of 20–70 CM (8–28 IN.) and has bright red flowers.

The cotyledons of young seedlings of *Paeonia tenuifolia* are raised above the ground when the seed germinates, whereas in most other species of peony (with the exception of *P. brownii*) they are retained in the seed as storage organs (Saunders and Stebbins, 1938).

Paeonia veitchii

This pretty peony looks very similar to *Paeonia anomala*, but usually has at least two flower buds instead of the one in *P. anomala*. Hong De-Yuan and Pan Kai-Yu (2004) treat *P. veitchii* as a synonym of *P. anomala*, but the presence of more than one flower to a stem seems constant in the species and justifies keeping them separate.

The plant is native to Gansu, Shensi and Sichuan Provinces in China, where it grows in subalpine meadows and scrub at altitudes of 2400–3000 M (7900–9800ft.). It forms a compact clump and has stems measuring up to 60 CM (24 IN.) high. The leaves are bronzy green when they are young, but turn dark green as they age, with a line of small bristles along the midrib and main veins; they are pale green and glabrous beneath. Each leaf is divided into 8–9 oblong or elliptic segments, which are drawn out into a long acuminate tip. The leaf segments measure 5–15 CM (2–6 IN.) long and 0.5–2 CM (0.2–0.8 IN.) wide. The flowers are described as being peony purple, but they also occur in shades of magenta and pink, with yellow anthers and pink filaments. The carpels are densely tomentose. There is also a very rare white form, var. *alba*. It is diploid (2N=10).

Paeonia veitchii var. *woodwardii* is a slightly smaller plant, which grows to a height of 30 CM (12 IN.). It was first collected in 1912 by George Fenwick-Owen, who found the plant growing in a tub at the Choni Monastery in Gansu Province. It was named after Robert Woodward, who first grew it from seed and was killed in the Second World War. Var. *woodwardii* is endemic to Gansu and Northwest Sichuan Provinces.

Both the species and var. *woodwardii* are happy growing in most garden soils, but do best in full sunshine; the latter is particularly suitable for a rock garden.

Most botanists consider that *P. beresowskii* is a synonym of *P. veitchii*. The plant was originally described by Komarov in 1921 and is said to have deeply notched petals and cream-coloured stigmata.

Paeonia veitchii var. *woodwardii* is more readily available than the typical form of the species and slightly smaller.

Paeonia veitchii is compact and smaller than most peony species, which makes it an ideal plant for the rock garden.

The Chinese peony was originally called *P. albiflora* (the name means white flower) but was renamed after it was discovered that it had previously been called *P. lactiflora*.

Chapter 5
Cultivars of *Paeonia lactiflora*

Paeonia lactiflora was first introduced into Europe towards the end of the eighteenth century and has given rise to several thousand cultivars. It is one of the easiest peonies to grow and will tolerate a wide range of soil conditions. While it grows best in fertile, well-drained slightly calcareous soil, it can also be grown in sandy loam or heavy clay. It is not suitable for planting in areas that are prone to flooding and the roots will quickly die if the soil remains waterlogged. However, it has proved to be an excellent garden plant and is widely cultivated for the production of cut flowers. The species is valued for its ability to produce a wide range of different flower types, many of which are highly perfumed.

The Chinese peony was first described as *Paeonia lactiflora* in 1776 by the German botanist Peter Pallas (1741–1811) who found it growing in Russia's Lake Baikal Province (Pallas, 1776). However twelve years later in 1788 he seems to have forgotten about his earlier encounter when he renamed another specimen *P. albiflora*. The plant was known by the latter name for more than a century, but the error was discovered and the original name took precedence. The decision to revoke the original name caused uproar in horticultural circles and many gardeners and nurserymen could not understand why it was necessary. Some nurseries refused to accept the new name and for many years they continued to list the plant as *P. albiflora*.

George Anderson's 1817 monograph is an invaluable source of information about the early introductions of this species into the United Kingdom. The first plant appears to have been 'Fragrans', which was introduced in 1805 by Sir Joseph Banks and, as the name suggests, had strongly fragrant flowers. This was followed in 1808 by 'Whitleyi', a double cultivar with white crown-shaped flowers, and in 1810 by the watermelon red 'Humei'. These three plants are thought to be Chinese cultivars, but Anderson says that some of the plants introduced into the U.K. were grown from wild-collected seed. While further plants were imported in subsequent years from China, these three plants were widely distributed around Europe and it seems likely that they are the ancestors of most modern cultivars of this species.

The Start of Peony Breeding

Paeonia lactiflora (*Shao-yao*) has been cultivated in China for many centuries, but it has never approached the popularity of the tree peony. The plant was initially grown for its medicinal properties and it only started to be appreciated as an ornamental during the Sung Dynasty (AD 960–1279), when production was concentrated in the city of Yangchow and there were approximately forty cultivars. According to the *Chhün Fang*, which was written in the eleventh century AD (in Needham *et al.*, 1986): "It grows in clusters about 1 to 2ft high, each stem having three branches and five leaves resembling those of the *mu-tan* but narrower and longer. The flowers bloom in the early summer, red, white, purple, etc. in colour. The yellow ones are generally considered to be the best. There are single (*tan*) varieties, double ones (*chhien yeh*) and piled-up double ones (*lou tzu*). The seeds are like those of the tree-peony but smaller." Pallas is thought to have introduced *P. lactiflora* into Europe in *circa* 1784, but there is no record of his plants being used to produce new cultivars. Modern peony breeding seems to have started when French breeders acquired plants from Great Britain. The first person to produce his own seedlings of *Paeonia lactiflora* was Nicolas Lemon (1787–?), who lived in Porte St. Denis, near Paris. In 1824 Lemon introduced the famous 'Edulis Superba' and 'Grandiflora Nivea Plena', both of which are still widely grown.

Modeste Guerin (?–1866) started introducing new cultivars in 1835, after acquiring further peonies from China and Japan. Guerin's work is considered important because he was able to introduce yellow shades into his lactifloras, which included 'Grandiflora Lutescens', with blush-coloured guard petals and a yellow centre, and 'Triomphe de Paris', which had white flowers with a yellowish heart (Harding, 1993).

In 1850 Jacques Calot (?–1875) acquired the peony collection of the Comte de Cussy, a French aristocrat and keen amateur gardener, who had imported plants from China and is thought to have bred his own cultivars. Calot produced three extremely popular peonies, namely 'Duchesse de Nemours', 'Philomèle' and 'Reine Hortense'. In 1872 Calot's collection was purchased by Felix Crousse (1840–1925), who lived in Nancy. Crousse introduced many of the former owner's plants as well as his own, including 'Avalanche', the eternally popular 'Monsieur Jules Elie' and 'Felix Crousse'. In 1849 Victor Lemoine (1823–1911) acquired Crousse's collection and went on to produce 'Sarah Bernhardt', probably the most successful peony of all time, and several other outstanding plants such as 'Primevère', 'La France' and 'Solange'.

Auguste Dessert (1859–1929) spent most of his life in the town of Chenonceaux, where he worked with his grandfather Etienne Mechin (1815–1895), who had earlier purchased Modeste Guerin's collection. Dessert and Mechin produced a very large number of magnificent plants, among them 'Germaine Bigot', 'Laura Dessert' and 'La Fiancée'.

The English Perspective

The English nursery of Kelway and Son was once one of the largest in the world, supplying a wide range of vegetables and ornamental plants. The nursery at Langport in Somerset was first established in 1851 by James Kelway (1815–1899) and in its heyday employed approximately 400 people. Kelway and his descendants bred delphiniums, peonies and many other plants. The company supplied most of the large estates in the United Kingdom, but went into decline after the First World War, when Britain's aristocracy were subject to punitive death duties. The Kelways introduced approximately 500 cultivars of Chinese peony including the famous 'Baroness Schroeder', 'Lady Alexandra Duff' and 'Kelway's Glorious'. These plants have stood the test of time and they remain extremely popular.

James Kelway claimed he had crossed the peony from the Island of Steep Holm (*P. mascula* subsp. *mascula*) with the Chinese peony (Paul, 1890). This is impossible to prove without gene sequencing, but there is no doubt that several of his early cultivars do have very dark magenta flowers and unusual foliage, rather different from that of most *P. lactiflora* cultivars. Several people, including Arthur Saunders, have disputed Kelway's claim, but if it is true then he was the first person successfully to cross two species of peony.

Breeding in the U.S.A.

Peonies are extremely popular in the U.S.A. and it is now the main centre for peony breeding. A large number of cultivars were raised during the twentieth century but the industry started in 1856 when M. A. Terry (1826–1909) purchased approximately thirty cultivars of *Paeonia lactiflora* from William Prince, a nurseryman based in Flushing, New York. Terry collected the seed from his plants and according to Wister (1995) raised several thousand seedlings. A contemporary of Terry was John Richardson (1798–1887) of Dorchester, Massachusetts who was raising peonies in 1857.

In the twentieth century the most important breeders were Robert Tischler, who introduced 'Douglas Brand'; Orville Fay who was responsible for several popular hybrid peonies, such as 'Paula Fay' and 'Prairie Moon'; and William Bockstoce (1876–1963), who bred 'Diana Parks' and 'Bess Bockstoce'. Myron Bigger earned his living by growing cut flowers, but won Gold Medals from the American Peony Society for the double red 'Kansas' and pink Japanese peony 'Westerner'. In Minnesota Oliver Brand (1844–1921) and his son Archie (1871–1953) introduced fifty-three cultivars, many of which have been very successful commercially; they include the popular 'Krinkled White' and the salmon pink 'Hansina Brand' which won the APS Grand Champion Trophy on three occasions.

In Sarcoxie, Missouri, Gilbert Wild and his family raised approximately forty cultivars, including 'Cherry Royal', and marketed several peonies on behalf of other breeders. Among them were Edward Auten (1881–1974), who introduced many fascinating hybrid peonies such as 'Chocolate Soldier' and 'Chief Justice'; Colonel Jesse Nicholls (1874–1961), who introduced 'Opal Hamilton' and 'Hit Parade'; and Dr. Earle White (?–1966), who was responsible for the yellow hybrid 'Claire de Lune'. Gilbert H. Wild and Son was for many years the largest peony nursery in the world and still sells substantial numbers of peonies and daylilies.

Thousands of other cultivars of *Paeonia lactiflora* have been raised during the past 150 years and there is not space for me to discuss all of those responsible; however to interested readers I recommend *Peonies* by A. Rogers (1995). The emphasis has now moved towards the breeding of hybrid peonies and intersectional hybrids, but breeders such as Roy Klehm are still introducing exciting new cultivars of *P. lactiflora* (see chapter 12).

Klehm and Don Hollingsworth have introduced a large number of peonies during the past ten years, but unfortunately very few of them are widely available yet. They have not only introduced new flower colours but have also improved stem strength, which makes them more suitable for cutting.

The speed of propagation is the main barrier to the rapid distribution of new peonies. Until recently it was not possible to micropropagate peonies and this limited the speed at which new cultivars could be introduced into the trade. Most herbaceous peonies are still propagated by division and it may take between ten and fifteen years before a new peony becomes readily available.

While the majority of breeders are currently concentrating on producing hybrid peonies, there is no doubt that *Paeonia lactiflora* still has plenty of potential for producing new cultivars.

The Character of the Flower

If the Chinese peony, *Paeonia lactiflora*, has a disadvantage it is the absence of a red pigment. Plant catalogues often describe Chinese peonies as having deep red flowers, but this is wishful thinking. The main pigment in this species is magenta, which appears in different hues. Flowers with small amounts of pigment appear pink, while those with large amounts are a deep purplish red. When the pigment is completely absent the flowers are white. The flower colour can vary considerably depending upon the quality of the light and it can also vary depending upon the amount of minerals in the soil in which the plant is growing. The best time to view peony flowers is in the early morning or late afternoon when the light is warmer. The yellow light brings the petals to life and imparts a warm glow to the centre of the flower.

In cultivars with double flowers the stamens and carpels are often transformed into petal-like structures, which are referred to respectively as staminodes and carpelodes. Staminodes are very common in semi-double and double lactifloras and are often edged with golden yellow pigment. This is derived from the transformation of the anthers and while these structures rarely produce viable pollen, they retain the yellow pigmentation of the functioning organs. Staminodes are often yellow towards their base and this imparts the golden yellow glow to the centre of many peony flowers. Carpelodes often have a light green base, and in white-flowered cultivars this imparts a green hue to the heart of the flower.

Chinese peonies make superb cut flowers and the French bred many new cultivars for this purpose towards the end of the nineteenth century. 'Sarah Bernhardt' is the most popular peony for cutting and many hectares are grown in Holland for this purpose. It is one of the cheapest peonies to purchase because it has been available for many years and the roots can be sold when plants are too old for commercial flower production. However, while it has beautiful, double, shell pink flowers, the stems are extremely weak and cannot support the weight of the fully developed blooms. The problem is not restricted to 'Sarah Bernhardt' and many nineteenth century cultivars of *P. lactiflora* have similarly weak stems. Aware of this problem Charles Klehm set out to breed peonies with strong stems, specifically for the cut-flower trade. These "Estate Peonies" do not need to be staked and some, such as 'Chiffon Parfait' and 'Dinner Plate', are far superior to 'Sarah Bernhardt'.

The Names

It was quite common in the nineteenth century for peonies to be named after prominent members of the aristocracy, who were often sufficiently flattered to buy large numbers of the plants. However, this could be a rather ephemeral association because the plants were often renamed when someone fell out of favour. It is quite common to find older cultivars from France and Britain sharing the same name; this can cause some confusion because one plant may be single, while the other is double. Many of these duplications have been resolved by the American Peony Society, but the date of introduction is not always recorded and this makes it difficult to determine which cultivar has priority. There is no doubt that some of the early cultivars are extremely good garden plants and bear comparison with most of their more recent cousins, however there are many others that should have been consigned to the compost heap years ago.

Cultivar Descriptions

The Chinese peonies are excellent garden plants and will bring a touch of elegance to any border. Some cultivars, such as 'Festiva Maxima' and 'Edulis Superba', were first raised over 150 years ago and represent extremely good value. However, if you are thinking about buying some Chinese peonies I would strongly advise you to visit a specialist nursery, where you will be able to see a large number of plants in flower. Peonies live for a long time and will only reach their prime when they are four or five years old.

The great majority of the descriptions I have made from living plants, however peony flowers vary according to the age of the plant, where it is planted and the mineral content of the soil. Fragrance can often be difficult to detect on wet windy days, but is very prominent when the weather improves. Cultivars of *P. lactiflora* are notoriously difficult to identify; if you are uncertain about a plant's identity the only way of being certain is to compare it with another of known identity.

For every entry in the Catalogue of Cultivars the name is followed by the breeder and the date of introduction where known. More details of flower forms, colour and times of flowering are given in chapter 2. Each description ends with the flowering season and the approximate height of a mature plant.

Catalogue of Cultivars

'Abalone Pearl' (Krekler, 1978)

Single with pearl pink flowers, golden yellow anthers and long pale yellow filaments. The carpels are hirsute with purple styles and sit on top of a purple-coloured staminoidal disc. Early season, 70 CM (28 IN.).

'Adolph Rousseau' (Dessert and Mechin, 1890)

Double flowers have large cardinal red petals with a satiny texture that alternate with rings of golden yellow stamens. The latter have short yellow filaments, which become red towards the base; some are developed into narrow staminodes. The carpels are pale green with pink styles. The fragrance is rather clinical. The plant is tall growing and free flowering, with dark green foliage and red-tinged stems, but needs staking. Midseason, 95 CM (3.1 FT.).

'Algae Adamson' (Kelway, 1893)

This is a pretty, bomb-shaped lactiflora with deep pink guard petals, which surround a ring of pale pink inner petals, slightly flushed with magenta. Some flowers have a further group of deep pink petals, which match the shade of the guard petals and unfurl from the centre. The outer carpels are slightly flattened, foliaceous and purple in colour with a yellow centre. The inner carpels are much smaller and tomentose. It is a moderately sized peony with strong fragrance, but rather weak stems. Midseason, 80 CM (32 IN.).

'Alice Harding' (Lemoine, 1922)

This popular double lactiflora has flesh pink guard petals and creamy white inner petals. The flowers have a sweet fragrance and open flesh pink, but the colour quickly fades in sun. It is said that Victor Lemoine, the plant's breeder, thought that 'Alice Harding' was his best introduction. Midseason, (1 M (3.3 FT.)

'Angel Cheeks' (Carl G. Klehm)

A delicately-coloured bomb-shaped peony with large, pale pink guard petals and a central raised mound of deep pink petaloids, which is surrounded by a collar of pale yellow petals. The flowers are slightly fragrant. Midseason, 70 CM (28 IN.).

'Auguste Dessert' (Dessert, 1920)

This is a very decorative semi-double lactiflora with strongly silvered, deep pink petals with streaks of magenta. There are two concentric rings of yellow stamens, with yellow filaments and small, purple, tomentose carpels with purple styles. The carpels sometimes develop into carpelodes. The flowers have a spicy fragrance. Mid to late season, 75 CM (30 IN.).

'Augustin d'Hour' (Calot, 1867)

Widely regarded as a landscape plant, this vigorous lactiflora has bomb-shaped flowers with deep magenta guard petals surrounding a mound of equally sized, deeply divided inner petals. There are no stamens. The carpels are green with extended styles, which are flattened and stained with magenta. The flowers become heavily silvered in sunshine and have little fragrance. Midseason, 1 M (3.3 FT.).

'Aureole' (Hollis, 1905)

Flowers are of Japanese form with deep magenta-pink guard petals and a centre of ivory white petaloids with wavy pink tips. Some of the outer petaloids may be tipped with yellow and appear to be partly functional. The carpels are pale green with magenta styles. As the flower ages the staminodes elongate and turn white with bright yellow bases. The carpels turn deep purple and have vivid magenta styles. This is a robust, rather pretty plant with deep green leaves and strong red stems, and no apparent fragrance. Early to midseason, 95 CM (3.1 FT.). Synonym 'Anne Lady Brocket'.

'Baroness Schroeder' (Kelway, 1889)

Raised at the end of the nineteenth century, 'Baroness Schroeder' is still one of the best peonies. The globe-shaped, double flowers open blush pink but the colour quickly fades to snow white. The very large flowers have a pleasant fragrance and their strong stems make them good for cutting. Mid to late season, 90 CM (3 FT.).

'Barrymore' (Kelway)

A pretty, pale pink Japanese-form lactiflora with cup-shaped flowers and a centre of golden yellow staminodes with gold edges. The scented flowers have pale green carpels with white styles. The guard petals are slightly wavy and fade to white in the sun. Side buds are very rare. Recommended. Late midseason, 85 CM (34 IN.).

'Boule de Neige' (Calot, 1867)

Large semi-double flowers, which open blush pink, fading to milky white, with long wavy staminodes borne on thin yellow filaments. On young flowers the staminodes have a pale yellow line down the centre. The large purple carpels have magenta styles, and the outer petals are very large and nicely rounded. The fragrant flowers are borne on strong stems and there are a lot of side buds. Midseason, 85 CM (34 in.).

'Bower of Roses' (Kelway, 1931)

Semi-double or Japanese flowers with deep magenta-pink, notched guard petals which contrast well with the coral pink inner petals, or staminodes. The inner petals lose their colour with age, becoming almost white with blush hints. The carpels are purple with long, pointed, magenta-coloured styles. Some of the flowers are almost double with large magenta carpelodes in the centre. It has strong stems and a slightly spicy fragrance. One of the last peonies to be introduced by the Kelway family. Early season, 1 M (3.3 FT.).

'Bowl of Beauty' (Hoogendoorn, 1949)

Justifiably popular, this Japanese-form peony has very large fuchsine rose guard petals and masses of upright creamy yellow staminodes, golden yellow at the base with wavy tips. The flowers, held on strong stems, can measure up to 30 CM (12 IN.) across and have pale pink carpels with magenta styles. Mid to late season, 90 CM (3 FT.).

'Calypso' (Andrews, 1925)

A bright and cheerful peony of Japanese form, it has large magenta-pink guard petals with deep magenta veins. In the centre are masses of yellow-tipped, magenta and buff staminodes each with a yellow streak down the middle. The carpels are green at the base and ivory white at the top, with ivory styles. Side buds are present and flowers have a slight fragrance. Mid to late season, 95 CM (3.1 FT.).

'Cascade' is a very underrated crown-shaped lactiflora with masses of white petals.

'Cascade' (Kelway)

This superb double peony is very under-rated and deserves to be more widely grown. Deep blush pink buds open to display crown-shaped flowers with nicely rounded, pale blush pink guard petals surrounding a collar of very narrow pale yellow staminodes. As the flower ages a crown of large, wavy, white petals develops from the centre. The carpels are green at the base, pink at the top with white styles. It has a few side buds. The flowers can be very large—up to 15 CM wide by 18 CM high (6 × 7 IN.)and fade to milky white in strong sunshine. It is only let down by a lack of fragrance. Mid to late season, 90 CM (3 FT.).

'Charlie's White' (Carl G. Klehm, 1951)

The substantial, pure white bomb-shaped flowers have large guard petals, surrounding a raised mass of smaller petals. The inner petals are golden yellow, imparting an attractive golden glow to the middle of the flower. It looks rather like a white version of 'Monsieur Jules Elie' and flowers at the same time. A very vigorous, strong-stemmed plant with slightly fragrant blooms, 'Charlie's White' has been very successful commercially and is widely grown as a cut flower. Early season, 1.2 M (4 FT.).

'Cheddar Charm' (Roy Klehm, 1985)

Bred in the Midwest of the U.S.A., this attractive anemone-form peony has masses of forked golden yellow staminodes, surrounded by a double ring of wavy white guard petals. Small white petals occur occasionally among the staminodes. The blooms are delicately fragrant and have strong stems. Midseason, 90 CM (3 FT.).

'Cheddar Cheese' (Carl G. Klehm, 1973)

'Cheddar Cheese' looks rather like a white plate with a pile of grated cheese on top. The slightly scented, double flowers have very large creamy white guard petals and a wide, rather flat mound of cheddar yellow staminodes. These are slightly wavy, with a firm texture and forked tips. Most of the carpels are converted into creamy white petals, which erupt from the centre of the flower, but a few remain with ivory white styles. The staminodes are bright yellow at the base, imparting a golden glow to the centre of the flower. The rather large, dark green leaves have red petioles. Midseason, 1 M (3.3 FT.).

'Chiffon Parfait'.
(Credit: Roy Klehm)

'Cheddar Charm'.
(Credit: Roy Klehm)

'Cherry Royal' (Wild, 1967)

The double, deep magenta-red flowers are almost crown-shaped and have a slight depression at the top. There are no stamens. Midseason, 80 CM (32 IN.).

'Chiffon Parfait' (Carl G. Klehm, 1981)

This peony is best described as a greatly improved 'Sarah Bernhardt' and deserves to be more widely grown. Bred by crossing 'Monsieur Jules Elie' with 'President Taft', it has massive ball-shaped flowers with numerous pale salmon pink petals. The flowers are fragrant and have strong stems, which makes it good for cutting. Very late season. 85 CM (34 IN.).

'Circus Clown' (Wild, 1970)

A vigorous Japanese-form lactiflora that has deep magenta-pink guard petals and a bold centre of wavy butter yellow staminodes. The central staminodes are broader and marked with pink stripes. It has pale green carpels and creamy white styles. Midseason, 90 CM (36 IN.).

'Claire Dubois' (Crousse, 1886)

Fragrant, crown-shaped double flowers have pale pink guard petals. The inner petals are paler, narrow with pointed tips and surmounted by larger pink petals. Several carpels are converted into pink carpelodes, but one or two remain—these are pale green and glabrous, with ivory or pink tips. With its strong stems this old variety makes a good cut flower. Late season, 95 CM (38 IN.).

'Comanche' (Bigger, 1957)

This is a truly outstanding plant, very free flowering, and one of my favourite Japanese lactifloras. Flowers have extremely bright magenta-pink guard petals and a centre of amber yellow, wavy-tipped staminodes. The staminodes are themselves surrounded by a ring of semi-functional stamens. The magenta-flushed carpels are topped by magenta styles. Midseason, 90 CM (3 FT.).

'Cora Stubbs'.
(Credit: Roy Klehm)

'Cora Stubbs' (Krekler)

This is a very popular Japanese-form lactiflora, with pale magenta guard petals and a tight mound of short, creamy white and pale pink staminodes. The staminodes have pale yellow stripes running along the centre. The very fragrant flowers have green carpels and magenta styles. Midseason, 110 CM (44 IN.).

'Cornelia Shaylor' (Shaylor, 1919)

The double flowers are a massive dome of pale pink petals, surrounded by enlarged blush-coloured guard petals. The flowers fade to white in strong sunshine, but the guard petals retain some colour. Blooms are held on strong stems and have a slight fragrance. Midseason, 90 CM (36 IN.).

'Couronne d'Or' (Calot, 1873)

An attractive double lactiflora and one of the last to flower in summer with large ivory white guard petals surrounding a mass of smaller inner petals. Golden yellow stamens impart a golden glow to the centre of the flower and its central petals are splashed with carmine-red. It is good for cutting and has green carpels with pink styles. Late season, 1 M (3.3 FT.).

'Daisy Coronet' (Roy G. Klehm, 1995)

In recent years Roy Klehm has introduced a number of interesting new peonies with "daisy-style" flowers. In 'Daisy Coronet' they are rather small, measuring 5.0–7.5 CM (2–3 IN.) across, with very narrow tapering pink petals. A ring of pale yellow stamens and large dark red carpels occupies the centre. Early season, 56 CM (22 IN.).

Roy Klehm has introduced several new peonies with narrow petals, such as the outrageous 'Daisy Coronet'.
(Credit: Roy Klehm)

'Dawn Pink' (Sass, 1946)

Many people consider this one of the very best single pink peonies. It has extremely large, single, China rose flowers with a nicely rounded boss of golden yellow stamens and green carpels with purple styles. The medium green leaves have a decurrent lamina that extends along the petiole. Early to midseason, 90 CM (36 IN.).

'Desire' (Brand, 1923)

An ideal peony for smaller gardens, with semi-double, pinkish magenta flowers. The stamens are golden yellow with short filaments in the centre, becoming longer towards the outer part of the flower. The petals are slightly wavy with crimped edges and streaked with magenta. The carpels have developed into small pink petals, or carpelodes, and are mixed with stamens. Some flowers are crown-shaped with the stamens developed into petals, but all are extremely fragrant. Mid to late season, 60 CM (24 IN.).

'Diana Drinkwater' (Kelway)

This bomb-shaped lactiflora has extremely thick stems. The buds give no hint of the lovely rose-scented flower that lies within, which looks like many layers of pink crêpe paper. The guard petals are pink, large and nicely rounded. On top lies a mass of coral pink petals surmounted by a crown of silvered, deep pink petals. The carpels are purple with bright purple styles. Remove the old flowers as they fade; if left in place they distort the younger ones as they develop. It is worth removing the side buds if you want perfect blooms. Mid to late season, 105 CM (3.4 FT.).

Most cultivars of *Paeonia lactiflora*, such as 'Diana Drinkwater', have sidebuds, which extend the flowering period. However, they tend to distort the flowers and should be removed if you want the blooms for cutting.

'Dinner Plate'.
(Credit: Roy Klehm)

'Dinner Plate' (Carl G. Klehm, 1968)

This is aptly named, for the massive double, deep pink flowers, measure up to 20 CM (8 IN.) across. The outer petals are very large, forming a ruff around a depressed centre of small pink petaloids. The central stamens are converted into small, semi-functional, pink and yellow staminodes. Carpels are absent, or converted into small pink carpelodes. This extremely elegant, rose-scented peony has very strong stems and makes a great impact as a cut flower; it is far superior to the better-known 'Sarah Bernhardt'. Late season, 85 CM (34 IN.).

'Do Tell' (Auten, 1946)

A striking Japanese lactiflora with speckled shell pink guard petals and masses of wavy, cream, rose pink and purple staminodes, all of which are bright yellow at the base. It has pale green carpels with creamy white styles. Awarded an APS Gold Medal in 2004. Midseason, 80 CM (32 IN.).

'Doreen' (Sass, 1949)

One of the most reliable Japanese-form lactifloras, this cultivar has fuchsia pink guard petals and masses of rose pink staminodes with wavy golden tips. The carpels are green with magenta styles. The flowers are slightly fragrant and the leaves are light green. Late season, 80 CM (32 IN.).

'Dr. Alexander Fleming' (breeder unknown)

A fully double lactiflora with deep pink flowers, fading slightly towards the edges, opening from fuchsia purple (67B) buds. The central petals may be tightly curled up into a ball, even when the flower is mature, and they alternate with concentric rings of golden stamens. Some flowers may be semi-double with green carpels and purple styles. Sweetly fragrant and attractive to bees, this peony is the result of a cross between 'Bunker Hill' and 'Sarah Bernhardt'. Midseason, tall growing to 1.2 M (4 FT.).

'Duchesse de Nemours' (Calot, 1856)

'Duchesse de Nemours' may be a very old cultivar but it is extremely beautiful, still widely available and well worth growing. It is a free-flowering, crown-shaped lactiflora with rich creamy white flowers, touched with a hint of yellow. The outer petals are large and well rounded with a slight notch at the tip, surrounding a circle of smaller petals, surmounted by an erupting crown of large white, slightly incurved petals. The carpels are absent or rudimentary, as are the stamens. Deliciously scented and with attractive green foliage. AGM. Midseason, 80 CM (32 IN.).

'Edulis Superba' (Lemon, 1824)

One of the oldest cultivars in commercial production, 'Edulis Superba' is still one of the best double peonies available. It is free flowering and produces masses of deep magenta-rose (66D), crown-shaped flowers with large, nicely rounded guard petals. The crown of the flower is composed of a mass of silvered magenta-pink petals with yellow "roots", surrounded by a collar of narrow, pale pink petaloids. There are no stamens and the tomentose carpels are usually quite small, with tapering green styles. The flowers have a sweet fragrance and are good for cutting, but the stems are rather weak. Highly recommended. Early to midseason, 95 CM (3.1 FT.).

'Emma Klehm' (Carl G. Klehm, 1951)

A compact growing, fully double lactiflora with large heather pink (68B) flowers. The petals tend to fade in bright sunlight, but the colour remains in the depths of the flower. Carpels and stamens are absent, transformed into petals. Very late season, 80 CM (32 IN.).

'Emma Klehm' is a reliable lactiflora, with double heather-pink flowers.

'Evening World' (Kelway, 1928)

This unusual peony of Japanese form is easily mistaken for the better-known 'Bowl of Beauty'. The outer guard petals are pale pink and heavily flushed with magenta, but fade in bright sunlight. The staminodes are quite broad and wavy, pink with a hint of blush and surround yellowish green carpels with ivory-coloured styles. The best time to see the flowers is in the early evening when the low sun makes them appear lavender with a pink centre. This is a truly wonderful peony and deserves to be better known. Free flowering, mid to very late season, 90 CM (3 FT.).

At dusk the magenta-pink flowers of 'Evening World' appear to be transformed to a wonderful shade of lavender.

'Fairbanks' (Auten, 1945)

A Japanese-form flower composed of very large milky white guard petals and masses of narrow, twisted, milky white staminodes. The outer staminodes are partially functional with thin thread-like filaments. It has long pale green carpels with cream styles. Plants are very vigorous, but the stems are rather weak and need supporting. Very late season, 95 CM (3.1 FT.).

'Feather Top' (Wild, 1970)

This is an unusual Japanese-form peony with alternating layers of petals and staminodes, surrounded by large magenta guard petals. The staminodes are streaked with pink and have bright yellow tips. In the centre of the flower there are a few pink carpelodes, which are surrounded by yellow staminodes and finally another ring of magenta staminodes. Midseason, 90 CM (3 FT.).

'Felix Crousse' (Crousse, 1881)

This is one of the most widely available cultivars of *P. lactiflora*. It has large, double, globe-shaped, magenta-carmine flowers, with tomentose pink carpels, purple styles and yellow stamens with short filaments. It has an appealing fragrance, but the petals lack substance and the flowers tend to flop when cut. Midseason, 1 M (3.3 FT.).

'Festiva Maxima' (Miellez, 1851)

This ethereal white peony may have been introduced over 150 years ago but it has few peers. The double flowers are pale pink when they open, but quickly fade to creamy white in sunshine, with sulphur yellow depths. They are globe-shaped and have a centre of tall, recurved petals, marked with distinctive red splashes, which are surrounded by a ring of smaller petals, encircled by large white guard petals. The pale green carpels have creamy white styles and are surrounded by very narrow staminodes. I highly recommend this peony, which is good for cutting and has very fragrant flowers. Midseason, 1 M (3.3 FT.).

'Flamingo' (Andrews, 1925)

A semi-double lactiflora with heavily silvered, deep pink flowers; the outer guard petals are deeply notched. The inner petals are narrow towards the centre of the flower, becoming rather "feathery" towards the top. The upper part of the flowers tends to become bleached in strong sunlight. The carpels are purple, although some may be developed into petal-like carpelodes. 50 CM (20 IN.).

'Florence Ellis' (Nicholls, 1948)

The buds of this beautiful double lactiflora are splashed with carmine-red, but they open to display large, flesh pink flowers. The outer parts of the highly fragrant flower fade in strong sunshine, but the depressed centre remains pink. Plants have strong stems and large dark green leaves. Midseason, 70 CM (28 IN.).

The flower buds of 'Gainsborough' open to reveal Japanese form blooms, but as they age the centre is filled by a mass of pink and buff petals.

'Gainsborough' (Kelway, 1933)

This flower goes through an amazing metamorphosis. Salmon pink buds open to a Japanese form flower, with deep pink guard petals and buff-coloured, lance-shaped staminodes with a yellow stripe down the centre. With age the outer petals become much paler. The staminodes continue to grow into narrow, wavy, pure white petals, sometimes flecked with magenta. The glabrous purple carpels spread out to form a star in the heart of the flower. Quite a performance. The fragrant flowers are borne on strong stems. Early to midseason, 1 M (3.3 FT.).

'Gardenia' (Lins, 1955)

A sweetly fragrant, double peony with large, crown-shaped, milky white flowers, which develop from neat pink buds. The crown consists of a mass of white petals, some streaked with pink, mixed with small functional stamens. In the centre are a few white carpelodes, but there are no carpels. Early midseason, 85 CM (34 IN.).

'Gay Paree' (Auten, 1933)

This is one of the most striking of all anemone-form lactifloras and a splendid cut flower. It has bright cerise-pink guard petals and masses of staminodes with notched edges. The staminodes are deep pink in the centre with creamy white edges but they fade quickly in bright sunshine, turning pale pink or even white. Flowers can be anemone or Japanese form. Midseason, 75 CM (30 IN.).

'Gazelle' (Kelway)

A semi-double lactiflora with deep pink, globe-shaped flowers. The outer petals are heavily striped on the outside with red and notched at the tips. Golden yellow stamens are scattered throughout. The stems are reasonably strong but it needs staking. It is a free flowering, fragrant peony with many side buds. Early to midseason, 90 CM (3 FT.).

'Genevieve' (Kelway, 1925)

A single-flowered lactiflora with large magenta petals and enlarged, flattened stamens. The filaments are yellow, supporting dagger-shaped anthers with yellow edges and a magenta centre. The carpels are dark green, with twisted pink styles. The petals become silvered in sunshine. The flowers have a slight fragrance. Midseason, medium height.

'Gene Wild' (Cooper, 1956)

The double flowers open pale soft pink, but fade to creamy white with rose pink depths. The inner petals are often splashed with carmine-red. The carpels are very small or developed into carpelodes and surrounded by a ring of golden yellow stamens. It forms a low growing plant. Midseason, 60 CM (24 IN.).

Paeonia lactiflora 'Gilbert Barthelot' has rather flat, semi-double or double, magenta-pink flowers.

'Gilbert Barthelot' (Dorriat, 1931)

A semi-double or double lactiflora with magenta pink flowers. Plants of this variety can have rather flat, semi-double flowers with a single whorl of petals, surrounding a central boss of golden stamens. However, mostly the flowers are fully double with a second set of petals, which unfurl from the centre of the stamens. The flower thus ends up with a secondary ring of stamens. The tomentose carpels with purple styles may be very small or completely absent. The flowers are fragrant, carried on strong stems with side buds. Midseason, 90 CM (3 FT.).

'Grandiflora' (Richardson, 1883)

The flesh pink buds open to form very large semi-double or double flowers with milky white petals. Young flowers have a touch of blush, but this fades as the flower matures. Flowers have a spicy fragrance and no carpels. One of the last peonies to flower. Late season, 90 CM (3 FT.).

'Heartbeat' (Kelway)

A Japanese-form lactiflora with deep purple guard petals, deeply notched and surrounding a mass of narrow purple staminodes. The carpels are pale green with creamy white styles or partially developed into carpelodes. Pleasing foliage, strong stems, but the flowers may not be to everyone's taste. Mid to late season, 90 CM (3 FT.). Synonym: 'Helicon'.

'Heirloom' (Breeder unknown)

A semi-double to double lactiflora, the flowers open lilac-pink, but the inner petals fade in bright sunshine and become almost white. The guard petals remain pink, while the central petals are mixed with several thread-like staminodes. Carpels may or may not be present. The flowers vary in colour with semi-double blooms predominantly pink, while those with more petals have a white centre. This variety is strongly fragrant and free flowering; it has strong stems but needs staking. A pretty plant. Mid to late season, 70 CM (28 IN.).

'Helen Hayes' (Murawska, 1943)

A fully double, bomb-shaped lactiflora with very large magenta-pink flowers (66B becoming 66C) and a delicious rose-like fragrance. Carpels are absent and the stamens are reduced to vestigial pink staminodes with yellow tips. Mid to late season, 88 CM (35 IN.).

'Henri Potin' (Doriat, 1924)

The Japanese-form flowers have rose magenta petals surrounding stiff buff-coloured staminodes, which are green at the base, becoming pink in the middle and pale yellow at the top. A few of the staminodes are developed into pink petals, which are held above the flower, and the tomentose carpels are purple with dark purple styles. The flowers produce a massive amount of nectar. Late season, 70–85 CM (28–34 IN.).

Bomb-shaped flowers, such as 'Helen Hayes' may not develop their typical shape until they are a couple of days old. Younger flowers may appear semi-double while the central petals are developing.

'Highlight' (Auten-Wild, 1952)

Large, double, velvety, dark red flowers with golden yellow stamens scattered among the petals. It has very small white carpels with pink styles, surrounded by a few stamens. Late midseason, medium height.

'Ingenieur Doriat' (Doriat)

A rather disappointing peony, for the buds hold a promise that is not fulfilled when the flowers open. The semi-double or double, slightly scented flowers have pinkish purple petals, which alternate with rings of golden yellow stamens. The inner petals are derived from stamens and have a yellow stripe, while others are partially functional. The upper petals become silvered in strong sunshine. Midseason, 75 CM (30 IN.).

'Inspecteur Lavergne' (Doriat, 1924)

This peony is widely grown and readily available, but I have to admit that I find it rather uninspiring. It has globe-shaped flowers composed of many small, deep, white-rimmed, crimson-red petals surrounded by large, crimson-red guard petals. The carpels are often transformed into green and purple carpelodes. Mid to late season, 78 CM (31 IN.).

'Jan Van Leeuwen' (Van Leeuwen, 1928)

This popular peony of Japanese form has a small centre of narrow, golden yellow staminodes, surrounded by pure white guard petals. It has pale green carpels and cream-coloured styles. The leaves are rather different from other lactifloras, which suggests it might be a hybrid with another species. The flowers are fragrant and suitable for cutting. Midseason, 90 CM (3 FT.).

'Jean E. Bockstoce' (Bockstoce, 1933)

An appealing plant with strong stems and claret red anemone-form flowers where all of the stamens are developed into petal-like staminodes. The carpels are pale green with a touch of purple on the styles. Early season, 85 CM (34 IN.).

'June Rose' (Jones, 1938)

Large globe-shaped semi-double flowers open purplish pink (67A), but then turn deep pink (67C). The flowers retain their colour in bright sunshine, but the outer petals become slightly silvered. Very small carpels have magenta styles and the stamens are scattered among the petals in the centre of the flower. The flowers have a pleasant fragrance. Midseason, 78 CM (31 IN.).

'Kansas' (Bigger, 1940)

'Kansas' is a distinctive peony with deep fuchsia purple (67B) globe-shaped double flowers. The petals are strongly marbled on the inside and retain their colour in strong sunshine. It has very small green carpels and red styles. The strong stems make it a good cut flower. Awarded a Gold Medal by the APS. Midseason, 90 CM (3 FT.).

'Kathleen Mavoureen' (Kelway)

Very strong stems support flamboyant, deep pink, crown-shaped flowers with large emarginate petals. The blooms open deep magenta-pink, becoming heavily silvered as they age. The stamens are absent or reduced to narrow pink staminodes. It has red carpels with erect, pointed, purplish red styles. The flowers are pleasantly fragrant. Midseason, 70 cm (28 in.).

'Kelway's Brilliant' (Kelway, 1928)
'Kelway's Brilliant' is an unusual Japanese lactiflora, quite outstanding in bright sunlight, when the flowers seem to glow with an inner light. Deep purple guard petals surround a mass of sword-shaped orange-purple staminodes. The staminodes have a bright yellow line down the centre and become broader towards the middle of the flower. The carpels are pale green with pale purple, recurved styles. Flowers are fragrant, but there are rarely side buds. It is not widely grown outside the U.K., but deserves to be. Mid to late season, 90 cm (3 ft.).

'Kelway's Brilliant' is a striking Japanese form peony with a mass of sword-shaped staminodes and bright purple guard petals.

'Kelway's Circe' (Kelway, 1916)
A Japanese-form lactiflora, with deep magenta-pink guard petals, enhanced by a silvered edge. There are a large number of staminodes in the centre of the flower, which are magenta when they are young with buff-coloured tips. As they become older the staminodes become broader and ribbon-like, tapering and pink. They are yellow at the base and approximately 6 cm (2.5 in.) long. The carpels are deep purple, glabrous, except for a few long scattered hairs, and have purple styles. A delightful peony with strong stems and pleasantly fragrant flowers. Midseason, 90 cm (3 ft.).

'Kelway's Fairy Queen' (Kelway, 1927)
The flowers of this pretty lactiflora appear single when they open, but then a mass of curly petals emerges from the centre to make them semi-double. The petals are coral pink but fade towards the edges, while the inner ones are surrounded by a ring of golden yellow stamens. The carpels are yellowish green with pink styles. The flowers have a wonderful, rather sweet fragrance. This is a very underrated cultivar that deserves to be better known. Mid to late season, 78 cm (31 in.).

'Kelway's Glorious' (Kelway, 1909)
This is one of Kelway's most highly regarded peonies and has been widely grown since its introduction. It produces masses of highly fragrant white flowers with a yellow centre. The outer petals are very large and turned upwards, as are those in the centre of the flower that surround a tuft of very narrow staminodes. It has green carpels and purple styles. The majority of the stamens are converted to staminodes, but a few semi-functional ones remain. Mid to late season, 1 m (3.3 ft).

'Kelway's Lovely' (Kelway, 1905)

A delightful semi-double lactiflora, whose young flowers have large, deep pink, nicely rounded guard petals, surrounding a neat mound of almost salmon pink inner petals. These are streaked with magenta and yellow at the base with a pale yellow stripe on the underside. As the flowers age the colour of the inner petals fades, making the contrast with the guard petals even greater. In some flowers the upper petals are larger and the form becomes crown-shaped. Stamens are absent, while the carpels are pale green in colour with bright purple styles. The flowers have a definite rose fragrance, and are borne on strong stems. Late season, 1.05 M (3.4 FT.).

Paeonia lactiflora 'Kelway's Lovely' is a pretty plant with semi-double flowers and a strong rose fragrance.

The Japanese peony 'Kelway's Majestic' has masses of narrow staminodes, surrounded by large, bright pink guard petals.

'Kelway's Majestic' (Kelway, 1928)

A peony of rather striking Japanese form with broad, magenta-pink guard petals and masses of creamy yellow staminodes, which have purple tips and a pink stripe down the centre. The flowers are fragrant with pale green carpels and purple styles. Midseason, 1 M (3.3 FT.).

'Kelway's Rosemary' (Kelway, 1916)

Flowers of Japanese form with large peony purple guard petals and wavy spear-shaped staminodes. The tips of the staminodes are slightly wavy and either silvered or look as though they have been dipped in orange paint. The pale green carpels have purple styles, with a strong demarcation between the two. Midseason, 90 CM (3 FT.).

'Kelway's Scented Rose' (Kelway, 1934)

This is a semi-double lactiflora with magenta-pink petals. The outer petals are large, well rounded and enclose a ring of large yellow stamens. In the middle of these lie a second clump of petals and a heart of golden yellow stamens. The carpels are pale green with pink styles. Of moderate height, it has coarse foliage and flowers over a long period. Mid to late season, 1 M (3.3 FT.).

'Kelway's Supreme' (Kelway, 1891)

It is surprising that this lovely plant is so little known. It produces masses of fragrant single or semi-double flowers, with whorls of pale pink petals and a centre of golden yellow stamens. It flowers for a long period of time, with lots of side buds and is good for cutting. Mid to late season, 1 M (3.3ft).

'Kelway's Venus' (Kelway, 1917)

Many bomb-shaped flowers take some time to develop their full potential, and 'Kelway's Venus' is no exception. The buds appear to be developing into a Japanese type of flower, with pale pink guard petals, but further small petals gradually develop in the centre. Eventually the flower develops into a tall bomb-shape, surmounted by an enormous mound of pale yellow wavy edged petals. The mound is crowned by a neat ring of creamy white petals and a heart of pale yellow, narrow staminodes. It is very pretty, but has only a little scent. Midseason, 1 M (3.3 FT.).

'Krinkled White' (Brand, 1928)

One of the most beautiful of the single white lactifloras, the flowers are composed of slightly crinkled, milky white petals and a small tuft of golden yellow stamens. The pale green carpels have creamy white styles. It makes a good cut flower. Early season, 78in (31 IN.).

'La Belle Helene' (Kelway, 1915)

A semi-double lactiflora whose flowers open pale pink, but turn milky white as they mature. Some of the petals are strongly streaked with red. The inner petals alternate with the small number of yellow stamens. The purple carpels are very small, with pink styles. The flowers are fragrant, but have weak stems. Midseason, 90 CM (32 IN.).

'La Lorraine' (Lemoine, 1901)

This beautiful peony has a reputation of being slow to establish. It has semi-double or double flowers with large guard petals, which surround a mound of wavy, spoon-shaped inner petals. The flowers open with pale pink guards and buff-tinged inner petals, but the colour fades after a day or so and the central mound becomes creamy white. The staminodes have a bright yellow base, surrounding large pinkish purple carpels with wavy, reddish purple styles. It forms a large bushy plant, with very strong stems and glossy foliage, but the flowers have little fragrance. Midseason, 1 M (3.3 FT.).

'La Perle' (Crousse, 1886)

The opening buds are very attractive, so it is slightly disappointing when they unfurl to reveal an untidy semi-double bloom. The pale pink outer petals are streaked on the outside with crimson and fade to creamy white in bright sunshine. The inner petals alternate with rings of golden yellow stamens. The carpels are very small, purple with pink styles. A free-flowering plant with fragrant flowers and strong stems. Midseason, 80 CM (32 IN.).

'Lady Alexandra Duff' (Kelway, 1902)

This peony should be in everyone's collection to enjoy the very beautiful double flowers, with lavender-pink outer petals and small white inner petals. The central petals are often marked with splashes of carmine-red. It has strong stems, with side buds and these can develop into semi-double or double flowers. The flowers are very fragrant. 'Lady Alexandra Duff' is best purchased from a specialist nursery, because there are several inferior forms on the market. Midseason, 90 CM (3 FT.).

'Lady Orchid' (Bigger, 1942)

This fully double lactiflora has large flowers with masses of soft lavender-pink petals and nicely rounded guard petals. There are no carpels and the stamens are transformed into deep pink staminodes, which are yellow towards the base. It is free flowering and slightly fragrant. Mid to late season, 75 CM (30 IN.).

'Langport Beauty' (Kelway)

A dark, beetroot red single lactiflora with a mound of yellow anthers borne on long filaments, which are yellow at the top and reddish at the base. The carpels are also beetroot red, with magenta styles. Flowers have no noticeable fragrance. Midseason, 95 CM (3.1 FT.).

'Langport Triumph' (Kelway, 1905)

A very under-rated peony that deserves to be more widely grown because its flowers are extremely decorative. They are fully double and crown shaped with pale magenta guard petals and numerous pink and buff, crinkly inner petals. The carpels are purple and green with bright magenta styles. It has strong stems with side buds, but only a slight fragrance. Midseason, 1 M (3.3 FT.).

'L'Eclatante' (Calot, 1860)

This semi-double lactiflora has cherry pink flowers with large, guard petals, notched at the tip. The upper petals become silvered in sunshine. The carpels are purple, tomentose with magenta styles. The flowers are pleasantly fragrant, and only let down by their weak stems. Midseason, 90 CM (3 FT.).

'Lemon Queen' (Origin unknown)

A Japanese-form lactiflora with creamy white guard petals and wavy, twisted lemon yellow staminodes, which fade to pale yellow with ivory tips as the flower ages. The carpels are pale green with yellow styles. Midseason, 90 CM (3 FT.).

'Lorna Doone' (Kelway, 1905)

The young flowers of this bomb-shaped lactiflora have pink guards, a pale yellow centre and a slightly pink crown. As the flowers mature the large rounded guard petals pale and the ring of inner petals can be appreciated. They are creamy white and yellow edged with deeply forked tips, broad at the base and narrowing to a fine wavy point. Mixed in with them are very narrow, ribbon-like petals. The top of the bomb is composed of a few very large white petals surrounding a depressed centre of many very small tapering petals streaked with crimson. Late season, 90 CM (3 FT.).

Paeonia lactiflora 'Lotus Queen' has Japanese form flowers with milky white guard petals.

'Lotus Queen' (Murawska, 1947)

A pretty Japanese-form flower with milky white guard petals, its outer stamens are normal but the inner ones are developed into wavy, creamy yellow staminodes with crinkled tips. The pale green carpels have cream-coloured styles or are developed into a tuft of creamy white carpelodes. Midseason, 85 CM (34 IN.).

'Love Mist' (Origin unknown)

This cultivar bears two types of flowers: the smaller are Japanese in form with creamy white guard petals, while the larger are fully double. The small flowers have pale yellow staminodes and tiny carpels with beetroot purple styles. In contrast the larger flowers develop into a fully double crown shape with large cream-coloured guards and creamy white inner petals, becoming yellow towards the base. In these larger flowers the carpels are developed into carpelodes with purple tips. The flowers are slightly fragrant. Midseason, 78 CM (31 IN.).

'Loving Cup' (Origin unknown)

A Japanese-form lactiflora with orchid pink guard petals, surrounding broad, ribbon-shaped staminodes with pink filaments. Some of the filaments are slightly broadened, while the others are unchanged and have large anthers with a pale yellow edge. There are a reduced number of carpels, but the two or three that survive are very large, tomentose and have pink styles. The staminoidal disc has cream lobes. Midseason, 70 CM (28 IN.).

'Madame Butterfly' (Franklin, 1933)

'Madame Butterfly' is a striking Japanese lactiflora with cyclamen purple guard petals. The forked magenta-pink staminodes fade to almost white, with magenta tips. It has yellowish green carpels and magenta styles. Midseason, 60 CM (24 IN.).

'Madame Calot' (Biellex, 1856)

This old cultivar has crown-shaped flowers with pale pink outer guard petals and creamy white, wavy inner petals, which can be very narrow. Some flowers can have a heart of blush pink petals, forming a flat crown. The carpels are pale purple with wavy, pink and purple elongated styles. The flowers have a spicy fragrance and are borne on strong stems. Late season, 75 CM (30 IN.).

'Madame Ducel' (Mechin, 1880)

Reliable and free flowering, this is a bomb-shaped lactiflora with strongly scented flowers. The central bomb consists of a large mound of small petals, which are creamy white at the base becoming lavender-pink towards the top, and surrounded by lavender-pink guard petals. The purplish green carpels have magenta-coloured styles. Early to midseason, 60 CM (24 IN.).

'Mademoiselle Leonie Calot' (Calot, 1861)

An attractive crown-shaped flower, its pale magenta guard petals have slightly ragged edges. In the centre is a ball of wavy, pink and buff staminodes, becoming golden yellow towards the base. The carpels are small, green at the base and cream towards the top, with pink styles. The flowers are very fragrant. Midseason, medium height. Synonym: 'Monsieur Charles Leveque'.

'Magic Orb' (Kelway, 1927)

A free-flowering peony that produces a large number of side shoots and masses of slightly fragrant crown-shaped flowers. These have large magenta guard petals with silvered edges and a central mass of buff-coloured staminodes. Those towards the outside are broader,

Paeonia lactiflora 'Magic Orb'.

streaked with magenta pigment and golden yellow at the base. There are up to 9 purple, slightly hairy carpels, with stiff upward-pointing magenta styles. Midseason, 1 M (3.3 FT.).

'Major Loder' (Kelway, 1927)
A pretty Japanese-form flower with magenta guard petals and golden yellow staminodes, which become orange at their wavy tips. The carpels are creamy yellow at the top and green at the base. The flowers are only slightly fragrant. Early season.

'Marie Lemoine' (Calot, 1869)
This elegant peony has very large, double, globe-shaped flowers. The overall impression is of a white flower with a strong lemon-yellow tint, reminiscent of a lemon meringue pie. Most of the stamens are converted into staminodes, but a few functional ones can be found among the petals. The strong stemmed flowers are sweetly scented and may have flecks of red on the central petals. Late season, 78 CM (31 IN.).

'Martha W.' (Spangler/Anderson, 1985)
The single flowers are slightly fragrant with bright pink petals and a large mass of golden yellow stamens. Plants may need to be staked in windy locations. 'Martha W.' produces profuse quantities of large seed and has proved invaluable as a seed parent for intersectional hybrids; it has been widely used by Roger Anderson in his breeding programme. Its parentage is unknown, but it may be a chance seedling of 'Monsieur Jules Elie'. This cultivar was originally called 'Martha Washington', but renaming was necessary when it was discovered the name had already been used for another peony. Early to midseason, 1 M (3.3 FT.).

'Minerve' (Dessert, 1908)
A single lactiflora with magenta flowers. It has many golden yellow stamens and pale purple carpels with magenta styles. It is short-growing with remarkably coarse foliage. Could it be a hybrid with *P. mascula* subsp. *mascula*? 70 CM (28 IN.) (Synonym 'Minerva').

'Miss America' (Mann-van Steen, 1936)
This semi-double lactiflora opens blush pink and then turns pure white, with a hint of yellow at the base of the petals. It has golden yellow anthers, bright yellow filaments and vivid green, glabrous carpels with cream-coloured styles, which provide a striking contrast to the white petals. The flowers are highly fragrant and the stems are strong. 'Miss America' is a truly wonderful peony and has received the APS Gold Medal on two separate occasions, indicative of its high quality. Early season, 90 CM (3 FT.).

'Mister Ed' (Roy Klehm, 1980)
This bomb-shaped lactiflora has fragrant flowers with deep rose pink outer petals, which fade towards the centre and become creamy white. The stamens are converted into narrow staminodes and mixed with the petals, both of which have yellow roots. Carpels

are usually absent and converted into small petals. 'Mister Ed' was produced by treating 'Monsieur Jules Elie' with colchicine (see Glossary). Early season, 70 CM (28 IN.).

'Monsieur Jules Elie' (Crousse, 1888)

Almost 120 years after it was first introduced, this beautiful peony is still one of the best available. It has very large light rose pink, bomb-shaped flowers with masses of smaller incurved petals in the centre. Stamens and carpels are absent; the latter have developed into narrow, wavy, pink or yellow carpelodes. The flowers retain their colour well in bright sunlight and are pleasantly fragrant. They are good for cutting but have rather weak stems. Plants are cheap to purchase and readily available. Early to midseason, 1.1 M (3.6 FT.).

'Mrs. Franklin D. Roosevelt' (Franklin, 1932)

At first sight the flowers appear single with a tight ball of petals in the centre. The ball gradually unfurls like a large pink water-lily to form a very beautiful double flower with rose pink petals, becoming paler in the centre. The colour fades to almost white in strong sunshine. It is fragrant, very floriferous and the strong stems make it an excellent cut flower. It is one of my favourite lactifloras. GM. Midseason, 85 CM (34 IN.).

'Music Man' (Wild, 1967)

The flowers of this double lactiflora are cone-shaped when young, but eventually they develop into large, deep magenta, crown-shaped blooms. There are one or two stamens in the centre of each flower. Midseason, 75 CM (30 IN.).

'Nancy Nicholls' (Nicholls, 1941)

This very appealing double lactiflora has symmetrical, well-shaped flowers, which open pale pink, but fade quickly to creamy white. A number of petals are streaked on the outside with pink pigment. The majority of the stamens are turned into very narrow white staminodes and the few surviving are only partly functional. Carpels are absent. It has strong stems and a very pleasant fragrance. Mid to late season, 90 CM (3 FT.).

'Neon' (Nicholls, 1941)

An aptly named Japanese-form lactiflora with dazzling pink guard petals, surrounding a pompon of gold-tipped, bright pink staminodes. The carpels are bright green with purple styles. Midseason, 1.1 M (3.6 FT.).

'Nick Shaylor' (Allison, 1931)

Double flowers open blush pink, with a hint of yellow in the depths and gradually fade to white with a blush pink centre. The guard petals are often streaked with carmine on the reverse and streaks can also occur on the central petals. The flowers are not fragrant. The American Peony Society has awarded a Gold Medal to this highly regarded peony on two occasions. Very late flowering, 85 CM (34 IN.).

'Nymphe' (Dessert, 1913)

There are many single lactifloras, but this is one of the most elegant, with large flesh pink petals and a tight mound of yellow stamens. The flowers are fragrant and have green carpels with magenta styles. Late season, 65 CM (26 IN.).

'Opal Hamilton' (Nicholls-Wild, 1957)

This is an extremely attractive Japanese-form lactiflora, with very large, well-rounded lilac-pink guard petals. The outer threadlike staminodes have a yellow base and deep pink tips, while the inner are much larger, yellow and pink in colour with a toothed tip. The yellowish green carpels have cream styles. Midseason, 1 M (3 FT.).

'Mrs. Franklin D. Roosevelt' has received a Gold Medal from the American Peony Society.

The flowers of 'Nancy Nicholls' open pink, but eventually fade to white in sunshine.

'Nymphe' is one of the best of the single pink lactifloras, with large saucer-shaped flowers.

'Ornament de Passifs' (Crousse, 1893)

Pretty deep pink petals produce a fully double flower with silvered edges and a small central cluster of golden yellow stamens with similarly coloured filaments. The stamens are intermixed with the petals. The flowers are highly fragrant. Mid to late season.

'Paul M. Wild' (Wild, 1964)

It seems unlikely this plant is a pure lactiflora because it has rich melon red flowers. The flowers are fully double, with large rounded guard petals surrounding numerous small petals; carpels and stamens are absent. It makes a superb cut flower. Midseason, 95 CM (3.1 FT.).

'Peppermint' (Nicholls-Wild, 1957)

The double flowers open blush pink with a hint of yellow in the centre and fade to white after a few days. The outer petals and some of the inner ones, which are much narrower, are streaked with carmine. It has green carpels with purple styles, which are surrounded by golden stamens. Late midseason, 85 CM (34 IN.).

'Peter Brand' (Seit, 1937)

This is a tall, fully double lactiflora with deep ruby red flowers, which become more purple with age. The inner petals are deeply divided with almost spoon-shaped tips. Yellow stamens are scattered throughout the flower; their filaments are yellow at the top and reddish towards the base. Young flowers have a soft satiny texture, with slight fragrance. The foliage develops good autumn colour. Midseason, 95 CM (3.1 FT.)

'Peter Pan' (Kelway, 1907)

The single flowers are composed of magenta petals with dark magenta veins surrounding a centre of golden yellow stamens. The carpels are purple, tomentose with magenta styles. Plants have strong stems, rather coarse foliage and flowers with a similar scent to *P. mascula* subsp. *mascula*; 'Peter Pan' may be a hybrid with this species. Midseason, 75 CM (30 IN.).

'Philomèle' (Calot, 1861)

This is a rather elegant anemone or crown-shaped peony, with large lavender-pink guard petals and a centre of buff and lavender-pink petaloids. Young plants have anemone-shaped flowers with a depressed centre of narrow buff-coloured petals, but stronger growing, mature plants may develop crown-shaped blooms with lavender-pink central petals—the crown may not appear for several days. The carpels are very small with pink styles. It has strong stems and fragrant flowers. Midseason, 80 CM (32 IN.).

'Pink Formal' (Nicholls-Wild and Son, 1953)

When young the flowers of this fully double peony are wrapped into a tight ball. Mature flowers have creamy white petals in the centre, but there are no stamens or carpels. As the flowers age they become milky white, but a hint of pink remains in the depths. Late midseason, 90 CM (3 FT.).

'Pink Parfait' (Carl Klehm, 1975)
This attractive plant is quite similar in character to the eternally popular 'Sarah Bernhardt', but it has much stronger stems. The substantial, fully double, soft pink flowers have large, nicely rounded guard petals and a mound of smaller petals in the centre. The carpels and stamens are converted into petals, which retain a hint of yellow at the base, imparting a golden glow to the centre. The flowers are slightly fragrant and ideal for cutting. Midseason, 95 cm (3.1 ft.).

'Pink Princess' (Breeder unknown, 1985)
One of the best-selling single pink peonies; its petals are covered with tiny specks of pigment. The flowers fade in bright sunshine, but remain pink in shaded areas. The mass of golden yellow stamens with short yellow filaments surround purplish green carpels with purple styles. In mature plants the carpels may be converted into pink carpelodes. The flowers are slightly fragrant. This plant was originally sold as 'Pink Dawn', but the name had already been taken by another peony. Midseason, 95 cm (3.1 ft.).

'Primevère' (Lemoine, 1907)
A lovely anemone-form peony with creamy white guard petals and a large mass of lemon-yellow staminodes, which fade to white as the flower matures. The flowers are very fragrant. Midseason, 88 cm (35 in.).

'Raspberry Rumba' (Roy G. Klehm, 1995)
This is a rather unusual single lactiflora because the slightly wavy white petals are strongly marked by raspberry red stripes. It has green carpels with dark red styles and golden yellow anthers. The spoon-shaped petals are deeply notched at the tips. Midseason, 80 cm (32 in.).

'Raspberry Sundae' (Carl G. Klehm, 1968)
This superb bomb-shaped peony is aptly named. Pale pink guard petals, which quickly fade to white in bright sunshine, surround a collar of pale yellow lance-shaped staminodes, with greenish yellow roots. As the flower matures a large plume of pale pink petals erupts from the centre, until it forms a large globe-shaped mass. Young flowers may have no trace of pink and can appear Japanese-form until the central petals emerge. The flowers are highly fragrant and carpels are absent or rudimentary. Midseason, 70 cm (28 in.).

'Red Rover' (Kelway)
This tall single lactiflora has large, peony purple flowers and a small centre of golden yellow stamens. The carpels are hairy with magenta styles. It has a spicy fragrance. Midseason.

'Reine Hortense' (Calot, 1857)

One of the oldest peonies in cultivation, this beautiful plant has very large double, pale rose pink flowers with substantial guard petals. In the centre are a few white carpelodes surrounded by a ring of short yellow stamens. Further stamens are scattered throughout the rest of the flower. The fragrant flowers fade to pure white in strong sunshine. They are good for cutting. Midseason, 83 CM (33 IN.).

'Sarah Bernhardt' (Lemoine, 1906)

This is by far the most popular peony in cultivation and it is widely grown as a cut flower. The fragrant, fully double, "apple blossom" pink flowers fade in bright sunshine, but remain deep pink in the depths. Carpels are usually absent or, if present, very small with magenta styles and stigmata. The golden yellow stamens are mixed with the petals. Despite its popularity, I cannot recommend this plant because it has such weak stems. Mid to late season, 95 CM (3.1 FT.).

Paeonia lactiflora 'Shirley Temple' has wonderful, creamy white flowers.

'Top Brass' has a collar of yellow petals topped with pink.

'Shirley Temple' (origin unknown)

The deep pink buds become blush pink as they open and finally develop into large, globe-shaped, fully double, creamy white flowers with blush pink outer petals. The centre is filled with very narrow white staminodes, becoming yellow towards the base. The carpels are very small and have extended magenta styles. It makes a good cut flower with strong stems and fragrant blooms. The peony was raised by crossing 'Festiva Maxima' with 'Madame Edouard Doriat'. Mid to late season, 83 CM (33 IN.).

'Solange' (Lemoine, 1907)

Victor Lemoine raised many beautiful peonies, but this one has few peers. The very large double, creamy white flowers have amber tints and a deep salmon pink heart. They develop from the blush-coloured buds and may take several days to open fully. Opinions on the fragrance vary; some people find it unpleasant. The foliage provides fine autumn colour and the flowers are good for cutting. Very late season, 85 cm (34 in.).

'Suzanne Dessert' (Dessert and Mechin, 1890)
Pale pink, double and very pretty, this cultivar has flat, crown-shaped flowers, with a centre of small pink petals mixed with golden-yellow anthers on short filaments. It is a free flowering plant with strong stems, but little fragrance. Midseason, 95 cm (3.1 ft.).

'Thérèse' (Dessert, 1904)
This peony is interesting because its flowers pass through a complete metamorphosis as they develop. Young flowers open saucer-shaped and semi-double, with magenta-pink outer petals and a ring of golden yellow stamens surrounding a tight ball of unfurling petals. The ball gradually expands to form a fully double flower with masses of small irregular blush pink petals, often splashed with carmine-red. The flowers are very fragrant with white carpels and pink styles. Midseason, 78 cm (31 in.).

'Top Brass' (Carl G. Klehm, 1968)
This is a very striking peony, with a large collar of canary yellow petaloids sitting on top of ivory white guard petals. Pale pink petals erupt from the centre of the flower. The carpels are insignificant or developed into wavy pink carpelodes. It is very vigorous. Midseason, 1 m (3.3 ft.).

'Translucient' (Kelway)
The large single flowers are very pale pink and some of the petals are deeply notched. The colour eventually fades to leave elegant creamy white flowers with a bold centre of golden yellow stamens and dark purple carpels with salmon pink styles. Tall growing and very pretty, the flowers have a slight spicy scent. Early to midseason, 90 cm (3 ft.).

'The Mighty Mo' (Wild, 1950)
The double carmine-red flowers often exhibit a flower-within-a-flower form. A central ring of stamens enclose a tuft of petals, within which is a further small dome of stamens. It has tiny green carpels with red styles. The long stems make it good for cutting. Early season, 70 cm (28 in.).

'Vogue' (Hoogendoorn, 1949)
A extremely beautiful fully double lactiflora with soft pink flowers that are very large and fragrant. It is good for cutting. Midseason, 85 cm (34 in.).

'Vogue'

'White Cap' (Winchell, 1956)

This is one of the most striking Japanese-form lactifloras because its deep beetroot purple guard petals contrast so strongly with the staminodes. The latter are buff with a pink centre when the flowers open but quickly fade to creamy white and have toothed tips. The carpels are pale green with creamy yellow styles. Midseason, 80 CM (32 IN.).

'White Ivory' has very large double flowers and strong stems.
(Credit: Roy Klehm)

'White Ivory' (Roy G. Klehm, 1981)

An elegant fully double lactiflora, with large ivory white flowers and a large number of golden yellow stamens scattered throughout. It is tall growing and has strong stems with as many as five buds to a stem. Flowers have little fragrance. Midseason, 75 CM (30 IN.)

'White Rose of Sharon' (Kelway, 1886)

A Japanese-form flower with pure white guard petals and a mound of wavy yellow staminodes. The carpels are very large, yellow-green with small white styles. It has strong stems. Early to midseason, medium height.

'White Wings' (Hoogendoorn, 1949)

The single pure white flowers have petals with slightly serrated edges. The buds have purple stripes on the outside, but the colouring fades quickly in sunlight to leave a pure white bloom. The flowers have pale green carpels with magenta styles and are slightly fragrant. Late season, 83 CM (33 IN.).

'Whitleyi' (Whitley, 1808)

According to many gardening books, including Graham Stuart Thomas's erudite *Perennial Garden Plants* (Thomas, 1976), 'Whitleyi Major' was introduced in 1808 and has single white flowers. However, I have discovered that this is an error and the plant that was introduced in 1808 under the name 'Whitleyi' was actually a double peony with crown-shaped flowers and pink guard petals. George Anderson (1818) described 'Whitleyi' as having "flowers full double, having the outside petals reddish, and the inside petals pale straw-coloured. The whole becoming nearly white."

The error, if that is what it is, seems to have occurred in England during the latter part of the nineteenth century, because Paul (1890) includes 'Whitleyi' among his list of single peonies. We cannot be certain what happened to the original plant, but it was highly regarded in the early nineteenth century and appears to have been widely grown. It is unlikely that 'Whitleyi' is extinct because peonies are so long lived and gardeners tend to retain attractive plants, even if they have lost their name. According to Peyton (1943) 'Whitleyi' was marketed in the United States as 'Queen Victoria'.

'Whitleyi Major' (origin unknown)

The origins of this plant are rather obscure, but it starts to appear in British nursery catalogues at the end of the nineteenth century and may be a synonym of 'The Bride', which is credited to Dessert (1902). Kelways' records describe it as being "ex Alba Grandiflora", but this is impossible to substantiate and James Kelway's statement that

'Whitleyi Major' is a dependable single lactiflora with attractive white flowers and dark green foliage.

'Wiesbaden' has double flowers with the inner petals mixed with concentric rings of golden yellow stamens.

'Whitleyi Major' and 'Whitleyi' are synonyms (Kelway, 1954) is also clearly erroneous. There are at least two clones of this plant available in the nursery trade; the most common is described as follows. The single flowers have a blush tint when they open, but quickly become pure white in sunshine. It has nicely rounded egg-shaped petals, an attractive centre of yellow stamens and green carpels with white styles. The young shoots appear at an acute angle to the stem and the foliage turns a wonderful shade of red in autumn. Early season, 95 CM (38 IN.).

'Wiesbaden' (Goos-Koenemann, 1911)

Masses of rose-scented flowers open at the beginning of the summer. The double blooms have large, magenta-pink guard petals surrounding masses of smaller flesh pink petals. The stamens alternate with the inner petals, forming a series of concentric rings. A few of the stamens are converted into narrow pink staminodes, supported by broad yellow filaments. The centre of the flowers is occupied by green carpels with pink styles. Early season, 80 CM (32 IN.).

'William F. Turner' (Shaylor, 1916)

The ruby red, semi-double flowers have satin-textured petals. It has bright yellow stamens scattered throughout the flower and numerous pale yellow carpels with small ruby red styles. A tall-growing peony with strong stems and a few side buds, which extend the flowering time. This plant was very highly regarded when it was first introduced. Midseason, 95 CM (3.1 FT.).

'Zuzu' is quite a distinctive semi-double peony. The petals become progressively smaller towards the centre of the flower.
(Credit: Roy Klehm)

'Zuzu' (Kreckler, 1955)

The very pretty, semi-double, saucer-shaped flowers are pale flesh pink with deeply notched petals that become smaller towards the centre of the flower. Its golden yellow stamens have short filaments and reddish purple carpels are topped by pinkish red styles. Flowers fade quickly in bright sunshine and become pure white. Midseason, 85 CM (34 IN.).

Chapter 6
Hybrid Herbaceous Peonies

As far as we know the first hybrid herbaceous peonies were bred by Victor and Emile Lemoine at the beginning of the twentieth century. Their early crosses include 'Mai Fleuri' (1905), 'Le Printemps' (1905), 'Avant Garde' (1907) and 'Messagère' (1909), which are hybrids between *Paeonia lactiflora* and *P. wittmanniana*. The greatest progress was made by Professor Arthur Saunders, who systematically crossed all of the species that he could obtain and laid the foundation for the development of modern peony breeding. More recently breeders have concentrated on developing hybrids with *P. wittmanniana* and *P. macrophylla* (but see chapter 4), with the intention of producing early flowering plants with pastel-coloured flowers. The majority of the hybrids are between *P. lactiflora*, *P. officinalis* subsp. *officinalis*, *P. peregrina* and *P. wittmanniana*.

Hybrid peonies flower over a long period of time, from early spring, when the majority of the species flower, to the early summer when the Chinese, or lactiflora, peonies are in bloom. The earliest are those descended from *Paeonia wittmanniana* and *P. mlokosewitschii*, such as 'Athena' and 'Avant Garde'; the hybrids with *P. peregrina* and *P. officinalis*, 'America' and 'Postilion', flower a few weeks later in the late spring; and a tiny proportion, such as 'White Innocence' bloom at the same time as the lactifloras.

These plants are usually very vigorous and have a wide spectrum of flower colours. They range from 'Paula Fay' with vivid, neon pink flowers, to 'Lavender', salmon pink 'Salmon Dream' and apricot-coloured 'Coral Sunset'. There are many hybrids with bright red flowers, such as 'America' and 'Scarlet O'Hara', and when fully grown they make wonderful specimens. The hybrids between *P. lactiflora* and *P. peregrina* exhibit the greatest range of colours, including true scarlet, pink, coral red, apricot and peach shades.

Many of the hybrids with *Paeonia peregrina* produce adventitious buds on the roots, and plants, such as the stunning 'Cytherea', will eventually spread to form a large diffuse clump. Some such as 'Lovely Rose' are quite breathtaking, producing massive coral pink flowers measuring up to 18 CM (7 IN.) across, while hybrids descended from 'Otto Froebel' often have a broad white stripe on the reverse of the petals.

Yellow Herbaceous Peonies

American peony breeders had always dreamt of producing an herbaceous peony with double yellow flowers. The most obvious candidate as a parent was *Paeonia mlokosewitschii*, whose flowers are the deepest yellow among the species. However this species does not grow very well in the United States and this may have contributed to its failure to produce viable offspring.

One peony breeder, Dr. Earle White, tried to cross *Paeonia mlokosewitschii* with *P. lactiflora* on several thousand occasions, but only produced one fertile seed. This grew to produce the extremely beautiful hybrid 'Claire de Lune', which has single, pale yellow flowers. The indefatigable Arthur Saunders also had little success in breeding the two species, although he did succeed in crossing *P. mlokosewitschii* with *P. broteroi*, *P. emodi*, *P. peregrina* and *P. mascula* (subsp. *mascula* and subsp. *triternata*). Ironically *P. mlokosewitschii* seems to hybridize quite frequently with other species in Europe. Few of the plants are named, but

an exception is 'Cousin Nora', which can be found growing in the Royal Horticultural Society's Gardens, at Wisley, in England. This plant is labelled as *P. mlokosewitschii* but it is clearly a hybrid with another species, probably *P. wittmanniana*. It has large, glaucous, obovate leaves and bowl-shaped, pale yellow flowers with large tomentose carpels.

It was only at the end of the twentieth century that peony breeders finally managed to produce the first hybrid herbaceous peonies with double yellow flowers. This was achieved by using third generation seedlings from Arthur Saunders' 'Silver Dawn', the result of a cross between *Paeonia obovata* var. *willmottiae* and *P. macrophylla*.

In the past ten years or so it has become apparent that the taxonomy of the Caucasian peonies is far more complex

'Cousin Nora'

right: The hybrid 'America' has received a Gold Medal from the American Peony Society.

than was previously thought (see chapter 4). Some forms of *Paeonia wittmanniana* var. *nudicarpa* (syn. *P. steveniana*) have quite yellow flowers, which approach the hue seen in *P. mlokosewitschii.*

Catalogue of Hybrids

Details of flower form, colour and flowering time are given in chapter 2.

'America' (Rudolph, 1976)

Widely considered to be the best of the single, red hybrids, 'America' has massive single, brilliant scarlet-red flowers, touched with a hint of magenta. The petals have a satin finish and are delicately pleated, surrounding a mass of golden yellow stamens and yellowish green carpels with white styles. Awarded a Gold Medal by the APS. ('Burma Ruby' × unknown). Early to midseason, 90 CM (3 FT.).

'Angelo Cobb Freeborn' (Freeborn, 1943)

This long-flowering hybrid has unusual double, coral red flowers, surrounded by nicely rounded guard petals. The flower is composed of masses of tightly curled petals. The stems are strong, but they still need staking in exposed situations. (*P. lactiflora* × *P. officinalis*). Midseason, 1 M (3.3 FT.).

'Archangel' (Saunders, 1950)

A very impressive plant which has large, glossy, dark green leaves and single creamy white flowers. The flowers have large, furrowed, greyish green, tomentose carpels and purple styles, surrounded by a large mound of golden yellow stamens. The stamen filaments are very long, pale yellow, becoming purple at the base, and situated on a large staminoidal disc with bright pink lobes. It needs plenty of space as it has a spread of 1 M (3.3 FT.). (*P. lactiflora* × *P. macrophylla*). Early season, 80 CM (32 IN.).

'Athena' (Saunders, 1960)

'Athena' is a quadruple hybrid between *P. lactiflora,* *P. macrophylla*, *P. mlokosewitschii* and *P. officinalis* and is one of the first to flower in spring. The single, ivory white, cup-shaped flowers have large rose pink flares, and tomentose pale green carpels with red styles and golden yellow stamens. Very early season, 75 CM (30 IN.).

The beautiful hybrid 'Athena' flowers very early in the year and has distinctive rose-pink flares.

'Auten's 1816' (Auten)

Many people think this plant celebrates some long-forgotten battle, but the truth is more prosaic; 1816 is the breeder's seedling number. The large bomb-shaped flowers are composed of masses of dark red petals. The carpels are green with long styles and there are no stamens present. The plant has strong stems but they are unable to support the weight of the heavy blooms and it needs staking. Early season, 75 CM (30 IN.).

'Avant Garde' was bred by Victor and Emile Lemoine and was one of the earliest hybrid herbaceous peonies.

'Avant Garde' (Lemoine, 1907)

This was one the first hybrid peonies to be produced. The large, single flowers are strongly marked with magenta-coloured veins and the petals are suffused with magenta pigment, which fades as the flower ages. It has tomentose, green carpels with erect, dark red styles and golden yellow anthers with very long purple filaments. It is a vigorous plant with glossy mid green leaves. The true plant can be difficult to find for there are a lot of similar hybrids which purport to be 'Avant Garde'. (*P. wittmanniana* × *P. lactiflora*). Early season, 110 CM (43 IN.).

'Belle Center' (Mains, 1956)

Almost identical to 'Buckeye Belle', but it flowers a fortnight later. The flowers are semi-double, cup-shaped, with mahogany-red petals and yellow stamens. Early season, 75 CM (30 IN.).

'Black Monarch' (Glasscock, 1939)

This vigorous hybrid has very double, dark red flowers (53A) with tightly curled petals. There are no stamens and the greenish yellow carpels have long tapering magenta styles. It is a similar colour to 'Belle Center' and 'Buckeye Belle' and looks stunning when backlit by sunshine. It resembles a very dark version of *P. officinalis* 'Rubra Plena'. (*P. officinalis* × *P. lactiflora*). Early season, 75 CM (30 IN.).

'Bright Knight' (Glasscock, 1939)

A vigorous hybrid with large single blood red flowers, which eventually fade to magenta-red with age. The yellow anthers have white filaments, which become pink towards the base and sit on a pale pink staminoidal disc. Originally called 'Black Knight', it has light green carpels and coral pink styles. Very early season, 95 CM (3.1 FT.).

'Brightness' (Glasscock, 1947)

Vivid scarlet-red flowers open from beautifully rounded, tulip-shaped buds. The flowers have pale green carpels and cream styles surrounded by yellow anthers, supported by similarly coloured filaments. The flowers are held well above the ground on strong, erect stems, making this a good specimen for the front of an herbaceous border (*P. lactiflora* × *P. peregrina* 'Sunbeam'). Early season, 65 CM (26 IN.).

'Buckeye Belle' (Mains, 1956)

An unusual hybrid peony with striking dark red (53A) guard petals surrounding masses of variously shaped staminodes. The latter range in shape from functional stamens to petal-like structures tipped by arrow-shaped anthers and completely formed petals. Its carpels are pale green and tomentose with red styles. This is a very free-flowering cultivar, whose flowers look stunning when backlit by sunshine. 'Belle Center' is almost identical, but flowers approximately fourteen days later. Early season, 85 CM (34 IN.).

'Burma Midnight' (Roy G. Klehm, 1980)

This pretty hybrid is a seedling of the well-known 'Burma Ruby'. It is stronger growing than its parent with deep red (60B) flowers, a small centre of yellow stamens, and pale green carpels with creamy white styles. It has strong stems, but the flowers lack any fragrance. Midseason, 95 CM (3.1 FT.).

The colour of 'Buckeye Belle' is transformed by late afternoon sunshine from deep brownish red to a rich blood red.

'Burma Ruby' (Glasscock, 1951)

An eye-catching hybrid with large, single, brilliant red flowers, which can look remarkably like those of an Oriental poppy. The flowers are fragrant and have a mass of bright yellow stamens. The award-winning 'America' is a seedling of 'Burma Ruby', but the parent is still one of the best single reds available. Highly recommended. (*P. lactiflora* × *P. peregrina* 'Sunbeam'). Early season, 70 CM (28 IN.).

'Cardinal's Robe' (Saunders, 1940)

Very large single, bright scarlet flowers and pilose pale green carpels, which are surrounded by large stamens with golden yellow anthers. (*P. lactiflora* × *P. peregrina*). Early season, 65 CM (26 IN.).

'Carina' (Saunders, 1944)

Semi-double with bright scarlet flowers and deeply dissected foliage, this hybrid is reminiscent of its *P. peregrina* parent. The flowers have a conspicuous staminoidal disc with red lobes, pale green carpels and red styles. The anthers are golden yellow, supported by yellow filaments. The reverse of the petals is speckled with purple pigment. If you live in an area where the summers are very hot, 'Carina' will benefit from a shady position. (*P. lactiflora* × *P. peregrina*). Early season, 70 CM (28 IN.).

'Carol' (Bockstoce, 1955)

A vigorous, semi-double hybrid with fragrant, deep crimson-red flowers; the large petals are neatly arranged in a rosette and it makes a superb cut flower. However the plant has a rather poor habit in the garden for the stems, although strong, are not well supported at the base and tend to flop. There are no stamens or carpels. Early season, 70 CM (28 IN.).

'Chalice' (Saunders, 1929)

This elegant plant was one of Saunders' first hybrid peonies. It has large creamy white flowers, with a mass of golden yellow stamens in the centre, green carpels and red styles. The plant is very substantial with massive dark green leaves. (*P. lactiflora* × *P. macrophylla*). Very early season, 1.2 M (4 FT.).

'Cherry Ruffles', raised by Don Hollingsworth, has long-lived bright cherry red flowers.

Dr. Earle White crossed *Paeonia lactiflora* with pollen from *P. mlokosewitschii* on several thousand occasions, until he eventually produced 'Claire de Lune'.

'Cherry Ruffles' (Hollingsworth, 1996)

This is a fairly recent introduction. Its bright semi-double, cherry red flowers are extremely long lasting and supported by very strong stems. The flowers have pink filaments, golden yellow stamens and tomentose carpels with pale pink styles. Each ruffled petal has a pale blotch on the reverse. The glossy, deeply dissected leaves have slightly curly margins. This is a vigorous and highly recommended plant. ([*P. officinalis* × *P. peregrina*] × *P. lactiflora*). Midseason, 75 CM (30 IN.).

'Chief Justice' (Auten, 1941)

Semi-double flowers have glossy dark, cherry red petals and masses of golden yellow stamens. The stamens have long red filaments and form a decorative ring around the pale green carpels. It flowers very late in the season, often at the same time as *P. lactiflora*. (*P. lactiflora* × *P. officinalis*). Late season, 85 CM (34 IN.).

'Chocolate Soldier' (Auten, 1939)

It is stretching the truth to say that this hybrid has chocolate-coloured flowers but they are certainly a very dark shade of brownish red (slightly lighter than 187A, becoming redder as they age). The flowers vary from Japanese form to fully double on one plant. Most are single with large yellow anthers and reddish purple filaments, sitting on a bright pink staminoidal disc. The large tomentose, creamy white carpels have red styles. The plant is very vigorous with strong stems and dark green foliage. (*P. lactiflora* × *P. officinalis*). Early season, 70 CM (28 IN.).

'Claire de Lune' (White, 1954)

The breeder of this peony went to incredible lengths to achieve this, his Holy Grail: a cross between *P. mlokosewitschii* and *P. lactiflora* 'Monsieur Jules Elie'. Dr. Earle White made 500 crosses every year for eight years and, while several seeds germinated, only this one survived to maturity. It has slightly crinkled, but nicely rounded, creamy yellow petals, bright yellow anthers and orange filaments. One of the first peonies to flower in the spring, it has large tomentose carpels and cream-coloured styles. Very early season, 80 CM (32 IN.).

'Commando' (Glasscock, 1944)

A dramatic double flower with glossy, mahogany-red guard petals and masses of staminodes with pointed tips. The carpels are green with coral pink styles (*P. lactiflora* × *P. officinalis*). Early season, 95 CM (3.1 FT.).

'Coral Charm' (Wissing, 1964)

This is an incredibly beautiful peony with semi-double, saucer-shaped, peach-coloured flowers, with an orange centre. The outer petals are rounded, flushed with magenta pigment and marked on the reverse with a narrow white flare, while the inner petals are narrower and deeply incised. The tomentose green carpels have bright magenta, sickle-shaped styles and are surrounded by large, golden yellow anthers with orange filaments. GM. Early season, 90 CM (3 FT.).

'Coral Fay' (Fay, 1973)

This plant was a bit of surprise when I first saw it, because I was expecting bright lipstick-red flowers. Instead those of 'Coral Fay' are semi-double with rather floppy crimson-red (57A) petals and narrow foliage, derived from its *P. tenuifolia* parent. The carpels are pale green with pink styles and surrounded by a ring of yellow stamens with yellow and orange filaments. The petals blow about in the breeze and are touched with coral pink. Plants are very vigorous but may need supporting. Early season, 95 CM (38 IN.).

In the last forty years several peonies have been introduced with coral pink flowers. Those of the aptly named 'Coral Sunset' quickly turn to apricot and finally yellow.
(Credit: Roy Klehm).

'Coral Sunset' (Wissing-Carl G. Klehm, 1981)

This is an extremely important peony because it introduced a new colour to the palette: apricot. When they open the flowers are more evenly coloured than those of 'Coral Charm', but they quickly change from coral pink with an orange centre, to apricot and finally yellow. 'Coral Sunset' has approximately fifty petals, green tomentose carpels and bright pink styles. A few of the stamens are turned into non-functional staminodes, while the remainder have golden yellow anthers and filaments. (*P. lactiflora* 'Minnie Shaylor' × *P. peregrina* 'Otto Froebel'). Early season, 80 CM (32 IN.).

'Cream Delight' (Reath, 1971)

This is a beautiful single hybrid with glossy dark green foliage and highly fragrant, creamy white flowers. It produces side buds and has pale green, tomentose carpels with pink styles. Early to midseason, 80 CM (32 IN.).

'Cytherea' (Saunders, 1953)

An unusual peony, because it is low growing and forms a large diffuse clump. The roots are rather slender and produce adventitious buds at their tips. The crimson-red, semi-double flowers are borne on stiff upright stems. It is popular as a cut flower and has been awarded a Gold Medal by the APS. (*P. lactiflora* × *P. peregrina*). Early season, to 60 CM (24 IN.).

'Dad' (Glasscock-Krekler, 1959)

One of the most vigorous hybrids, a semi-double whose glossy, cardinal-red flowers turn slightly purple in bright sunshine. The carpels are very large and tomentose, with bright pink styles. The flowers have strong stems and very few stamens. Early season, 95 CM (3.1 FT.).

'Dauntless' (Glasscock, 1944)

This single hybrid has rather strangely coloured flowers, which are dark ruby red with a hint of brown, almost the colour of 'Chocolate Soldier'. The flowers have pale green, tomentose carpels with cream-coloured styles, surrounded by yellow stamens with red filaments. The plant is very vigorous, but it bears few flowers. (*P. lactiflora* × *P. officinalis*). Early season, 90 CM (36 IN.).

'Dawn Glow' (Saunders-Hollingsworth, 1986)

This beautiful hybrid peony was originally included in the famous 'Silver Dawn' mixture, but its qualities were recognized and the plant was given a separate cultivar name. It forms a very large plant, which flowers early in the season and has massive glossy green leaves. The flowers have large creamy white petals and magenta flares; a conspicuous pink staminoidal disc supports large tomentose carpels with red styles. Early season, 90 CM (36 IN.).

'Defender' (Saunders, 1929)

An attractive plant, but there are several other hybrids that are just as good or even better. Nevertheless the Royal Horticultural Society has given it an Award of Garden Merit, which should signify that it makes a particularly good garden plant. It has very large dark crimson, cup-shaped flowers and green carpels with pink styles. The stamens have golden yellow anthers with yellow filaments, becoming red towards the base. The stamens sit on a conspicuous pink disc. (*P. lactiflora* × *P. officinalis*). Early season, 1.1 M (3.6 FT.).

'Delaware Chief' (Hollingsworth, 1984)

Don Hollingsworth has taken one of the most common peonies, *P. officinalis* 'Rubra Plena', and crossed it with a double lactiflora with deep red flowers. In doing so he has retained much of the character of the former, but has eliminated most of its faults. 'Delaware Chief' has very large, deep crimson-red, fully double crown-shaped flowers with well-rounded guard petals and a large mass of staminodes; stamens are absent. The flowers gradually turn reddish purple (57A) in bright sunshine and have a pleasant spicy fragrance. A highly infertile triploid, with large pale green carpels and pink styles. Early midseason, 70 CM (28 IN.).

'Diana Parks' (Bockstoce, 1942)

This richly coloured hybrid has very fragrant double flowers, with large, nicely rounded guard petals. The bright fire engine red flowers fade to crimson-red as they age. It has pale green carpels and creamy white styles (*P. lactiflora* × *P. officinalis*). Early season, 85 CM (34 IN.).

'Early Glow' (Hollingsworth, 1992)

One of the earliest flowering herbaceous hybrids, 'Early Glow' has single, pale yellow cup-shaped flowers flushed at the base with pink pigment. The petals are slightly fluted with notched tips. The stamens have golden yellow anthers and yellow filaments, becoming pinkish red towards the base. The large pale green carpels are furrowed and rather hirsute, and have deep red styles. This is a very vigorous spreading plant that produces plenty of side buds and flowers for over two weeks. ('Roselette's Grandchild' × 'Cream Delight'). Very early season, 75 CM (30 IN.).

'Early Glow' has pale yellow flowers and slightly fluted petals.

'Early Scout' is a hybrid between a cultivar of *P. lactiflora* and *P. tenuifolia,* and flowers extremely early in the year.

'Ellen Cowley' has wonderful buds, that open to reveal semi-double flowers.

'Early Scout' (Auten, 1952)

A vigorous hybrid with deeply divided dark green foliage and deep red (60A) single flowers, with slightly notched petals. The carpels are pale green, finely furrowed, tomentose with long reddish purple styles. It has golden yellow anthers and purple filaments, supported by a pink staminoidal disc. (*P. lactiflora* 'Richard Carvel' × *P. tenuifolia*). Early season, 60 CM (24 IN.).

'Early Star' (Hollingsworth, 1993)

Single pale yellow flowers, measuring up to 15 CM (6 IN.) across, with very large anthers and yellow filaments. It has a pink staminoidal disc, supporting pink, tomentose carpels with purple styles. The leaves are very large and slightly glossy. (Saunders seedling 4992 × *P.* 'Roselette's Grandchild'). Very early season, 85 CM (34 IN.).

'Ellen Cowley' (Saunders, 1940)

This extremely pretty hybrid has semi-double, cherry pink flowers with white flares on the reverse of the petals, inherited from its *P. peregrina* parent. The flowers have rather large carpels and pink styles, surrounded by a small number of yellow stamens. The leaves are deeply dissected. (*P. lactiflora* × *P. peregrina*). Early season, 70 CM (28 IN.).

'Eventide' (Glasscock, 1945)

The single, bright rose red flowers have glossy petals. The colour fades towards the edge of the petals and a bold white stripe runs down the inner and outer surface. In the centre there are green carpels and coral pink styles, surrounded by golden yellow anthers with greenish yellow filaments. (*P. lactiflora* × *P. peregrina* 'Sunbeam'). Early season, 85 CM (34 IN.).

'Famie' (Saunders-Krekler, 1955)

An anemone-form hybrid with large orchid pink guard petals surrounding similarly coloured staminodes; the latter have a white line running down the middle. The centre of the flower is occupied by small, pale green carpels with cream-coloured styles. It was named after William Krekler's mother. Early season, 80 CM (32 IN.).

'Fire Bird' (Auten, 1956)

A fully double hybrid whose outer petals are dark cherry red on the outside, becoming almost mahogany-red towards the centre. The green carpels have small red styles. It has strong stems, but they need to be supported with canes. (*P. lactiflora* × *P. officinalis*). Early season, 90 CM (3 FT.).

'Firebelle' (Mains, 1959)

This vigorous hybrid peony has semi-double, bright scarlet-red flowers, supported by strong stems. The carpels are pale green with a pink-magenta style surrounded by long yellow anthers on short yellow filaments. It makes a good cut flower. Early season, 85 CM (34 IN.).

'Garden Peace' (Saunders, 1941)

Originally called 'Peace', this single-flowered hybrid with large glossy leaves has rather waxy, creamy white petals and a conspicuous pink staminoidal disc, topped by green carpels with purple tops and large purple styles. The flowers are pleasantly fragrant and the sidebuds enable it to have a long flowering period, but it needs to be staked. It is a back cross, produced by taking a hybrid between *P. lactiflora* and *P. officinalis* and crossing it with another *lactiflora*. Early season, 85 CM (34 IN.).

'Golden Glow' (Glasscock, 1935)

This pretty hybrid peony has single flowers, with glossy scarlet-orange flowers. The carpels are pale green with cream or pink styles, surrounded by a mound of bright yellow stamens. The glossy green leaves have emarginate tips. (*P. lactiflora* × *P. peregrina* 'Otto Froebel'). GM. Early season, 65 CM (26 IN.).

'Halcyon' (Saunders, 1948)

This unique plant has single, pale blush flowers with striking lavender-coloured flares at the base of the petals. It has yellow anthers on red filaments and light grey, tomentose carpels with red styles. 'Halcyon' was produced by crossing 'Ozieri Alba', a plant that Saunders had raised from seed, with a cultivar of *P. lactiflora*. Saunders was very excited to have produced a hybrid with lavender flares, but disappointed when he discovered the nursery that had supplied the original seed had lost the records of its parentage. Very early, 60 CM (24 IN.).

'Honor' (Saunders, 1941)

'Honor' is extremely beautiful and deserves a place in every garden. A hybrid between *P. lactiflora* and *P. peregrina* 'Otto Froebel', it has single, or occasionally semi-double Bengal rose (75B) flowers with a nice ring of golden yellow anthers and long greenish white filaments. The tomentose, pale green carpels have creamy white styles and sit on top of a conspicuous white staminoidal disc. The flowers are slightly fragrant. Midseason, 90 CM (36 IN.).

'Huang Jin Lun'
(Credit: David Root, Kelways)

'Huang Jin Lun' (China, origin unknown)

Perhaps the most enigmatic peony of all, 'Huang Jin Lun' is quite unlike any other in existence. The plant has bright green foliage, yellow roots and double yellow flowers and has been sold under various synonyms, including 'Goldmine', 'Golden Wheel', 'Minuet', 'Oriental Gold', 'Yokihi' and 'Aurea'.

'Huang Jin Lun' is thought to have originated in China and, according to Langhammer (1997), was first recorded during the Tang Dynasty (*circa* AD 800) when one was given to the Chinese Emperor. There is no further mention of the plant until approximately 200 years ago when it was rediscovered by Zhao-De-King, a breeder of herbaceous and tree peonies during the Qing Dynasty. In 1954 Louis Smirnow offered the plant for the first time in the United States under the name 'Oriental Gold', after acquiring it from Japan (the Japanese are thought to have obtained it when they invaded China during the 1930s). Smirnow registered the plant with the American Peony Society in 1974 and says that he obtained it from Japan in 1960, where it was known as 'Yokihi'.

Nothing else was heard about it until 1997 when White Flower Farm offered the plant as 'Golden Wheel' in their mail-order catalogue.

The bright yellowish green stems and foliage have no trace of red or purple pigmentation, and on the underside of the leaves are scattered long hairs. It appears to be related to *Paeonia lactiflora*, because it has a line of papillae along the edge of the leaf, which is good diagnostic feature for that species. The most likely explanation is that it is an ancient hybrid between an extinct or undiscovered species of peony with yellow flowers and *P. lactiflora*. It has a reputation of being difficult to grow and is still very expensive. It would be an exciting candidate for gene sequencing. Midseason, 90 CM (3 FT.).

'Illini Belle' (Glasscock, 1941)

'Illini Belle' and 'Illini Warrior' (below) are both named after Native American Indian tribes who lived on the upper reaches of the Mississippi River (the name is pronounced *Ill-eye-ni*).

'Illini Belle' has rather symmetrical, semi-double, ruby red flowers (53B) and glossy petals. The golden yellow stamens have purple filaments and surround pale green carpels with pink styles. Although the flowers are very pretty, the plant is slightly let down by the foliage and the stems need to be supported. Early season, 80 cm (32 in.).

'Illini Warrior' (Glasscock-Falk, 1955)
The very beautiful single or semi-double tulip-shaped flowers are cardinal red and have green carpels, with cream or salmon pink styles. The petals have a glossy surface similar to that of satin and slightly serrated tips. The parents of this pretty peony are unknown, but the presence of a pale line on the reverse of the petals suggests that *P. peregrina* might be one of them. It is very vigorous with fragrant flowers and has a nice mound of golden-yellow stamens, but the tall stems need support. Early season, 1 m (3.3 ft.).

The hybrid 'Illini Warrior' is named after the Native American Indians who used to live on the upper reaches of the Mississippi River.

'Janice' (Saunders, 1939)
This dainty hybrid has single, coral pink flowers held on very strong stems. The petals have a white centre. Golden yellow stamens surround yellow-green carpels, with cream-coloured styles. (*P. lactiflora × P. peregrina*). Midseason, 58 cm (23 in.).

'Jenny' (Breeder unknown)
I went through a lot of soul-searching before including this peony but it is so beautiful that I felt that it should be described, even though it is very difficult to find. 'Jenny' is a vigorous hybrid with glaucous mid-green foliage and pure white single flowers, with a large ring of yellow anthers on slender purple filaments, which become white towards the top. The upper surface of the leaves is lightly hairy, while underneath they are greyish green and more densely hairy. The petals are tinged with magenta towards the edge, which becomes more pronounced when the plant is grown in shade. It has three almost glabrous carpels and reddish purple styles. Early season, 80 cm high.

'Lavender' is the closest that anyone has come to producing a blue peony. The flowers have a strong magenta cast when they are young but quickly fade in strong sunshine to reveal this beautiful lavender colour.

'Lavender' (Saunders, 1939)
This cross between *P. coriacea* and *P. lactiflora* is the closest anyone has come to developing a peony with blue flowers. 'Lavender' originally had six or seven siblings, known collectively as the Lavender Strain, but it is not known how many of these still

survive. The single flowers are magenta-lavender when young, but as they mature they do indeed become lavender in colour. The leaves are purplish green with acuminate tips and wavy margins. Early season, 55 CM (22 IN.).

'Le Printemps' (Lemoine, 1905)

The large single flowers are pale creamy white with yellow veins, pale yellow anthers and white filaments, which become reddish purple towards the base. The carpels are green with reddish purple styles. 'Le Printemps' is another of the Lemoines' hybrids between *P. lactiflora* and *P. wittmanniana*, a vigorous plant with mid-green foliage similar to that of *P. wittmanniana*, and flowering in early spring. Early season, 80 CM (32 IN.).

'Legion of Honor' has very deep scarlet-red flowers, with a distinctive ring of yellow stamens.

While Roger Anderson is best known for his intersectional hybrids, he also raises hybrid peonies, such as 'Lime Phosphate'. The flowers open lime-green, but fade to yellow and have a vanilla fragrance.

'Legion of Honor' (Saunders, 1941)

Another fascinating hybrid from Arthur Saunders' stable, 'Legion of Honor' has single or semi-double flowers of an intense scarlet-red, without the slightest sign of pink, and a conspicuous ring of yellow anthers borne on cream filaments. The pale green tomentose carpels have recurved pink styles. Plants have wiry stems and bright green foliage. (*P. lactiflora* × *P. officinalis*). Early season, 70 CM (28 IN.)

'Lil' Sweetie' (Krekler-Roy G. Klehm)

A vigorous hybrid with attractive finely divided, dark green foliage and single, deep purplish red flowers (60B), which become redder as they age (61B). The stamens have golden yellow anthers and thin greenish yellow filaments, and the small tomentose carpels are greenish pink with reddish purple styles. Very early season, 75 CM (30 IN.).

'Lime Phosphate' (Anderson, 1999)

This is a rather unusual hybrid peony with Chartreuse-green (1D), semi-double, saucer-shaped flowers, which fade quickly to pale yellow. In some years the flowers are very double, but all have a pleasant vanilla fragrance. The inner petals are mixed with narrow yellow staminodes; beyond these are yellow stamens with yellowish green filaments. The carpels are greyish green, tomentose, and with red styles. Plants have a very robust habit with strong stems and distinctive, rather wrinkled, dark green leaves. Early season, 75 CM (30 IN.) with a similar spread.

'Lorelei' (Hollingsworth, 1996)

Bomb-shaped, double flowers which have a slight, rather spicy fragrance and a unique colouration. They open deep pink with a hint of orange, gradually turning to apricot and then buff where the petals are exposed to the sun; the depths of the flower remain deep pink. The glabrous bright green carpels have flattened, bright pink styles. (*P. lactiflora* 'Belleville' × 'Good Cheer'). Early to midseason, 70 CM (28 IN.).

'Lovely Rose' (Saunders, 1942)

This is such a beautiful plant, with massive semi-double flowers measuring up to 18 CM (7 IN.) across. They open carmine-rose fading to pale pink with a darker marbling, and there is a white blotch on the outside of the petals, towards the base. The flowers have golden stamens and pale green carpels with pink styles. It forms a diffuse clump of wide-spreading stems. (*P. lactiflora* × *P. peregrina*). Early season, 75 CM (30 IN.).

'Mai Fleuri' (Lemoine, 1905)

Raised in the early twentieth century by Victor Lemoine, this delicately coloured hybrid has white flowers flushed with blush pink and deep violet veins. (*P. lactiflora* × *P. wittmanniana*). Early season, 70 CM (28 IN.).

'Lovely Rose' is very vigorous and may have flowers measuring up to 18 cm (7 in.) across.

'Many Happy Returns' (Hollingsworth, 1990)

Deep cardinal-red, anemone-form flowers have all of the stamens converted into petals. The slightly scented flowers retain their colour well in strong sunshine and have nicely rounded guard petals. Carpels are pale green with tapered pink styles. Plants are vigorous with strong stems and deeply dissected, undulating leaves. ('Good Cheer' × 'Nippon Splendor'). Midseason, 76 CM (30 IN.).

'Marie Fischer' (Fischer, 1973)

A robust strong-stemmed plant with single ivory white flowers, tinged with a hint of blush pink. There are a large number of stamens with golden yellow anthers and cream filaments, which become pink towards the base. The carpels are green, pilose, with purple styles. Early season, 84 cm (33 in.).

'May Music' (Saunders, 1973)

Appealing single, flesh pink flowers are marked with dramatic magenta flares. The stamens have pale yellow anthers and long magenta filaments, enclosing pale green, pilose carpels with magenta styles. Plants are inclined to have rather crooked stems. Early season, 80 cm (32 in.).

'May Treat' (Krekler, 1978)

A pretty semi-double hybrid with large coral-pink flowers. It has yellow anthers and filaments, encircling green carpels with salmon pink styles. The petals are green at the base. Early season, 90 cm (36 in.).

'Melissa' (Anderson, 2005)

This beguiling peony is one of the deepest yellow double hybrids available and is named after my daughter. The deep sulphur yellow (2C) flowers are semi-double or double and have deeper yellow depths. Large, nicely rounded guard petals surround a ruff of smaller rounded petals and narrow yellow staminodes, which are arranged in a series of circles around the carpels. The carpels themselves are rather small, pale green and tomentose with pale pink styles. A few golden yellow anthers on delicate white filaments are present. It forms a fairly compact plant with glossy, bright green leaves. Early season, 65 cm (26 in.).

'Montezuma' (Saunders, 1943)

Saunders found that the cross between *P. lactiflora* and *P. peregrina* was very successful and produced many exciting hybrids. 'Montezuma' is one of the best, with tulip-like buds and single or semi-double, fragrant, dark scarlet flowers (46A). The petals have serrated tips and, like many *peregrina* offspring, have a broad white stripe on the outside of the petals. The tomentose carpels are greyish green and have salmon pink styles. Early season, 90 cm (3 ft.).

'Moonrise' (Saunders, 1949)

No one could have expected that a cross between *P. lactiflora* and *P. peregrina* would have produced such an extraordinarily beautiful peony. 'Moonrise' is an F2 hybrid with cream-coloured buds and creamy yellow single flowers. It has pleasant light green foliage with 11–13 leaflets. The fragrant flowers have golden yellow stamens and green carpels with cream-coloured styles. Early season, 70 cm (28 in.).

'Nova' (Saunders, 1950)

This is one of Saunders' most interesting crosses, between two Caucasian species, *P. macrophylla* and *P. mlokosewitschii*. 'Nova' is the best known, but its sibling 'Nova II' is also a desirable plant. Both have pale yellow flowers with very large leaves.

'Nova' is a very vigorous F2 hybrid with thick stems and is one of the first hybrids to flower in the spring. It has single, cup-shaped, pale yellow (8D) flowers with a very large mass of golden yellow stamens and an ivory white staminoidal disc. The stamens have large anthers and yellow filaments, becoming reddish orange at the base. Tetraploid and highly fertile. Very early season, 85 CM (33 IN.).

'Nova II' (Saunders, 1950)

'Nova II' is similar to 'Nova', with single, pale yellow flowers. The petals are flushed pale pink at the base and there are two, sometimes three, large, heavily tomentose, pale green carpels with ivory-white styles. It has golden yellow anthers on pale yellow filaments, which are tinted orange at the base. The flowers have a spicy fragrance and erect stems, which grow approximately 45 degrees from the vertical. The stems and underside of the leaves are slightly pubescent. Very early season, 90 CM (3 FT.).

'Papilio' (Saunders, 1950)

'Papilio' is a very vigorous peony with peach-coloured (26D) flowers. The underside of the petals is very strongly marked with bright red (58B) veins and on the inside the petals are flushed purple at the base. The carpels are pale green, tomentose and grooved with erect pinkish red styles. The anthers are golden yellow, very large, with short yellow filaments. The flowers are rather small for such a vigorous plant and have no fragrance. The stems and underside of the leaves are slightly pubescent. It is a quadruple hybrid between *P. lactiflora*, *P. macrophylla*, *P. mlokosewitschii* and *P. peregrina*. Early season, 85 CM (34 IN.).

'Paramount' (Krekler, 1978)

This is a fast-growing hybrid peony with single, rose red (58B) flowers and glossy emarginated leaves. The petals have a large white blotch on the inside and outside. It has green carpels and pink styles, surrounded by golden yellow anthers on long yellow filaments. Early season, 85 CM (34 IN.).

'Patriot' (Saunders, 1943)

This is a dramatic peony with single, bright crimson-red flowers, golden yellow stamens and reddish orange filaments. The carpels are yellowish green with cream-coloured styles. It has a large bright pink and white staminoidal disc. (*P. lactiflora* × *P. macrophylla*). Early season, 90 CM (3 FT.).

'Paula Fay' has extremely bright neon pink
flowers—but they are not to everyone's taste.

'Paula Fay' (Fay, 1968)

This is a popular F2 hybrid with rather waxy, semi-double, extremely vivid pink (57A) flowers. It has yellow anthers and filaments and green carpels with salmon pink styles. 'Paula Fay' is a vigorous plant with light green foliage and fragrant flowers, however their bright colour is not to everyone's taste. It makes a eye-catching garden plant and improves with age, flowering for up to two weeks. The stamens turn black if they are damaged by late frosts. GM. Early season, 90 CM (3 FT.).

'Pink Angel' (Christenson, 1948)

An appealing hybrid with large, single, blush pink flowers, strongly flushed towards the base of the petals with magenta pigment. The golden yellow anthers have very long filaments, which are violet at the base and white towards the top. The dark red carpels are tomentose with long, dark red, sickle-shaped styles. It forms a broad spreading plant, measuring up to 1 M (3.3 FT.) across, with strong stems and large elliptic leaflets. It is well worth growing, although slightly let down by the rather chemical smell of the flowers. (*P. wittmanniana* × unknown F2 hybrid). Early season, 70 CM (28 IN.).

'Pink Hawaiian Coral' (Roy G. Klehm, 1981)

This very beautiful hybrid has semi-double coral pink flowers. It has two rows of nicely rounded guard petals, with a bold white stripe on the outside and a centre of numerous wavy staminodes. The staminodes are very variable, some of them are quite broad, while others are narrow and wavy; a few of them have functional anthers. The carpels, creamy white when young, turn green and have coral pink styles. (*P. lactiflora* 'Charlie's White' × *P. peregrina* 'Otto Froebel'). Early season, 90 CM (3 FT.).

'Postilion' (Saunders, 1941)

'Postilion' is an extremely vigorous hybrid with large dark green leaves, strong stems and highly fragrant flowers. The semi-double flowers are bright scarlet-red with a touch of orange and occasionally have a "flower within a flower", with a small tuft of wavy petals emanating from the centre of the carpels. Further stamens and carpels can be found within these petals. This is one of the best red hybrid peonies, but the tall stems need support to prevent them from falling. (*P. officinalis* 'Sultan' × *P. lactiflora*). Early season, 90 CM (3 FT.).

'Prairie Moon' (Fay, 1959)

A particularly lovely peony with translucent petals produced by crossing 'Archangel' with 'Laura Magnuson'. The flowers are single, pale yellow, with a mound of bright yellow stamens and green carpels with creamy white styles. Highly desirable—even the buds are beautiful. Rather expensive to buy, but well worth the cost. Early season, 80 CM (32 IN.).

'Red Red Rose' (Saunders, 1942)

A semi-double peony with a very symmetrical flower composed of rather stiff, deep blood red petals, marked on the reverse with a paler stripe. The anthers are golden yellow with red filaments and surround yellowish green carpels with purple styles. It has very strong stems and beautiful buds. (*P. officinalis* × *P. peregrina*) Early season, 85 CM (34 IN.).

'Requiem' (Saunders, 1941)

'Requiem' is a substantial and free-flowering plant with tall stems, large glossy, dark green leaves and milky white flowers with yellow-green carpels and pink styles. The anthers are golden yellow, supported by yellow filaments becoming pink towards the base. The flowers have a pink staminoidal disc and a spicy fragrance. One of Arthur Saunders' best-known hybrid peonies, this is the result of backcrossing a hybrid between *P. lactiflora* and *P. macrophylla* with *P. lactiflora*. Midseason, 93 CM (37 IN.).

'Requiem' is one of Arthur Saunders' best-known hybrid peonies. He raised it by backcrossing a hybrid between *P. macrophylla* and *P. lactiflora* with another cultivar of *P. lactiflora*.

'Reward' (Saunders, 1941)

One of the earliest hybrid peonies to flower, 'Reward' has single, slightly fragrant flowers with glossy, ruby red petals. It has yellow anthers and very short filaments, which are pale yellow at the top and pink towards the base. The carpels are tomentose and topped by dark red styles.

At the base of the stamens is a distinctive bright magenta disc. (*P. lactiflora* × *P. peregrina*). Early season, 70 CM (28 IN.).

'Royal Rose' (Reath, 1980)

Young buds look like those of an artichoke, and form a series of concentric triangles. They open to semi-double, Neyron rose (55B/C) flowers with large yellowish green carpels and salmon-pink styles. It has golden yellow anthers and yellow filaments. (*P.* 'Paula Fay' × *P.* 'Moonrise'). Early season, 85 CM (34 IN.).

'Salmon Beauty' (Glasscock-Auten, 1939)

The elegant bomb-shaped flowers are composed of large, rounded rose red guard petals and masses of toothed staminodes with yellow margins. The carpels are yellow-green with creamy white styles. It needs staking. (*P. lactiflora* × *P. officinalis*). Midseason, 86 CM (34 IN.).

'Salmon Chiffon' (Rudolph-Roy G. Klehm, 1981)

An attractive single peony with cup-shaped flowers, which are salmon pink on the inside and deeper pink on the outside. The stamens have golden yellow anthers and yellow filaments, while the carpels are pale green with bright pink styles. It is of uncertain parentage, but is probably a seedling of 'Lovely Rose'. It is fragrant, early season, 76 CM (30 IN.).

Young plants of 'Salmon Dream' tend to have single flowers, but may be double on more established specimens.

'Salmon Dream' in maturity with double flowers.

'Salmon Dream' (Reath, 1979)

A wonderful plant, which has few peers. The flowers are deep salmon pink when they open with a magenta cast, but as they mature this colouration disappears and the petals become pure salmon pink with paler edges. The petals have a white flare on their reverse towards the base. On young plants the flowers are single, but as the peony matures they are more likely to be semi-double. Once the outer petals have opened the inner petals emerge in clusters among the stamens and grow quickly to fill the middle of the flower. It has tomentose carpels with salmon-pink styles and yellow stamens. It forms a very good-looking, compact plant with glossy green leaves and strong erect stems. ('Paula Fay' × 'Moonrise'). Early season, 85 cm (34 in.).

'Scarlet O'Hara' (Glasscock-Falk, 1956)

Breeders always face a very difficult task when they choose a name, but few new plants can have been so aptly named as 'Scarlet O'Hara', with its vigour and vivacious, bright scarlet-red flowers. The flowers are fragrant and have nicely rounded petals, large golden yellow anthers with yellow filaments, green carpels and salmon pink styles, and a pink staminoidal disc. There are a lot of single red hybrid peonies, but few can compare with this outstanding plant, with its vigour and strong stems. (*P. lactiflora* × *P. officinalis*). Early season, 90 cm (3 ft.).

Aptly named 'Scarlet O'Hara' has vivacious, bright scarlet-red flowers.

'Sprite' (Saunders, 1950)

A very vigorous peony with strong stems that bear fragrant single flowers. The petals are pale, creamy white in colour, flushed at the edges with magenta—the overall effect is of a pink and pale yellow flower. It has pale green, tomentose carpels with a grooved surface and red styles, golden yellow anthers and very short yellow filaments. It is very early flowering. [*P. lactiflora* × (*P. tenuifolia* × *P. mlokose-witschii*)]. Early season, 1 m (3.3 ft.).

'Starlight' (Saunders, 1949)

The flowers are single, sulphur yellow (8D) with a hint of pink at the base of the petals and borne on slightly pubescent stems. The carpels are pale green and tomentose, the anthers golden yellow and carried on rather short filaments, which are yellow at the top and pinkish orange at the base. The flowers have a slight spicy fragrance and open very early in the year. A quadruple hybrid between *P. lactiflora*, *P. officinalis*, *P. mlokosewitschii* and *P. macrophylla*. Early season, 1 m (3.3 ft.).

'Steve Nickel' (Krekler, 1980)

The single, bright China rose flowers have white flares at the base of the petals. The pilose, green carpels have bright pink styles and sit on top of an ivory white staminoidal disc. The stamens have golden yellow anthers and long pale yellow filaments. A vigorous plant with dark green foliage. Early season, 90 cm (3 ft.).

'Sugar 'n' Spice' (Rogers, 1988)

This recently introduced hybrid has very large, flesh pink flowers, measuring up to 23 CM (9 IN.) across. The petals, which become rather wavy with age, have a paler margin and a reticulate pattern of magenta. The centre of the flower is filled with a large mass of golden yellow stamens with pink filaments. The tomentose green carpels have greyish purple styles. It forms a very large, vigorous plant with massive, glossy green leaves, but needs some support. Early season, 1 M (3.3 FT.).

'Tranquil Dove' (Saunders)

A single-flowered hybrid with slightly curled white petals which are edged with lavender. The stamens have golden yellow anthers on magenta-coloured filaments, which become white towards the top, and the pink tomentose carpels have red styles. With its glossy green foliage it makes an attractive garden plant, but spots of lavender-coloured pigment sometimes spoil the flowers. Early season, 65 CM (26 IN.).

'Vivid Glow' (Lyman Cousins, 1986)

This vigorous hybrid peony has single, rose Benghal flowers, with a white line on the reverse of the petals. The stamens have yellow filaments, while the green carpels have magenta styles. It was originally called 'Vivid Salmon Glow'. Early season, 1 M (3.3 FT.).

'White Innocence' (Saunders, 1947)

'White Innocence' is one of Arthur Saunders' greatest achievements, produced by crossing P. lactiflora with P. emodi. It is the latest hybrid peony to flower and the tallest. There are several single flowers to a stem, each composed of 10 deeply notched, snow white petals and a small centre of golden yellow stamens. The white staminoidal disc partly encloses the pale green furrowed carpels which have white styles. Late season, 1.5 M (5 FT.).

Chapter 7
Chinese Tree Peonies

Tree peonies are among the oldest plants in the world and have made an indelible impact upon the world's art. The Chinese have been growing these lovely shrubs for approximately one thousand six hundred years and it is still easy for us to imagine the sense of awe that Europeans must have felt when they first saw them over three hundred years ago. The flowers were many times larger than those of a rose, and they must have seemed incredibly exotic. Most of us still have that feeling when we look at a mature plant, covered with dozens of flowers. On the face of it tree peonies appear to be rather delicate, but they can tolerate low temperatures in the winter when they are dormant and will withstand summer drought.

A mature tree peony, such as 'Qing Long Wo Fen Chi' (**Green Dragon in a Pink Pool**) may have a hundred or more flowers when it is mature.

History

Tree peonies are endemic to China, where they have been grown as medicinal plants since at least the Han Dynasty (206 BC–AD 220). The first reference to their medicinal use was found in a medical book, excavated in 1972 from a tomb in Gansu Province (Lianying *et al.*, 1998). Carved on sheets of bamboo and dated to the first century AD the book refers to the bark of tree peony roots being used to prevent blood clotting. Two centuries later the *Wu shih Pên Tshao*, which was written in AD 235, says that "The root is the thickness of a finger, and black, this is where the dangerous active principle resides. The fruits and seeds should be picked between the second and the eighth months, and when dried in the sun can be eaten. They lighten the body and promote longevity."

We do not know how long the Chinese have been growing tree peonies as ornamental plants, but they first appear in paintings as early as the fourth century AD. The earliest record of cultivated varieties comes from the time of the Sui Dynasty (AD 581–618), when tree peonies were grown in the imperial gardens in Xiyuan (now Luoyang). Most of them were probably collected from the wild and included plants with white, red or pink flowers. The tree peonies were so highly regarded that the Emperor Yang Ti issued a decree placing tree peonies under his personal protection.

During the reign of the Tang Dynasty (AD 618–907) China became a prosperous and peaceful country. Chinese nurserymen and private gardeners started to collect all of the species of tree peony that were available and experimented with them until they discovered how to graft them. Cultivation seems to have started in the old capital of Changan (now Xi'an in Shensi Province) and then spread to other provinces, where breeding continued and in some cases the plants were crossed with other wild species that were endemic to that region.

While open pollination must have taken place and new cultivars arose naturally it also seems likely that the Chinese would have quickly learnt how to pollinate the plants artificially and produce their own seedlings. One of the leading horticulturists of the time, Sung Shan-Fu (AD 713–755), is said to have produced a thousand varieties and made a plantation of "tens of thousands of them" for the emperor at his summer palace at Li Shan (Needham *et al.*, 1986).

Tree peonies gradually spread to the rest of China, so that by the time of the Song Dynasty (AD 960–1279) they were among the most popular of all garden plants in China. The main centre for tree peony cultivation at this time was Luoyang, where the Chinese started to produce cultivars with double flowers. The majority of the plants were named after the family that raised them and some of the ancient plants, such as Yao's Yellow, have survived to the present day.

The most important historical account of tree peonies grown in China is Ouyang Xiu's *Lo-Yang Mu-Tan Chi* (*Account of the Tree-Peonies of Luoyang*), which was written in AD 1034. He says:

> Most Loyang households have tree-peony flowers, but few of the plants grow into big
> trees, because without grafting the most elegant blooms are not produced. Early in

the spring Loyang people go out to the Shou-an Shan and cut small scions for sale within the city, cuttings which are called 'mountain combs'. The townsfolk cultivate the soil around their homes, making little bordered garden plots in which they plant the cuttings, and then when autumn comes they are grafted. The most famous practitioner of this art was a man called Mên the Gardener (Mên Yuan Tzu) and among the rich families there were none who failed to employ him. A single graft of the Yao yellow is worth 5000 cash. Contracts are made in the autumn, and when spring comes and the flowers appear, then the full payment is remitted (to the grafter). Loyang people are deeply attached to this variety and loth to allow the spread of its cultivation. If privileged patricians or high officials come looking for this flower they are likely to be given a graft which has been killed by dipping in hot water. [from Needham *et al.*, 1986]

Ouyang Xiu relates how tree peonies could be grafted or grown from seed and describes twenty-four varieties that were grown in Luoyang, including plants with red, yellow, purple and white flowers. The Chinese continued to breed tree peonies, so that by the early seventeenth century the author Xue Fengxiang is able to describe more than 260 cultivars in his book *Mudan Shi* (*History of Tree Peonies*) (Haw, 2001). In *circa* AD 1600 the Chinese discovered that tree peony cultivars grew better if they were grafted onto the rootstocks of wild tree peonies (Hsüeh Fêng-Hsiang, 1610).

Tree peonies now grow in public places throughout northern and central China, north of the Yangtze River (the Great River). They are deep within the Chinese psyche, and widely represented in traditional and contemporary propagandistic art because they symbolize prosperity. A potted tree peony is considered to be the perfect New Year's gift in China because it represents prosperity, good fortune and love. In the nineteenth century the Dowager Empress Ci Xi (AD 1835–1908), the country's penultimate imperial ruler, declared the tree peony the national flower of China. During the Cultural Revolution, which started in 1966, the cultivation of tree peonies was banned. The Chinese were forbidden to grow them for ornamental purposes, but most of the cultivars survived because the people claimed that they were growing the plants for medicinal purposes. In 1994 a poll was held to choose a new national flower, but the popularity of the tree peony is firmly rooted, because it still came top.

Horticultural Sharp Practice

Chinese tree peonies have been one of the best-kept secrets in the horticultural world. The Chinese have always been extremely wary of foreigners and during the latter part of the eighteenth century they did their best to prevent Europeans from obtaining their national flower.

European traders were well established in China by the end of the eighteenth century, but were restricted to trading posts, such as Canton and had little opportunity to explore the interior. The first cultivars that reached Europe have been criticized because they have very double flowers that hang between the leaves. Regardless of their political system the Chinese have always proved to be astute businessmen and, tempted by sufficient money, a few of them would have been willing to provide the Europeans with some tree peonies. The traders were probably happy with their purchase, but the Chinese appear to have had the last laugh because they supplied them with some of the worst plants. Some Chinese traders were even more devious because they boiled the tree peony roots in water to prevent them from growing.

In 1656 the Dutch East India Company sent traders from their base in Canton to the imperial capital Peking, where they saw tree peonies for the first time. The Europeans described the plants as being like roses but without thorns and having flowers that were twice as large (Haworth-Booth, 1963). The first tree peony to be grown in Europe was obtained by Dr. Alexander Duncan on behalf of Sir Joseph Banks, the first Director of the Royal Gardens at Kew (later the Royal Botanic Gardens). The plant arrived in 1789 and was followed by further specimens in 1794 and 1797. The original plant thrived at Kew and was reported as being 8 FT. high and 10 FT. across (2.5 × 3 M). Sadly it was destroyed in 1842 during the construction of a new building.

One of the most interesting specimens to be imported arrived in 1802 on board a ship called *Hope*. This had semi-double white flowers with deep purple flares at the base of the petals and a deep purple sheath. The plant was named *Paeonia papaveracea* and for many years it was believed to be the ancestral peony. The plant was painted by Clara Maria Pope in 1821 and is still one of the most beautiful paintings of any peony.

The arrival of the plants caused great excitement in Britain but further tree peonies proved hard to obtain. The main problem the British faced was that they were restricted to Macao and were not allowed to travel into the interior of China. Macao was too hot for tree peonies to grow and the plants were imported from the cooler parts of the country. The tree peonies started to arrive in the spring, but by this time the traders from the British East India Company had returned home (Sabine, 1826).

In 1806 the British East India Company obtained four paintings of tree peonies, painted in Canton by Chinese artists. With the help of John Reeves, the Royal Horticultural Society obtained copies of these and a later painting of a double yellow tree peony. Joseph Sabine, the Secretary of the Royal Horticultural Society, did not believe that the yellow tree peony existed and said "the existence of a Yellow Moutan, is altogether disbelieved by those best capable of forming a judgment [sic] on the subject." (Sabine, 1826). Sabine says the plant was called 'Wong Moutan Fa', and it has been suggested that the illustration is actually of **Yao's Yellow** ('Yao Huang'), which has creamy yellow flowers and certainly existed at that time. Among the other paintings in the "Reeves Collection" is a portrait of a tree peony with orange flowers. This would appear to have been a figment of the artist's imagination, but it is always possible that such a peony did exist and has since been lost.

In 1834 the Royal Horticultural Society commissioned Robert Fortune, the famous plant hunter, to collect plants from China. Fortune's contract makes fascinating reading:

It is needless to particularise at much length the plants for which you must enquire.
It is however desirable to draw your attention to—
The Peaches of Pekin, cultivated in the Emperor's garden and weighing 2 lbs.
The Plants that yield tea of different qualities.
The circumstances under which the Enkianthi grow at Hong Kong, where they are
    found wild in the mountain.
The Double Yellow Roses of which two sorts are said to occur in Chinese gardens
    exclusive of the Banksian.
The Plant which furnishes rice paper.
Peonies with blue flowers, the existence of which is, however, doubtful. [Wilson, 1943]

Fortune made a total of four trips and in 1846 returned with twenty-five different tree peonies. These were planted in the Society's garden at Chiswick, London, where they started to flower in 1847. One of the plants was thought to have wisteria blue flowers, but when it bloomed for the first time they were lilac. The tree peonies were propagated by British and European nurserymen and soon became highly fashionable. E. H. Krelage, a Dutch nursery, was offering 190 cultivars in 1867 and by the late 1890s the French nursery Louis Paillet was listing 337. The final collection from China was made in 1890.

Chinese tree peonies were widely grown in Europe during the nineteenth century and several nurseries raised their own seedlings, many of which had very double flowers. However, when Japanese tree peonies started to become available in the latter part of the nineteenth century, the Chinese cultivars started to fall from favour. A number of the old varieties continued to be grown, particularly in France, and a few, such as 'Reine Elizabeth' are still available.

Renaissance

China was a closed society for much of the twentieth century and during this time little information reached the West about tree peonies. A colossal number of tree peonies were lost during the Cultural Revolution because they were seen by the Communist regime to represent the bourgeoisie. However, many were also preserved by Chinese claiming they were keeping them for medicinal purposes.

David Furman, of Cricket Hill Garden in Connecticut, first discovered Chinese tree peonies through reading Chinese literature and poetry. In 1964 he saw a series of Chinese stamps illustrated with paintings of tree peonies and then an article in a Chinese magazine called *China Reconstructs*, which showed pictures of tree peonies growing in a commune in China. He wrote to the magazine and asked where the peonies grew, but his letters to the nurseries remained unanswered. In the late 1980s David's wife, Kasha, read an article written by an official from the Parks Department in Luoyang, and wrote to enquire whether it would be possible to purchase some plants, with the intention of buying ten, but the nursery wrote back saying they would have to take 200. The Furmans sent the money, not knowing whether they would ever see the extremely expensive plants. They also bought a few tree peonies from a trading company in Shanghai, but they proved to be inferior and some never bloomed. Louis Smirnow had imported a few tree peonies from China a few years before, but in several cases the nurseries accepted the payment, but failed to ship the plants.

The first shipment consisted of five cultivars, which arrived during a snowstorm in December 1989 and David and Kasha had to remove the snow from the ground in order to plant them. The plants proved to be extraordinarily hardy and the majority survived to grow in the spring, spurring the Furmans to find better suppliers and investigate which were the best plants to purchase. Since then they have made purchases every year, gradually increasing their range of tree peonies. In 1993 they established Cricket Hill Garden and have spent the past twelve years assessing and increasing the range of cultivars. During this time they have established good working relationships with several Chinese sources and gradually improved the quality of the plants. They have managed to check cultivars are true to name and have also found which tree peonies are most suitable for American gardens.

The Furman's nursery is the only display garden in the U.S.A. that shows the complete range of Chinese tree peonies currently available. To date they have assessed approximately three hundred cultivars, but they only offer around seventy-five, having discarded many that are slow growing, shy flowering or otherwise unsuitable. They have learnt much from their dealings with the Chinese, including that it is possible to propagate tree peonies by layering, which was previously thought impossible. One of their most important contributions has been to ensure that plants are true to name, and their garden remains a unique reference collection. In the past eight years several other companies have started to import tree peonies from China, ranging from well-established peony nurseries to companies that trade entirely on the Internet.

Tree peonies have had a more chequered history in Europe. Chinese tree peonies became extremely fashionable when they were first introduced and were widely grown by the British aristocracy. Towards the end of the nineteenth century Japanese tree peonies started to be introduced and they seem to have been more popular and easier to obtain than their Chinese counterparts, which had to be propagated by European nurseries. While a number of nurseries succeeded in raising their own cultivars of tree peony from seed the majority imported the plants directly from Japan and gave them European names. In the early twentieth century Kelways, the British peony nursery, listed over a hundred tree peonies in their catalogues, but it seems likely that the great majority of their plants were actually Japanese cultivars that had been given English names. Demand for tree peonies gradually declined in Europe after the First World War and ceased with the advent of the Second World War, when trade with Japan came to an abrupt halt. In the U.K. antagonism towards the Japanese continued for many years after the Second World War, but sales started to increase again towards the end of the 1950s. In the early 1960s Michael Haworth Booth, who wrote a book about tree peonies, had a substantial collection of tree peonies at his home in Surrey, England. Unfortunately the plants were devastated by an attack of botrytis and he never managed to rebuild the collection. The French nursery of Pivoines Rivières, which was established in 1849, is currently the only company in Europe that propagates tree peonies and is still introducing new cultivars, such as 'Isabelle Rivière' and 'Jaqueline Farvacques'. Chinese tree peonies enjoyed a brief renaissance in Europe at the end of the 1990s, but Japanese tree peonies sell in larger quantities because they produce flowers on one-year grafts. At the time of writing the demand for American hybrid tree peonies is showing a significant increase, fuelled by increased availability and greater publicity.

The distinction between Chinese and Japanese tree peonies

From a botanical perspective the distinction between Chinese and Japanese tree peonies is completely artificial and many single and semi-double Chinese tree peonies look very like their Japanese cousins. However, Chinese cultivars show a much greater diversity in flower form, habit and leaf shape, the result of crossing several species over hundreds of years. By contrast the Japanese tree peonies seem to have been bred from a smaller number of ancestral species and the gene pool does not seem to have increased since the plants were first imported from China in the eighth century AD. Because of this, Japanese tree peonies are more uniform and have similar foliage. Chinese tree peonies appear to be more vigorous overall and many double cultivars are extremely fragrant, whereas Japanese tree peonies tend to become more vigorous only when they have developed their own root system, and most cultivars have little or no fragrance. Some people believe that Chinese cultivars may be more susceptible to late spring frosts than Japanese cultivars, but this may be because they flower a couple of weeks earlier. In Japan tree peonies are often disbudded to prevent the weight of the flowers from damaging the plant.

Many of the plants sold as *Paeonia rockii* are actually F1 hybrids between *P. rockii* and another species, "Gansu Mudan". These can be distinguished from the true species by their vigorous growth and larger leaflets. The flowers vary and can have differently shaped flares and coloured filaments. The original specimens of *P. rockii* 'Rock's Variety' were probably selected from wild plants because they have attractive pink buds and better-shaped flowers than the others.

The Chinese tree peony Pea Green ('Du Lou') is highly prized in China, but the distorted green flowers are probably the result of a genetic abnormality. The plant is rather flaccid and produces few flowers and while it is unique, it is difficult to justify growing it as a decorative plant. The cultivar 'San Bian Sai Yu' (Better than Jade with Triple Magic) is a much better plant, producing attractive flowers from its green buds.

Tree Peonies in China

It has always been thought that it was only the Japanese who grafted tree peonies and that the Chinese either grew them from seed or divided them. However it now appears that this is incorrect because while the cheaper plants are divided the most expensive are grafted (David Furman, *personal communication*). Cultivars with dark flowers tend to be slower growing and these are also grafted. Some older plants just fall apart when they are dug up and this makes them very easy to propagate. The Chinese are now actively breeding tree peonies and a large number of new cultivars have been introduced since the 1960s. There are now more than 800 cultivars available, ranging from singles to plants with fully double flowers.

China is a huge country with temperate, subtropical and tropical zones and because tree peonies have been bred for so long they have become adapted to the local climate where they have been raised. Chinese scientists have determined that there are four different cultivar groups, which are restricted to different geographical areas of China (Lianying *et al.*, 1998), and these are listed below. While this scheme has merit it is likely that tree peonies have a far more complex ancestry, which includes most of the existing wild species and possibly others now extinct. It also seems probable that the Chinese have used *Paeonia delavayi* in their tree peony breeding, but this may be difficult to prove without gene sequencing.

Central Plains Cultivar Group

The group developed in the middle and lower reaches of the Yellow River and includes over 500 cultivars. This is the most important group commercially, because the plants are very adaptable and available in a wide range of colours. The group was bred mainly from *Paeonia spontanea*, *P. rockii* and *P. ostii*.

There are approximately six hundred cultivars of "Gansu Mudan". They originate from Northwest China and are hybrid descendants of *Paeonia rockii* with other species. 'Hei Xuan Feng' (**Black Tornado**) has large flares at the base of its petals.

Northwest Cultivar Group

Peonies that evolved in Gansu, Qinghai, Shaanxi and Ningxia Provinces are very resistant to cold and drought. The plants appear to have been bred from *Paeonia rockii* and *P. spontanea* and have a dark flare at the base of the petals. They are often called "Gansu Mudan".

Southern Yangtze Cultivar Group

Developed mainly from *Paeonia ostii*, which grows along the banks of the Yangtze River, the group includes cultivars from the Central Plains Cultivar Group that can adapt to a hotter climate and their hybrids with *Paeonia ostii*. Over a hundred cultivars were known in the early nineteenth century, but only twenty to thirty have survived. They are tolerant of heat and high humidity.

Southwest Cultivar Group

The majority of the tree peonies that are grown in Tibet and the provinces of Sichuan, Yunnan and Guizhou seem to be descendants of the Central Plains and Northwest Cultivar Groups. They are based upon *Paeonia rockii*, *P. spontanea* and *P. ostii*, however, the ancestry is very uncertain and it is possible that it includes the genes of other species. In the twelfth century there were approximately one hundred cultivars, but only ten have survived to the present time. The plants are tall and sturdy and their large flowers have a dark flare or reddish mark at the base of the petals.

Growth

Many catalogues and books suggest that Chinese tree peonies can grow to as much as 3 M (10 FT.) high and have a similar spread. This is misleading, for while they are certainly capable of achieving this size it may take fifty to sixty years. The size given at the end of the description of each peony is an indication of how large the plant can be expected to become after approximately ten years. Of course, the growth rate depends to a great extent upon the soil conditions, climate and whether the plant is situated in shade or full sunshine. Some cultivars grow extremely quickly, while others are less vigorous.

Tree peonies can be grown successfully in most parts of Europe, but botrytis can be a serious problem in those areas that have an Atlantic climate, such as the British Isles. The British climate is notorious and while it benefits from mild winters, the springs are often wet and frosts can still occur in the month of May. Peony blight (*Botrytis paeoniae*) can be a serious problem in wet springs and may devastate a collection of peonies unless preventative action is taken. Recent changes in European legislation have led to the withdrawal of many horticultural chemicals and at the time of writing there is no systemic fungicide available in the United Kingdom for the control of botrytis. In the British Isles *Moutan* tree peonies usually flower from the end of April to the middle of May and hybrid tree peonies (*P. ×lemoinei*) from the beginning to end of May, although this may be delayed by as much as a fortnight in cold weather. In the South of France tree peonies flower approximately two weeks earlier than in the British Isles.

Opinions differ on how Chinese tree peonies perform in the United States. The Furmans believe that the Chinese plants will grow successfully throughout the U.S.A. and are hardy in U.S.D.A. zones 4–9. However, Don Hollingsworth, who lives in Missouri, believes that Japanese tree peonies grow better in the Midwest than Chinese. It is self evident that Chinese tree peonies are a relatively recent introduction to the U.S.A. and it may be some time before the situation becomes clear.

Flowering and flower types

Tree peonies may not produce flowers typical of the cultivar until they are several years old; young plants have a tendency to develop single blooms and fully double flowers may not appear until the plant is five or more years old. Double-flowered cultivars may continue to produce the occasional single flower, even when a plant is ten or more years old. Black-flowered cultivars or those with very dark flowers seem to grow very slowly, although the reason for this is unknown.

While herbaceous peonies flower at different times during the season, the distinction is not so marked with tree peonies. Flowering time depends more upon position—whether they are grown in full sun or shade—and the prevailing climatic conditions. In the State

These Chinese parasols perform a dual function; they protect the flowers from the effects of heavy rain and reduce the bleaching effect of the sun. The photograph was taken at Cricket Hill Garden in Connecticut, U.S.A.

of Connecticut Chinese tree peonies start to flower between 10 and 20 May, but this can vary by at least a fortnight, depending upon the weather.

The majority of peonies exhibit their most intense colour when the flowers are young and just opening. The colour can fade in strong sunshine, but you can reduce this if you provide some shading. The traditional method of shading is with umbrellas decorated with Chinese paintings, and these also give protection from heavy rain, which can damage the delicate flowers. It is possible to extend the flowering period for most cultivars by placing several plants in different locations in the garden. Plants in shade may flower between seven and ten days later than the same cultivar growing in full sunshine.

The Chinese recognize eight forms of tree peony flower, according to the number of petals and the origin of the plant. These terms are rarely used in the West, but you may find them referred to in nursery catalogues and Chinese books.

Single
Flowers have a single set of petals, normal stamens and carpels.

Lotus
In this type of flower there are four to five whorls of petals, which slightly overlap. Both lotus and chrysanthemum forms (see below) are considered semi-double in the West. The stamens and carpels are normal.

Chrysanthemum
These flowers have six whorls of petals, which gradually decrease in size towards the centre. The stamens may be normal or converted into staminodes.

Rose
The petals are slightly longer than in the chrysanthemum form, and they gradually become smaller towards the centre of the bloom. The stamens are converted into staminodes, while the carpels may be normal or converted into carpelodes.

Anemone
The flowers have two or three whorls of normal petals, but the stamens are converted into masses of long, narrow staminodes.

Crown
A raised dome of petals is surrounded by enlarged guard petals. Both the stamens and carpels are developed into petaloids. The term is also used in the West.

Globular or "silk ball"
All parts of the flower, including the stamens and carpels, are converted into petals. The bloom looks like a fluffy ball. Some very large flowers within this group, such as Purple Kudzu Scarf, are referred to by the Chinese as the "thousand-petal" form. They are very heavy and may lie on the ground when fully developed. This is not a desirable characteristic, but the plants are better able to support the flowers when they are fully grown and have stronger stems. The term "thousand-petal" is an exaggeration, because there are rarely more than three or four hundred petals.

Proliferate
Some cultivars of tree peony appear to have a flower within a flower, which the Chinese refer to as being proliferate.

Flowering time
It has become a convention to state whether peonies flower in the early, middle or late season. While this is very useful with herbaceous peonies, it does not have any direct value for *Moutan* tree peonies. Chinese and Japanese tree peonies flower at the same time but the flowering time depends upon the geographical location, prevailing climate and position in the garden.

Some Chinese tree peonies, such as 'Jia Ge Jin Zi' (Purple Kudzu Scarf), have very heavy flowers, which cannot be supported by the stems.

Fragrance

Fragrance, always difficult to describe, varies with the age of the flower and the time of day and the temperature. Tree peonies with single flowers rarely have much fragrance, but semi-doubles and doubles can be remarkably fragrant, with the scent drifting several metres on a still warm day. The majority of tree peonies have a rather spicy scent, but some have a sweet fragrance, similar to that of roses, and others can be best described as having a chemical, rather artificial smell.

Names

The Chinese language cannot always be translated directly into English and some peony names can have several interpretations. Care should therefore be taken when buying plants, because the same cultivar may be listed under several different names by various nurseries. It has been suggested that many of the tree peonies were named when the Chinese had a more liberal attitude towards sex and love, and the names often have a sexual connotation. Chinese names are usually written in traditional characters, which have been used in China for more than three thousand years. In 1958 the Chinese Government adopted the Pinyin zimu system as the standard way of translating traditional characters into Roman. In the following descriptions the first name (in quotation marks) is the Pinyin for the plant and is equivalent to a cultivar. The second name is the transliterated English name and equivalent to a trade designation. The transliterated name may not always be a direct translation of the Chinese name, particularly if the original was disparaging towards westerners or particularly bloodthirsty!

Catalogue of Cultivars

'Bai Xue Ta' (Snow White Pagoda)

This is a very vigorous crown or globe-shaped peony with bright green foliage on a robust, healthy-looking bush. It produces pure white flowers without flares and they have a slight spicy fragrance. A purple sheath surrounds pale green carpels with pinkish red styles. The golden yellow anthers have white filaments flushed purple at the base. Height 70 CM (28 IN.), spread 1.2 M (4 FT.) after 10 years.

'Cong Zhong Xiao' (Smiling In The Thicket)

A very vigorous tree peony with large, bright green leaves and semi-double flowers, which are deep magenta-pink (66D) with raspberry red flares. Towards the centre petals are smaller with a few wavy carpelodes. The stamens are supported by very short purple filaments, which are mixed with small pink staminodes. Flower form ranges from flat, saucer-shaped, to a large bomb, with arching staminodes. These flowers have alternating layers of petals, stamens, arching staminodes, stamens and finally carpelodes. The remaining carpels are pale green, with raspberry red styles. Blooms may be rather hidden by foliage. Height 80 CM (32 IN.), spread 1.2 M (4 FT.) after ten years.

'Da Hu Hong' (Big Hu's Red or Grand Barbarian Red)

This is a low-growing shrub with broad, red-flushed foliage of rather waxy texture. The semi-double flowers have a slight spicy fragrance. They are deep magenta-pink (66c) with warmer overtones and have small violet flares at the base of the petals. The tomentose carpels have reddish purple styles and are surrounded by a purple sheath. It has golden yellow anthers on long purple filaments. Plants are usually sold as **Big Hu's Red**, because **Grand Barbarian** is a rather disparaging reference to Europeans! Height 60 CM (24 IN.), spread 1.2 M (4 FT.).

'Da Zong Zi' (Deep Dark Purple)

An extremely vigorous plant which has large, dark green leaves and strong branching stems. The very fragrant flowers range from single to extremely large, crown-shaped blooms with imperial purple (78A) petals and darker purple flares; crown-shaped flowers have a layer of small purple, narrow staminodes in the middle of a ring of yellow stamens with purple filaments. The carpels in the centre of the flower are green, tomentose with red styles and surrounded by a rudimentary purple sheath. Strictly speaking the Pinyin name should be translated as **Big Brown Purple**. Height 80 CM (32 IN.), spread 1.4 M (4.6 FT.) after ten years.

'Er Qiao' (Twin Beauty)

An unusual cultivar named after the Qiao sisters, who are famous characters in Chinese literature. The flowers are magenta-red or pink, or a combination of both. The petals have a small deep red flare at the base. The plant is said to grow to a height of 2.5 M (8 FT.), but will only reach 1.2 M (4 FT.) after ten years.

'Fen Zhong Guan' (Supreme Pink)

A low-growing, spreading shrub with mid-green leaves bear semi-double, rose pink flowers with coral overtones. The flower buds are slow to open, then the colour appears in minutes. A purple sheath surrounds green, tomentose

The vigorous 'Da Hu Hong' (**Big Hu's Red**) also has the less elegant name of **Grand Barbarian Red**, a less than complimentary reference to the early European visitors to China.

'Da Zong Zi' (**Deep Dark Purple**) is a very vigorous Chinese tree peony with imperial purple flowers.

'Fen Zhong Guan' (**Supreme Pink**) is one of the most popular pink tree peonies in China. Young plants have semi-double flowers, but these become crown shaped on older specimens. It is vigorous and forms a spreading bush.

carpels with upright purple styles. The majority of the anthers are functional, golden yellow and supported by purple filaments, the remainder are developed into small pink staminodes. Plants can be slow to flower. Height 60 CM (24 IN.), spread 1.2 M (4 FT.) in ten years.

'Feng Dan Bai' (White Phoenix) is widely grown in China as a medicinal plant. Some specimens may have conspicuous patches of magenta at the base of the petals, which is inherited from *Paeonia ostii*. 'Feng Dan Bai' is often sold as that species, but the plant is very variable, as is apparent from the above photographs.

'Feng Dan Bai' (White Phoenix)

This is a cultivated form of *Paeonia ostii* and selected plants may be offered as the species. It has slightly ruffled white flowers with pale purple flares at the base of the petals and a slight spicy fragrance. The carpels are green, tomentose, with bright red styles and enclosed by a purple sheath. The stamens are golden yellow, supported on long purple filaments, which are white at the top. The attractive greyish green leaves have very long leaflets, the laterals are lanceolate and the terminal divided into three lobes (trifurcate). The cultivated form is considerably more vigorous than the species, probably the result of hybrid vigour. Plants are mainly raised from seed for medicinal purposes in China, but a selection of the more decorative plants may be offered for sale as ornamentals. The roots are valuable and plants are sometimes offered for sale with these pruned. The plants will recover from this treatment. 'Feng Dan Bai' is widely cultivated in China for use in Traditional Chinese Medicine (TCM). The bark of the root is called Mu Dan Pi (Moutan Radicis Cortex) and is produced by boiling the roots in water until the bark can be removed with a sharp knife. Mu Dan Pi is used as a sedative, an anticonvulsant and an analgesic; it has an anti-microbial effect against *Escherichia coli*, typhoid, cholera, *Staphylococcus aureus* and *Streptococcus hemolyticus* (for further details please see Page, 1997). Height 1.5 M (5 FT.), spread 1.1 M (3.6 FT.) after ten years.

'Feng Dan Zi' (Purple Phoenix)

A very elegant tree peony with strong upright stems and long green leaflets with a distinctive sinuous margin. A solitary, single flower tops each stem with pale lavender (78D) petals and a spicy fragrance. The flowers retain their colour well, but become blotched with specks of magenta as they age. They are quite large, measuring approximately 18 CM (7 IN.) in diameter, with deeply notched petals. The pale green carpels, which have purple styles and a purplish red sheath, are surrounded by a compact ring of golden yellow anthers on deep violet filaments. This erect growing plant has an inverted, cone-shaped habit. Height and spread 1.2 M (4 FT.) in ten years.

'Gong Yang Zhuang' (Palace Dress)

A low-growing tree peony with a spreading habit and very pretty, semi-double, bowl-shaped flowers. The flowers are deep neyron rose (55B) with yellow overtones, the colour becoming more intense in the centre of the bloom. Petals have notched tips and small maroon flares. The tomentose green carpels have red styles and are surrounded by an attractive violet sheath, which is enclosed by long yellow anthers, supported on violet and white filaments. The mid-green leaves have rather narrow leaflets. Height 70 CM (28 IN.), spread 1.2 M (4 FT.) in ten years.

'Feng Dan Zi' (**Purple Phoenix**) has pale lavender flowers opening from tapering buds, and (**left**) handsome foliage .

'He Hua Ying Ri' (Lotus that Shines in the Sun)

This extremely vigorous tree peony has an erect habit, with strong upright shoots and large, bright green leaves. Large buds open to single, pale violet flowers, whose petals are strongly flushed at the base with violet and have similarly coloured veins. Carpels are yellowish green with bright red styles, enclosed by a maroon sheath. The golden yellow anthers are held on short violet filaments. The stems can grow up to 60 cm (24 in.) in one season and may be up to 1 cm (0.04 in.) in diameter. Most tree peonies tend to produce a small bush with rather weak stems, but plant breeders could use this cultivar to produce plants with a better, more upright habit. Height 1.2 m (4 ft.), spread of 1.3 m (4.3 ft.).

'He Huan Jiao' (Merry Charm)

Mid-green foliage on an upright, compact shrub bearing flowers that are semi-double, pale pink with deep reddish purple flares. The inner petals are narrower and deeply forked, while the outer ones are larger and entire. Attractive purple stamen filaments surround 10 tomentose mid-green carpels with red styles. The flowers have a slight spicy fragrance but are not very well shaped. Height and spread of 70 cm (28 in.) in ten years.

'Hei Xuan Feng' (Black Tornado)

An erect growing Gansu hybrid with striking, very dark purple (60a) globe-shaped flowers with a spicy fragrance and measuring up to 15 cm (6 in.) across. The petals are all of a similar size and surround yellow anthers, which are borne on short, reddish purple filaments. The carpels are usually multiplied (up to 15) and surrounded by strands of a rudimentary ivory white sheath. The leaves are dark green, with reddish brown petioles. Height 1.2 m (4 ft.), spread 1.4 m (4.6 ft.) in ten years.

'Hong Mei Ao Shang' (Plum Blossom facing the Snow Storm)

A spreading shrub with bluish green leaves, forming a low, flat, cone-shaped bush. It has single, shell pink (62d) flowers with a hint of violet at the base of each petal. The carpels are pale green, tomentose and surrounded by a bright red sheath. The yellow anthers are supported on violet filaments. Height 70 cm (28 in.), spread 1 m (3.3 ft.) after ten years.

'Hu Hong' (Hu's Family Red)

This well-known peony has a rather prostrate habit, with large, coarse, mid-green foliage. It bears large, deep rose Bengal (57d) flowers, which can measure as much as 16 cm (6.3 in.) across. The carpels are green with purple styles and surrounded by a deep purple sheath. The pale yellow anthers are quite large and supported by robust purple filaments. Height 50 cm (20 in.), spread 1.5 m (5 ft.).

'Hua Hu Die' (Multi-coloured Butterfly)

This pretty, semi-double tree peony has magenta-pink (66c) flowers and a slight spicy fragrance. The strongly silvered petals have deep magenta veins, nicely rounded edges and deep purple flares. These are offset by tomentose green carpels, with pink-edged,

'Hong Mei Ao Shang' (Plum Blossom facing the Snow Storm).

yellowish green styles. The stamens have golden yellow anthers and short white filaments. It has a very upright habit and deep green foliage. Height and spread 80 CM (32 IN.) after ten years.

'Huo Lian Jin Dan' (Fire That Makes the Pills of Immortality)

The striking semi-double or double flowers can measure up to 20 CM (8 IN.) across and have an unusual musky fragrance. They look silvery red in bud, but open to coral red with small purple flares at the base of the petals. The centre of the flower is filled with 10 silvery green tomentose carpels with purple styles and surrounded by a vestigial sheath, which is reduced to narrow purple strips. The anthers are very long, pale yellow and held on purple filaments. Height 60 CM (24 IN.), spread 1 M (3.2 FT.) after ten years.

'Jia Ge Jin Zi' (Purple Kudzu Scarf)

It is difficult not to be attracted to this tree peony, but the flowers are very heavy and lie on the ground when fully developed. They are very double, crown-shaped and deep lavender (80C, with 80B depths) with large rounded guard petals. The crown is composed of masses of small feathery staminodes. Carpels are almost absent, rudimentary or converted into lavender carpelodes. On opening flowers are an even deeper colour (80B) and have a strong rose fragrance. Height 70 CM (28 IN.), spread 90 CM (3 FT.) after ten years.

'Jin Xiu Qiu' (Ball of Charm and Beauty)

This tree peony has semi-double flowers with satin-textured, deep reddish purple (71B) petals, which are rather darker at the base. The tomentose carpels are green with red styles and surrounded by yellow anthers held on purple filaments. The flowers have a slight spicy fragrance. Height 80 cm (32 in.), spread 1 m (3.3 ft.) after ten years.

'Jiu Zui Yang Fei' (Tipsy Imperial Concubine)

This is an unusual tree peony, which, as the name suggests, looks slightly drunk. However, the Chinese have always admired plants with a weeping habit and they are much sought after. The shoots start to grow upright, but the outer ones then fall at a crazy angle. The

'Jin Xiu Qiu' (**Ball of Charm and Beauty**) has large, deep reddish purple flowers.

The imaginatively named 'Jiu Zui Yang Fei' (**Tipsy Imperial Concubine**) has made a virtue out of a bad habit.

The flowers of 'Lan Bao Shi' (**Blue Sapphire**) have been likened to a glittering star, with bright violet flares radiating out from the centre.

'Luoyang Hong' (**Luoyang Red**) is an old cultivar with magenta-red flowers.

flowers are strongly fragrant and very beautiful; opening from cone-shaped buds they are lavender (73B) at first, turning more purplish as they age. The outer petals are triangular, the inner ones narrower and elongated. The green, tomentose carpels with purple styles are enclosed by a pale lavender sheath, which remains intact until broken by the fertilized carpels. The yellow stamens are supported by white-tipped, violet filaments. Height 70 CM (28 IN.), spread 1.1 M (3.6 FT.) after ten years.

'Lan Bao Shi' (Blue Sapphire)
A vigorous tree peony that seems to have some *Paeonia ostii* in its blood. It has very striking semi-double flowers, which open pale violet with striking dark violet flares radiating out from the centre like a glittering star. The carpels are pale green with red styles, surrounded by a violet sheath. The stamens are yellow and borne on violet filaments. It is a low growing plant and appears to be very free flowering, with a slight spicy fragrance. Raised in Zhaolou, Heze, in 1975. Height 60 CM (24 IN.), spread 1.1 M (3.6 FT.).

'Ling Hua Zhan Lu' (Ling Flower Wet with Dew)
A spreading shrub with light green leaves and semi-double flowers held upright. These have an unusual scent—somewhat reminiscent of freshly harvested peas. The flowers have lavender petals (78D) and a deeper imperial purple (78A) centre; the central petals being much narrower than those to the outside. The tomentose carpels are pale green with cream tops and purple styles. The elongated yellow anthers are supported on violet filaments. The leaves are composed of elliptic lateral leaflets and a terminal leaflet with three lobes (trifurcate). Height 70 CM (28 IN.), spread 1 M (3.3 FT.) after ten years.

'Luo Han Hong' (Luo Han Red)
This is very vigorous, fast growing and free flowering with mid-green foliage, flushed at the edges with red pigment. The flowers are semi-double, vivid carmine-red (52B) with a hint of violet in the rather waxy petals, which become smaller towards the centre. The tomentose carpels have red styles and are surrounded by a purple sheath. The stamens are held erect on purple filaments with white tops. Height 40 CM (16 IN.), spread 80 CM (32 IN.) in ten years.

'Luoyang Hong' (Luoyang Red)
One of the best-known Chinese tree peonies, which lines the streets of the city of Luoyang during the annual tree peony festival. It is very vigorous with bright green foliage and semi-double, reddish purple flowers, opening cyclamen purple (74A) and becoming more magenta with age. It has up to 10 mid-green tomentose carpels with red styles, surrounded by a very rudimentary purple sheath, which is reduced in places to narrow purple strands. The golden yellow anthers are supported by short purple filaments. Height 90 CM (3 FT.), spread 1.3 M (4.3 FT.) in ten years.

'Qi Hua Xian Cai' (Colour of Exotic Flowers)

This vigorous, wide-spreading tree peony produces masses of very pretty, rose-scented, deep pink flowers. The flowers are rose-shaped when young and do not have any flares. The flowers have a very strong fragrance—it is literally a rose without thorns. The green carpels have purple-red styles and sheath, the colour of which is enhanced by the golden yellow anthers supported by violet filaments. This is one of the best semi-double pink tree peonies and deserves to be more widely grown. Height 75 CM (30 IN.), spread 1.4 M (4.6 FT.) after ten years.

'Qing Long Wo Fen Chi' (Green Dragon in a Pink Pool)

This is one of the very best single pink tree peonies, with mid-green leaves and shell pink (62D) flowers. The yellow anthers are supported by very long filaments, which are pale violet at the base, becoming white at the top. The carpels are very large, tomentose, with a dark purple sheath. It is very vigorous and free flowering, producing many branching stems. It has slight fragrance. Height 1.1 M (3.6 FT.), spread 1.4 M (4.6 FT.) after ten years.

'Qi Hua Xian Cai' (**Colour of Exotic Flowers**) has deep pink, rose-shaped flowers, which are produced liberally throughout the spring.

'Qing Long Wo Fen Chi' (**Green Dragon in a Pink Pool**) is one of my favourite tree peonies. It is very fast growing with pale green foliage and incredibly beautiful pale pink flowers.

'Qing Long Wo Mo Chi' (Green Dragon Lying on a Chinese Ink Stone)

Despite its enigmatic name this tree peony has attractive tulip-shaped, single flowers of deep imperial purple (78A with red tints) and even darker purple flares. It has green carpels with reddish purple styles and yellow anthers, supported by violet filaments. It is a vigorous plant with rather coarse mid-green foliage, flushed with red along the edges of the leaves. The flowers are slightly fragrant. Height 1.1 M (3.6 FT.), spread 1.4 M (4.6 FT.) after ten years.

'Qing Xiang Bai' (Elegant Fragrance in White)

The name reflects the fact that the flowers are very fragrant, lotus to crown form although younger plants have semi-double flowers. The buds are pale blush, but the colour fades as they open to pure white with a hint of pink at the base of the petals. The small green carpels have brownish red styles and are surrounded by golden yellow anthers on white filaments. A rather dwarf plant with greyish green leaves.

'Rou Fu Rong' (Hibiscus with a Pink Complexion)

Semi-double flowers with masses of pale pink petals, which become smaller towards the centre. The petals are quite distinctive with a fine magenta line around the perimeter and a deep magenta flare. The inner petals are spoon-shaped (spathulate) with a fringed edge, while the outer petals have a slightly toothed (denticulate) margin. The flowers have a slight spicy fragrance, and can have as many as 10 green carpels with purple styles and a purple sheath. The stamens have yellow anthers and violet filaments.

The unusual 'San Bian Sai Yu' (**Better than Jade with Triple Magic**) has green buds, which gradually open to reveal an extremely beautiful pale pink bloom with green tips to the petals.

'San Bian Sai Yu' (Better than Jade with Triple Magic)

The tight green buds of this attractive tree peony gradually open to reveal a large fully double, crown-shaped flower. The young petals are chartreuse green when they open, becoming pale pink with green tips. The petals are elongated with a deep violet heart, becoming paler towards the outside and strongly marked with bold violet flares. The outer areas are almost white with a hint of violet. It has green, tomentose carpels, with some converted into small carpelodes and surrounded by a rudimentary violet-coloured sheath. The guard petals are rounded and surmounted by a mass of narrow staminodes, the latter topped by larger erect staminodes. Slow to bloom.

'Shan Hu Tai' (Coral Terrace)

This is a very desirable plant with bright crimson-red (52A), semi-double, or occasionally fully double, flowers. The outer guard petals are large and rounded, pointing down, while the inner petals become smaller and more erect towards the centre of the flower. The petals have narrow, purplish brown flares, which extend one third of the way down. The flowers fade in strong sunshine and have a spicy fragrance. They have as many as 10 tomentose, pale green carpels with erect purple styles, surrounded by a rudimentary purplish maroon sheath. The stamens are yellow, held on purple filaments. Among the best of the Chinese tree peonies, it forms a spreading shrub with many new shoots at the base. Height 1.2 M (4 FT.), spread 1.4 M (4.6 FT.) after ten years.

'Shan Hu Tai' (**Coral Terrace**) is a striking plant, which makes a good focal point for a garden.

'Shou An Hong' (**Ruby Red**) is probably the most fragrant of all peonies and the scent can be detected several metres away.

'Shou An Hong' (Ruby Red)

This vigorous shrub is, perhaps, the most fragrant of all Chinese tree peonies; the scent of the crown-shaped flowers can be detected several metres away. It has ruby red petals (61A becoming 61B), with deep purplish black flares at the base and a white flare edged with magenta on the reverse. Most of the stamens have been lost, with only one or two remaining in the centre of the flower. The carpels are large, pale green, with reddish purple styles enclosed by a purple sheath or developed into carpelodes, with distorted petaloid surfaces. The rounded, mid-green leaves are rather coarse. Western nurseries face several problems when they import Chinese tree peonies, but one of the strangest is how to handle the occasionally controversial names. A more accurate translation of this plant's Chinese name is **Blood Table Red**, but Cricket Hill Garden has given it the more pleasant name of **Ruby Red**. Height and spread 80 CM (32 IN.).

'Wan Shi Sheng Se' (Colour of Eternity)

Intriguingly named, this broad spreading shrub has extremely large, goblet-shaped flowers held at 40 degrees. The flowers are very double, extremely fragrant and pale lavender with imperial purple flares (centre 78A, outer petals 78D). The tomentose carpels are pale green with elongated purple styles. The stamens are no longer functional, being transformed into wavy lavender-coloured staminodes. The Chinese classify this peony as a thousand-petal form, but this is poetic license; in reality the flowers have between 300–400 petals. It grows to form a bush with greyish green leaves and reddish brown-flushed petioles. Height 80 CM (32 IN.), spread 1.2 M (4 FT.) after ten years.

The flowers of 'Wan Shi Sheng Se' (**Colour of Eternity**) are extremely large and composed of several hundred petals.

'Wei Zi' (**Wei's Purple**) is a rather slow growing, dwarf plant with purple flowers.

'Wei Zi' (Wei's Purple)

A nicely formed bush with mid-green foliage, bearing double or crown-shaped cyclamen purple (74B) flowers with dark purplish red flares. The anthers are held upright on purple filaments. The carpels are pale green with pale yellow styles and surrounded by an ivory white sheath. Semi-double blossoms are also produced, with a ring of narrow, slightly wavy staminodes surrounded by a ring of stamens. It is not a very vigorous plant. Height 60 CM (24 IN.), spread 45 CM (18 IN.) after ten years. Slow to bloom.

'Wu Long Peng Sheng' (Black Dragon Holds a Splendid Flower)

A fast-growing, floriferous tree peony which flowers at an early age and produces semi-double blooms, with magenta-rose (64B) petals marked with red flares on the inside and a white blotch on the reverse. The spice-scented, saucer-shaped flowers have smaller inner petals and very small staminodes. Yellow anthers on fine purple-and-white filaments surround green carpels with red styles. The flowers often remain half open. Height and spread 1.5 M (5 FT.) after ten years.

'Xiang Yang Hong' (Red Facing the Sun)

This vigorous tree peony has bold ruby red (61A) flowers. The petals are very dark at the base, but lack flares and there is no fragrance. The tomentose carpels are ivory white with purple styles and surrounded by long yellow anthers with dark purple filaments. Height 1.2 M (4 FT.), spread 1.4 M (4.6 FT.) after ten years.

'Xiang Yang Hong' (Red Facing the Sun) has deep purplish red flowers with four whorls of petals. It is very vigorous and eventually forms a large erect bush.

'Yan Long Zi Zhu Pan' (Coiled Dragons in the Mist Grasping the Purple Pearl)

This large, extremely vigorous and free-flowering tree peony has semi-double ruby red (59A) flowers with satin-textured petals and a spicy fragrance. The guard petals are reflexed and the inner petals narrow, deeply notched and upturned. The light green, tomentose carpels have ivory white styles and are surrounded by a vestigial ivory white sheath. It has bright yellow anthers, held on long, purplish red filaments, which become white at the top. Height 1.2 M (4 FT.), spread 1.4 M (4.6 FT.) after ten years.

'Yao Huang' (Yao's Yellow)

The double, pale yellow flowers of this tree peony may look rather insipid when they are compared with modern hybrids, but it has extremely long history. The flowers are crown-shaped and measure approximately 12 CM (4.7 IN.) across by 16 CM (6.3 IN.) high with mimosa yellow (8D) petals for one morning only before they fade to creamy yellow.

'Yao Huang' is one of the oldest cultivars of peony in existence and has long been appreciated for its yellow flowers. According to Ouyang Hsiu (AD 1034) "Only three or four buds of the Yao yellow or the Wei variety are sent, packed solidly inside little bamboo crates filled with fresh cabbage leaves so that they will not be shaken and jarred on the envoy's horseback journey, all bound up and covered over."

'Yin Fen Jin Lin' (Glistening Silver Pink)

This peony has very double, crown-shaped, baby doll pink flowers, with a deeper coloured centre. It is low growing and bears its flowers on rather weak stems, but the blooms have a strong rose scent. It has mid-green leaves with red petioles. Rather let down by weak stems and heavy flowers. Height 40 CM (16 IN.), spread 90 CM (3 FT.) after ten years.

'Ying Luo Bao Zhu' (Necklace with Precious Pearls)

This tree peony has goblet-shaped flowers, filled with wavy staminodes and carpelodes. It looks like a glass filled with masses of feathers and has a spicy fragrance. The rhodamine pink (62A) petals become silvered in bright sunshine, but have deeper coloured, neyron rose (55A) depths. The rather ruffled central petals are held upright. It forms a low growing shrub, measuring 1 M (3.3 FT.) high by 1 M (3.3 FT.) in width. The flowers show well and are not hidden by the leaves, being held at an angle of 40 degrees. The petals have a white patch on the reverse.

'Yu Ji Yan Zhuang' (Beauty Yuji's Gaudy Dress)

Bright pink, semi-double (51A) flowers have a slight spicy fragrance. The rather narrow petals are marked with a faint purple flare which is barely obvious. Some of the stamens are converted into very narrow pink staminodes. It has five green carpels with purple, yellow-edged styles. The stamens are golden yellow with violet filaments.

'Zhi Hong' (**Rouge Red**) has very large coral pink and violet flowers.

'Zhi Hong' (Rouge Red)

This is one of the most difficult flowers to describe. They are semi-double or double, and an intense shade of coral pink (52B) with pale violet undertones and strongly flushed with pale violet in the middle. A large tuft of crinkled, wavy carpelodes in the centre is surrounded by golden yellow anthers on violet filaments. The plant is quite vigorous, flowering on upright strong stems. The flowers only have a slight spicy fragrance—but you can't have everything.

'Zhong Sheng Hong' (Ancient Red)

A slow-growing plant with semi-double, coral red (52A) flowers; each petal has a violet-purple flare at the base and a white patch on the reverse. The yellow carpels have reddish purple styles, surrounded by a purple sheath. The yellow anthers are supported on purple filaments. The flowers are produced at an early age and have a slight, spicy fragrance. Height 1 M (3.3 FT.), spread 1 M (3.3 FT.).

'Zhu Sha Hong' (Cinnabar Red)

This extremely eye-catching tree peony stands out in the garden because of its masses of semi-double, bright coral red flowers (52B) with narrow purple flares. The flowers can measure as much as 16 CM (6.3 IN.) across and have 10 green, tomentose carpels and reddish purple styles, surrounded by a rudimentary violet-coloured sheath. The golden yellow anthers are supported on long filaments, which are violet at the base becoming white towards the top. It is strong growing with mid-green foliage. Height 60 CM (24 IN.), spread 1.1 M (3.6 FT.).

'Zhu Sha Lei' (**Cinnabar Ramparts**) is very free flowering and makes a wonderful garden plant.

right: Chinese parasols protect tree peonies from bright sunshine and rain.

'Zhu Sha Lei' (Cinnabar Ramparts or Red Fortress)

Low-growing, but very vigorous tree peony that bears semi-double flowers with a slight spicy fragrance. The flowers have strongly incurved, magenta-pink petals, which are heavily flushed with magenta pigment. A violet sheath surrounds green tomentose carpels with red styles, and long, slender, golden yellow stamens have pale violet, white-topped filaments. Height 80 CM (32 IN.), spread 1.8 M (6 FT.) or more after ten years.

'Zhuang Yuan Hong' (Number One Scholar's Red)

The buds may have a hint of red, but the very double, bomb-shaped flowers are deep violet (80B with 80A depths). They have large guard petals, with smaller petals inside, surmounted by upright, incurved, larger petals. Stamens and carpels are absent; they have developed into deep violet (80B) staminodes and carpelodes. Mature flowers have a depressed centre.

'Etienne de France' probably originated in China, but was given a European name. The flowers are very double, with the petals becoming progressively smaller towards the centre of the flower.

Other Chinese-style tree peonies

'Etienne de France' (origin unknown)

This is almost certainly a Chinese cultivar that has been given a French name. The double pale pink flowers have petals that become progressively smaller towards the centre. The outer petals are well rounded with a deep notch, while those towards the centre are rather wavy and irregular. Each petal has a deep magenta flare at the base, with magenta veins radiating from the centre. The carpels in fully developed flowers are modified to wavy pink carpelodes, surrounded by golden yellow stamens on very thin white filaments. Less developed blooms have functional carpels with red styles. This lovely plant has rounded leaflets and reddish brown petioles.

'Isabelle Rivière' (A. Rivière, 1975)

A vigorous tree peony with strong, upright stems supporting slightly fragrant, single magenta flowers with deep purple flares. In the centre the pale green carpels are surrounded by a deep purplish sheath and yellow anthers with purple and white filaments. A pleasing plant, with rather large, somewhat coarse, greyish green leaves.

Beautiful tree peonies such as 'Isabelle Rivière' are still being produced in France by the long established Rivière nursery.

'Reine Elizabeth' was introduced towards the end of the ninteenth century. It is very reliable and has distinctive greyish green foliage.

'Reine Elizabeth' (Sénéclause, *circa* 1895)

'Reine Elizabeth' is classed as a Chinese tree peony, but it was raised in Europe. The pleasing, rather heavy double flowers have deep China rose (58C) petals, 58B where they are protected from sunlight, with warmer overtones of carmine-rose (52C). The outer petals are strongly marked with magenta pigment. The pale green carpels are tomentose with white hairs and have dark red styles. It has yellow anthers with purple filaments, which become white towards the top. The plant has distinctive, rather sparse, greyish green foliage. The terminal leaflet is tri-lobed, but the others are entire. There is also a distinctly orangey pink form with identical form and foliage. Height and spread 1.5 M (5 FT.). (Synonym: 'Queen Elizabeth')

Chapter 8
Japanese Tree Peonies

Japanese tree peonies have been grown in the West for over a century and they are familiar to many gardeners. Tree peonies are not native to Japan, but were introduced by Korean and Chinese monks during the eighth century AD and became known as botan.

The plants were originally grown for medicinal purposes, but gradually they found favour as decorative plants. In the middle of the sixteenth century the Japanese obtained further plants from China and according to Hashida (2002) they were grown in temples near Osaka and Kyoto. The Japanese preferred plants with upright flowers without flares and those with a small number of stamens, but as trade with the West increased, Japanese peony breeders started to select for plants that had more colourful flowers, with a larger number of petals.

The colours of the flowers range from bright scarlet, to purple, pale pink and purest white. One can only speculate on the origin of the tree peonies with bright scarlet flowers, because no one has ever discovered a wild species with such vivid colour. The most likely reason is that the original parent has long been extinct, although Roger Anderson has bred intersectional hybrids with bright red flowers by using *Paeonia potaninii* as the pollen parent.

Japanese tree peonies remained unknown in Europe until the German botanist Englebert Kaempfer (1651–1715) referred to them in his first book *Amoenitatum Exoticarum* (1712), which was written in Latin. Kaempfer was a doctor of medicine and he was given a remarkable degree of freedom to travel around Japan. He had two audiences with the Shogun, the military ruler of Japan, and was allowed to collect plants and draw them. The botanist Carl Thunberg (1743–1822) mentions tree peonies in 1775, but there are no collections until 1844, when Philipp Franz von Siebold (1796–1866), another doctor, acquired forty-two tree peonies from the Imperial Gardens of Kyoto and Tokyo, which he sold to Prince Frederick of the Netherlands. The tree peonies started to flower in 1848 and received a number of medals at flower shows. In 1866 L. Boehmer, a German nurseryman who was based in Yokohama, exported a few plants but to all intents and purposes commercial trade began around 1890. It is not known when the first Japanese tree peonies reached the United States, but Professor Charles Sprague Sargent (1841–1927), the first Director of the Arnold Arboretum, returned with a collection of dozen cultivars when he visited Japan in 1892 (Boyd, 1928).

Although tree peonies originated in China, very few plants were exported to the West and a substantial trade was only established towards the end of the twentieth century. By contrast the Japanese seem to have been quite happy to sell their tree peonies to Europe and the United States, and large numbers were exported at the end of the nineteenth century. Perhaps the best-known Japanese grower was the Yokahama Nursery Company, which produced catalogues beautifully illustrated with paintings of peonies and iris. The company was founded in 1890 by father and son team Uhei and Hamakichi Suzuki, and it produced its last English-language catalogue in 1934. Japanese exports reached a peak at the beginning of the twentieth century and continued into the 1930s, until the Second World War brought the trade to an abrupt end.

A number of well-known Japanese tree peonies are very similar to Chinese and only differ in minor ways. Many Japanese tree peonies are of considerable antiquity and it is quite possible that they are either identical to Chinese cultivars or at the most only one or two generations removed. Most Japanese tree peonies have single or semi-double flowers, delicate, deeply dissected leaves and less robust stems than their Chinese cousins. The uniformity of their habit and morphology suggests that they have a less complex ancestry than Chinese tree peonies and are probably descended from a smaller number of species. Several of the plants have purplish green foliage, which is quite rare among Chinese cultivars. Most Japanese plants appear to be of the Central Lowland type and there does not seem to be much genetic input from *Paeonia rockii*.

While the great majority of Japanese tree peonies originate directly from Japan, a number of breeders in the U.S.A. and Europe have raised their own cultivars. A large number of seedlings appear to have been raised at the start of the twentieth century, but because they have proved difficult to propagate they have never become widely available. Frederick Stern, the author of *A Study of the Genus Paeonia*, raised several tree peonies at his home in Sussex. Two of his plants, 'Sybil Stern' and 'Mrs George Warre', received awards from the RHS, but neither are of them are now commercially available. More recently Sir Peter Smithers, who lives in Switzerland, has raised a number of attractive plants such as 'Snow Storm' and 'Lydia Foote'. He has demonstrated that there is still considerable potential for breeding Japanese tree peonies and I am sure that other dedicated gardeners would achieve considerable satisfaction from raising their own plants.

American visitors to the United Kingdom are often surprised when they come across tree peonies with English names, such as 'Duchess of Marlborough', 'Cardinal Vaughan' and 'Glory of Huish'. Most people assume these plants have been raised in the U.K., but in the majority of cases they are Japanese cultivars that have been given English names. Many were supplied by the famous British nursery Kelways, which used to be one of the largest nurseries in Europe and counted Queen Victoria among its customers. It was common practice at the end of the nineteenth century to name plants after wealthy customers, and tree peonies appealed to the British aristocracy who were among Kelways' best clients. Some peonies appear to have had two or even three names—perhaps the result of someone falling from grace or not paying their account. The same applies to a number of cultivars from continental Europe, such as 'Reine Elizabeth'. It has always been assumed that these were raised in Europe, descendants of Robert Fortune's introductions, but it is quite possible that a few of them are actually Chinese plants that have been given European names. Kelways is now a smaller and leaner company, but the English names are now so well established that it would be impractical to revert to their original Japanese moniker. In recent years they have imported a much wider range of tree peonies and these are sold under their original Chinese or Japanese names.

The appearance of Robert Fortune's tree peonies from China in the middle of the nineteenth century created a considerable demand for the plants, but European nurseries quickly discovered that they could not keep up with demand. Very few western nurseries seem to have mastered the skill of grafting and they found it much easier to import grafted plants from Japan. The tree peonies arrived bare rooted and the nurseries could pot them up for sale to their customers. The lack of grafting skills in the West was one of the main reasons why locally bred tree peonies have failed to become commercially successful. Compared to China, grafting is a relatively recent innovation in Japan, and was unknown in that country until *circa* AD 1700.

The technique of grafting has allowed tree peonies to be mass-produced and sold at a reasonable price, but it does have some drawbacks. Grafted tree peonies make ideal plants for a nursery or garden centre because they will usually flower in their first season. The plants usually sell on sight, but the flowers are so large that it places a strain on the young plant, the buds having been initiated on the mother plant.

Grafted tree peonies often fail to flower in their second year because the plant is recovering from the stress under which it was placed during the previous year. It is therefore best to remove the flowers from a newly purchased tree peony and allow it to become established before flowering. However, as the plant becomes more established it will start to produce more flowers and by the third or fourth year it should bear several normal-sized blooms.

All Japanese tree peonies are grafted and produce less foliage than their Chinese counterparts when they are young. It is quite common for them to suffer from a degree of dieback in the spring, but new shoots will usually sprout from the base of the stem. This problem tends to become less obvious when the grafted tree peony has produced its own roots and has a stronger constitution. It is quite common for a tree peony rootstock to throw up suckers; these should be removed as soon as possible, because if they are left the rootstock is likely to reject the scion (tree peony shoots are dull and purplish green in colour, while those of a *lactiflora* rootstock are shiny and reddish purple). Some people believe that the rootstock becomes parasitic upon the young tree peony scion in order to survive and it should be removed when the scion has produced its own root system. The *lactiflora* rootstock is easily distinguished by its swollen and blackish brown roots, while those of the tree peony are yellowish brown and fusiform (tapering like a carrot).

There are several hundred cultivars of Japanese tree peony, but only fifty or so are readily available. The great majority are imported from Japan as bare-root plants and while they are usually of high quality, they may well be incorrectly labelled. One strange outcome of this is that some cultivars have two or three clones, which are quite different from one another. This presents a major problem for western nurseries because they have to flower the plants before they can sell them. For this reason I would suggest that you purchase Japanese tree peonies from an established nursery where you can see the plant in flower during the spring. In the United Kingdom the majority of tree peonies are purchased at flower shows. Buying the plants by mail order is a lottery, because while they are cheaper bought this way, you have no idea whether the tree peony will be true to name until it has flowered. Most reputable nurseries will replace a plant if it is not true to name. Single-flowered cultivars tend to be damaged more easily by inclement weather and may lose their petals after four or five days, while semi-double cultivars may last for as long as ten days.

The main differences between Japanese and Chinese tree peonies

- Japanese tree peonies are grafted, while Chinese are usually, but not exclusively, propagated by division.
- Japanese cultivars will normally flower during their first year, whereas Chinese plants may not flower until they are two to three years old. Chinese tree peonies may need lower temperatures during the winter to initiate the production of flower buds than Japanese tree peonies.
- Japanese plants are less bushy, but produce larger flowers when they are young and have brighter colours, including several shades of vivid red, whereas Chinese tree peonies have a wider range of foliage types and tend to form bushier plants, which readily sucker at the base.
- Japanese peonies are invariably single or semi-double, while Chinese plants can be single, semi-double or fully double.
- Few Japanese peonies have conspicuous flares, suggesting that *P. rockii* has not made much of a contribution to their gene pool.
- Chinese tree peonies also seem to be more disease resistant.

Catalogue of Cultivars

Japanese tree peonies tend to be less vigorous than Chinese and rarely grow to more than 2 M (6.5 FT.) high. I have not provided individual heights for the different cultivars because they have a similar habit and vigour. Plants grown in full sunshine will grow better than those in shade and those growing on their own roots will be healthier than those that still depend upon a rootstock. While Japanese tree peonies make wonderful garden plants, they have always had a reputation for being incorrectly labelled. John Wister vented his frustration when he made the following statement: "Our troubles have been multiplied by the carelessness or unscrupulousness of some Japanese nurserymen. The principal exporters of the 1910–1925 era would sell a collection of fifty varieties with fifty different labels and all but two or three plants would prove to be identical." The situation has greatly improved since Wister's time and most Japanese tree peonies are usually true to the name on the label.

A number of western nurseries have tried to propagate these peonies for themselves, but have discovered that they cannot compete with the Japanese wholesalers. Tree peony production is a cottage industry in Japan and many small growers supply the wholesalers. It is quite possible that the plants vary slightly from one supplier to another, but they are all sold under one name. 'Kamada-fuji' is one of the most beautiful of the Japanese tree peonies, but there appear to be at least two clones sold under this name, one with lavender-coloured flowers and the other with magenta. The same applies to 'Nigata Akashigata' and 'Akashi-gata', which should be two different cultivars, but are often treated as being interchangeable by the Japanese wholesalers.

The names of Japanese tree peonies are also a minefield, which has caused considerable grief to previous authors. It is quite common to find names spelt in several different ways, with some letters being interchangeable. Many Japanese tree peony names end in the word -*jishi*, which means lion, but this can also be spelt "jisi", while the prefix *Siti-* may become "Shichi-". Hyphenation also varies from one book to another. Finally it is not unknown for Japanese suppliers to miss out part of the name, so that 'Shimane Hakugan' may also be found labelled simply as 'Hakugan'. David Root, the Manager of Kelways, says that "This is like calling something a 'pie', without mentioning that it is an apple pie or a steak pie."

I have done my best to check that the following descriptions are true to name, but if any reader suspects that the plant has been incorrectly identified I would be please to hear from them.

'Akashi-gata' (Akashi Beach)

Tulip-shaped buds open to semi-double very large, shell pink flowers, which pale towards the edges and have diffuse magenta flares. The petals become progressively smaller towards the centre of the flower and have magenta veins. The carpels have deep pink styles and are enclosed by a beetroot purple (71A) sheath. There are a small number of golden yellow stamens with white filaments. It has mid-green foliage.

There is a lot of confusion between 'Akashi-gata' and 'Nigata Akashigata'. Japanese nurseries treat the names as being interchangeable, even though the plants are quite different in character.

'Akashi-gata' (**Akashi Beach**) has attractive shell pink flowers.

'Bifuku-mon' (Beautiful Gate)

The semi-double flowers have deep beetroot purple petals and a contrasting creamy white sheath, with warmer, reddish purple centre and bold black flares; the latter suggest an affinity to Chinese "Gansu Mudan" (hybrids of *P. rockii*). The stamens have pale yellow anthers, supported by beetroot purple filaments.

'Cardinal Vaughan'

This is a very vigorous double-flowered tree peony with large, deep purple buds. These gradually develop into large, deep purple flowers (71A) with glossy petals and green carpels, surrounded by a reddish purple sheath. The anthers are golden yellow with purple filaments. The leaflets have sharply pointed tips. Mature plants are low growing with wide spreading branches. It is widely grown in the British Isles and has been sold under this synonym for many years; its Japanese synonym is unknown. Early flowering.

above and right: In the United Kingdom 'Godaishu' (**Giant Globe**) has been sold for many years under the synonym of 'Mrs. William Kelway'.

right: The Chinese tree peony 'Yu Ban Bai' (**Jade Plate White**) looks very similar to 'Godaishu', but forms a more compact bush.

'Godaishu' (Giant Globe)

One of the most reliable of the white-flowered Japanese tree peonies, it has semi-double, creamy white flowers and a beautiful ivory white sheath, surrounding greyish green, tomentose carpels with pale yellow styles. The flowers appear on long bare stems before the leaves develop. There is a hint of pink at the base of the petals, which suggests that *Paeonia ostii* may be one of its parents, but the foliage is very different, glaucous and slightly coarse. (Synonym: 'Mrs. William Kelway').

'Haku-banriu' (Many White Dragons)

The very large leaves are reminiscent of a Chinese tree peony. The large white flowers have wavy petaloids and golden yellow anthers, supported by white filaments. The sheath is creamy white.

'Hana-daijin' (Magnificent Flower **or** Minister of Flowers)

Semi-double, beetroot purple (71A) flowers have petals with serrated tips and diffuse dark red flares at the base. The anthers are golden yellow with red filaments and surround green carpels with red styles and a deep red sheath. A pretty plant, but the flowers have little fragrance.

'Hana-daijin' (**Magnificent Flower**) has beetroot purple flowers.

'Hana-kisoi' (Floral Rivalry)

A popular cultivar and one that has been widely painted by European artists. It has very large flowers that are magenta-rose (65C) when they open, becoming paler in strong sunshine, and strong upright stems. The petals have denticulate edges and are suffused with magenta pigment. Slightly wavy filaments, white at the top and purple towards the base, support the golden yellow anthers. Its pale green carpels are enclosed by an ivory white sheath and topped by buff-coloured styles. The outside of the flowers can smell of fish, although inside they have a wonderful rose scent.

'Haruno-akenbono' (Spring Dawn)

The large pale pink flowers are single, goblet-shaped and fragrant. The petals have wavy margins with slightly notched edges and diffuse magenta flares, shading to dark magenta at the base. The yellow anthers have white filaments, which become deep purple towards the bottom. The pale green carpels with ivory white styles are surrounded by an ivory white vestigial sheath. The flowers often have 1–2 narrow staminodes in the centre. Plants have light green foliage and strong upright stems.

'Hatsu-garashu' (First Crow of the Year)
Double mahogany-red flowers (187B) with a black flare at the base of each of the satin-textured petals. The pale green carpels have salmon pink styles and are surrounded by a blackish red sheath. The stamens have yellow anthers and reddish black filaments. The flowers fade in bright sunshine to deep purple.

'Higure' (Dusk)
This free flowering Japanese tree peony has spiraea red (63B), semi-double flowers with slightly wavy petals. A cream-coloured sheath surrounds pale yellowish green carpels with cream-coloured styles.

'Hinode-sekai' (World of the Rising Sun)
Unusual semi-double, deep spiraea red (63B) flowers have a hint of scarlet-red in the centre, cherry red flares and wavy petal tips. The green carpels have coral pink styles and are surrounded by a pink sheath and yellow anthers with spiraea red filaments.

'Horakumon' (Invitation to Abundant Pleasure)
Semi-double, beetroot purple flowers have warmer reddish purple tones in the centre. The yellow-green carpels have salmon-coloured styles, surrounded by a pale purplish white sheath. Pale yellow anthers are held on purple filaments.

'Howki' (**Charming Age**) has deep cardinal-red flowers and a purple sheath.

'Howki' (Charming Age)
A free-flowering cultivar with double, deep cardinal red flowers. A large centre of green carpels with purple styles is surrounded by a purple sheath and yellow anthers with purple filaments.

'Kamata-fuji' (Wisteria at Kamada)

'Kamata-fuji', or 'Kamada-fuji', is a superb tree peony with unique colouring, red-tinged foliage and a sweet fragrance. The very long-lasting flowers are double and deep violet-mauve (78B) with magenta depths and a small reddish purple flare at the base of each petal. It has tomentose, pale mint green carpels with pinkish purple styles and enclosed by a rudimentary purple sheath. The anthers are yellow, supported by purple filaments with white tops.

'Kamata-nishiki' (Kamata Brocade)

Sometimes sold as 'Kamata-fuji' (above), but while 'Kamata-fuji' has uniform violet-mauve flowers, those of 'Kamata-nishiki' are magenta-purple, with strongly silvered petals. The green carpels have red styles and a reddish purple sheath, and the golden yellow anthers have red filaments.

'Kaow' (King of Flowers)

This is one of my favourite red tree peonies. The semi-double flowers are very large, deep strawberry red with mauve-purple flares and a reddish purple sheath. It is very reliable and free flowering.

'Kaow' (**King of Flowers**) is an extremely reliable tree peony. The deep red petals have mauve-purple flares.

'Kokuryu Nishiki' (Black Dragon Brocade)

Single, purplish red flowers (61B fading to 61C) are edged with white, each petal having a reddish purple flare at the base. The green carpels are enclosed by a deep, reddish purple sheath and have similarly coloured styles. The yellow anthers have purple filaments. This is an attractive plant with finely dissected foliage.

'Koshino-yuki'

This cultivar exhibits the interesting characteristic of a flower within a flower. The buds have a blush tinge when they open, eventually developing into an extremely beautiful, crown-shaped flower, but with little fragrance. The outer part is composed of slightly curled petals, which form a ruff around the centre. The outer petals have streaks of violet at their extreme base—the barest suggestion of a flare. A few of the stamens are flushed with magenta pigmentation, while others are developed into small pale magenta staminodes. The central part of the flower consists of an inverted cone of erect petals, filled

'Kokuryu Nishiki' (**Black Dragon Brocade**) has single, purplish red flowers with white-edged petals.

The Japanese tree peony 'Koshino-yuki' exhibits the interesting feature of having a flower within a flower.

'Mikunino-akebono' is an extremely elegant tree peony with fringed white petals. Flowers with fringed and entire petals can appear at the same time.

with tiny white petals and purple-streaked carpelodes, and is surrounded by a ring of golden yellow anthers, which impart a golden glow to the inner bloom. The carpels are very small, pale green and mixed with a number of short stamens. The petioles are red on the upper surface and carry large, rather coarse leaves.

'Kozan'

A semi-double tree peony, whose bright, cardinal red flowers have a hint of purple. The ruffled petals are glossy towards the centre. There are a few stamens with yellow anthers and purple filaments surrounding purplish green carpels with pink styles. The sheath is purple.

'Mikunino-akebono'

A very unusual tree peony in that its pure white, single flowers are fringed; the petals are deeply dissected and have a plicate surface. The sulphur yellow anthers have white filaments and surround a pale purple sheath, which in turn encloses a group of purple carpels with pink styles. The flowers are not always fringed and some may have entire petals. The foliage is rather coarse, greyish green and slightly glaucous, flushed with purple pigment. This is a very distinctive tree peony, which developed as a bud mutation of 'Mikuninoi-hata' (Hashida, 1990).

'Muregarasu' (Flock of Crows)

The single flowers open violet-purple (74B), becoming violet (78B) with red overtones, Large red flares are present and the outer petals are heavily streaked with white. The carpels have ivory white styles and are surrounded by a similarly coloured sheath. Long, robust filaments, which are white at the top and magenta towards the base, support long, golden yellow anthers.

'Muregarasu' (**Flock of Crows**) has large purple flowers with rather untidy outer petals and much smaller inner petals.

'Nigata Akashigata' has beautiful, translucent white petals and purple flares.

'Nigata Akashigata'

The semi-double flowers have a slight spicy fragrance and are freely produced, but their main attraction is the translucent white petals with conspicuous dark purple (64B) flares, the colour extending some way into the petals, which have crimped edges. Inside the flower golden yellow anthers with white filaments encircle the pale green carpels with yellowish white styles and a white sheath. Japanese nurseries treat the names of this and 'Akashi-gata' as interchangeable.

'Niigata-otomenomai'

Although this may have no English name, it is one of the prettiest of all Japanese tree peonies, bearing large, snow white, semi-double flowers with magenta flares and ruffled petals. The yellowish green carpels have yellow styles. It grows to form a tall and vigorous plant.

'Rimpo' (Bird of Rimpo)

Large, double, ruby red (60A) flowers have rather substantial, glossy petals. The outer petals are streaked with white and the flowers have spicy fragrance. The carpels have ivory white styles and a white sheath, which is surrounded by golden yellow anthers with ruby red filaments. Plants have rigid upright stems, reddish brown petioles and slightly glaucous greyish green foliage.

'Ryokimon'

The single, ruby red flowers have a similarly coloured sheath. Green tomentose carpels bear crimson-red styles, and are surrounded by yellow anthers on ruby red filaments.

'Shimadaijin'

This is a very vigorous and richly coloured tree peony with semi-double, imperial purple flowers and nicely ruffled petals. The sheath is also imperial purple and the yellow anthers are borne on purple filaments.

'Shimane Hakugan' looks beautiful when backlit by low sunshine.

The flowers of 'Shima-nishiki' (Island Brocade) are boldly striped with red and white. The Chinese cultivar 'Er Qiao' is very similar with pink and red flowers on the same plant.

'Shimane Hakugan'

This is a very elegant tree peony with extremely large, snow white flowers and large tulip-shaped buds. The carpels have dark red styles and are enclosed by an unusual, dark red, cone-shaped sheath. The stamens have golden yellow anthers and white filaments. A tall, vigorous plant with pleasantly fragrant flowers. It produces plenty of new shoots from the base. It looks absolutely beautiful when backlit by low sunshine.

'Shimane Seidai'

The very large, ruffled, deep pink flowers are extremely beautiful. The petals, flushed with magenta, have a redder base. A few of the carpels may be developed into deep pink, petal-like carpelodes, with the remainder enclosed by a deep red sheath. The flowers are fully double, the silvered petals partially obscuring the yellow anthers on filaments that are white at the top and purple towards the base. In sunlight the outer parts of the flowers become silvered but the depths remain deep pink. Highly recommended.

'Shima-nishiki' (Island Brocade)

One of the most unusual of all tree peonies because it is capable of producing pure red and variegated flowers on the same plant. The flowers are semi-double and when variegated have bold white stripes running the length of the petals, an effect caused by the absence of any pigment. The centre of the flower consists of a compact ring of golden yellow stamens on short purple filaments surrounding bright green carpels, which are enclosed by a dull purple sheath. The carpels have upright wavy styles. It forms a medium-sized shrub with large mid-green leaves, flushed at the edges with red pigment. Height 60 CM (24 IN.), spread of 80 CM (32 IN.) after ten years.

'Shin Shichifukujin' (**Seven Gods of Fortune**) illustrates the Japanese tendency to select for brighter colours than the Chinese and their preference for single or semi-double blooms.

'Shin Shichifukujin' (Seven Gods of Fortune)

The stunning semi-double flowers are of a colour best summed up as coral red with a hint of purple, as they cannot be adequately described using colour charts. The petals are strongly silvered, and each one has a diffuse violet flare at the base. The carpels are surrounded by a purplish red sheath and are topped by purple styles. The stamens have long filaments, which are white at the top and purple towards the base. This is a vigorous plant with very large flowers and a strong spicy fragrance.

'Shin-shimano-kagayaki'

The colouration of the semi-double flowers is difficult to describe. From a distance they appear bright crimson-red (53C), however closer inspection shows each slightly crinkled petal to have an iridescent, bright scarlet centre (44B) and a violet reverse; the colour changes as the flowers age. A dark red sheath surrounds pale green carpels with purplish red, scythe-shaped styles. The yellow anthers have deep red filaments. The leaves are mid-green, deeply incised with apiculate tips and the petioles bright reddish purple on the upper surface. A beautiful plant that stands out among other shrubs.

'Shin-tenchi' (New Heaven and Earth)

One of the best Japanese tree peonies, it bears very large flowers that are roseine purple when they open, with darker veins and deep purple flares. The colours fade in bright sunshine, gradually turning to orchid pink with a darker centre.

The Japanese tree peony 'Sumino-ichi' (**Deepest Ink**) has rigid, upright stems, somewhat reminiscent of Chinese cultivars.

'Sumino-ichi' (Deepest Ink)

Single, deep red (59B) flowers are purplish red on the outside and may have a white rim around the edge of the glossy petals. The tomentose, pale green carpels have red styles and are enclosed by a similarly coloured sheath. The stamens have yellow anthers and dark red filaments. Plants produce short, upright stems, reminiscent of *Paeonia delavayi*, which may be one of its parents.

'Taiheiko'

An extremely elegant plant with single, pale pink flowers (65B fading to 65C and eventually 65D), flushed in the centre with magenta. The petals are deeply notched (emarginate), with wavy tips. In the centre of the flower is a bold circle of golden yellow anthers, supported by long filaments, violet at the base becoming white at the top. A tapering, conical, ivory white sheath surrounds the carpels, which have pale yellow styles. It is a very vigorous plant with rather coarse, red-edged foliage. The flowers have a spicy fragrance.

'Taiyo' (Sun)

This peony has masses of very large, fully double flowers on strong erect stems. The flowers, which are slow to open, are cardinal red (53C) with a darker centre (53B), fading to 53C and taking on a steely blue hue as they mature. Each petal has small deep red flares at the base,

'Taiyo' (**Sun**) has bright scarlet-red blooms, borne on upright stems. The woody stems need a small amount of pruning to ensure that they are strong enough to support the large flowers.

a scarlet-red centre and is stained violet on the reverse. It has tomentose magenta carpels with flesh pink styles and enclosed by a creamy white sheath, which is stained at the apex with magenta-purple. The stamens have yellow anthers and reddish purple filaments. It is very vigorous and, without doubt, one of the best double red tree peonies.

'Yachiyo-tsubaki' (**Eternal Camellias**) is one of the most reliable Japanese tree peonies. It has beautiful shell pink flowers and purple-green foliage.

'Yachiyo-tsubaki' (Eternal Camellias)

One of the most reliable pink tree peonies, the lovely semi-double flowers are coral pink with a darker centre. The green carpels have magenta styles and are surrounded by a purple sheath. There are only a few pale yellow anthers, supported by purple filaments. Plants have distinctive, slightly glaucous, purple foliage.

'Yagumo'

The large, semi-double flowers are purplish red (61A) with a redder centre. The petals become smaller towards the centre of the bloom, where they are rather irregular and spoon-shaped with lobed margins. The petal surface is rather warty and tinged with a reddish iridescence. It has pale green, tomentose carpels with pink styles and a rudimentary, dark reddish purple sheath. The stamens have yellow anthers and purple filaments.

Other recommended cultivars

'Asahino-sora' (Sky at Sunrise)

Semi-double pale pink flowers with a reddish purple sheath.

'Azuma-kagami' (Mirror of the East)

A rather weak growing plant, with single dark red flowers and a compact centre of golden yellow stamens.

'Banzai-mon' (Gate of Cheers)

The flowers resemble those of 'Rimpo' (described above) with a series of white stripes along the outer petals.

'Fujino-mine' (Snow Clad Fuji)
Semi-double, pure white flowers.

'Gunpo-den' (Temple adorned with many Flowers)
Semi-double, large, reddish purple flowers have a reddish purple sheath.

'Hakuo-jishi' (King of White Lion **or** White-tailed Lion)
Appealing semi-double, pure white flowers with a hint of magenta at the base of the petals, and a white sheath.

'Hino-tobira' (Passage of the Sun)
An unusual tree peony with rather narrow, obovate petals. Its flowers are bright red with a red sheath.

'Impu-mon' (Gate of Impu **or** Gate of Opulence)
A short-growing tree peony with single, bright red flowers.

'Iwato-kagura' (Sacred Dance of Iwato)
Semi-double, with heavily silvered, purplish red flowers.

'Jitsu-getsu-nishiki' (Sun and Moon Brocade)
Semi-double, large, deep red flowers and white-edged petals. A red sheath encloses the carpels.

'Kagura-jishi' (Sacred Lion Dance)
Semi-double, deep red flowers are silvered and rather asymmetrical.

'Kenrei-mon' (Gate of Kenrei)
Large, purplish red flowers with very dark purple flares at the base of the petals.

'Naniwa-nishiki' (Naniwa Brocade)
Single red flowers with white-edged petals.

'Renkaku' (Flight of Cranes)
A very elegant tree peony with single, pure white flowers and a creamy white sheath. The petals are slightly translucent and take on an ethereal quality when backlit by the low evening sun.

'Yae-zakura' (Host of the Cherry Blossom)
A very beautiful semi-double tree peony with deep pink flowers, fading slightly after a few days in the sun. The sheath is reddish purple.

'Yoyo-no-homare' (Glory of Many Generations)
Single, bright red flowers have a red sheath.

Modern cultivars

We owe much to William Gratwick (1904–1988) for the production of some very special cultivars. Gratwick worked initially with Arthur Saunders, grafting his tree peonies. He subsequently established a nursery at Pavilion in New York State, where he started to breed his own plants, and later worked with Nassos Daphnis.

'Companion of Serenity' (Gratwick, 1959)
Very large pale pink semi-double flowers with ruffled petals and reddish pink flares, this lovely peony has an ivory white sheath and golden yellow stamens with purple filaments. Early season.

'Guardian of the Monastery' (Gratwick, 1959)
An extremely elegant, single-flowered tree peony with large mauve petals, marked by very large maroon flares. The pale green carpels have cream-coloured styles and are surrounded by a creamy white sheath. There are a small number of yellow anthers with white filaments.

'Kishu Caprice' (Sasaki, 1988)
The semi-double, pale mauve flowers with dark imperial purple flares look rather like those of a magnolia with their nicely rounded petals. The sheath is imperial purple and surrounded by golden yellow anthers with purple filaments.

'Red Rascal' (Gratwick)
The single cardinal red flowers have a brighter red centre and darker red flares. A dark pink sheath encloses green carpels with pink styles and yellow anthers have red filaments. The flowers are held well above the foliage.

Chapter 9
Hybrid Tree Peonies

Many years ago, while I was studying botany, I was given an extremely useful piece of advice—if you say something is impossible you will almost certainly be proved wrong. I am sure that there are many scientists who wish that they had followed this advice. One person who should have heeded it was Maxime Cornu, an eminent French horticulturist, who famously said that the yellow tree peony, *Paeonia lutea*, would come to nothing as a garden plant. He must have been very embarrassed when he discovered a few years later that Professor Louis Henry (1853–1903) had named his hybrid tree peony 'Souvenir de Maxime Cornu'.

While there are thousands of beautiful plants in cultivation, horticulturists had always dreamt of producing a tree peony with bright yellow flowers. Until the twentieth century the only one that came close to this target was the ancient cultivar 'Yao's Yellow'. Chinese artists had portrayed this plant as having deep yellow flowers, but in reality they were creamy yellow and this colour faded after a day or so in bright sunlight.

The first successful cross between a *Moutan* tree peony and *P. lutea* is usually credited to Victor and Emile Lemoine, who introduced 'L'Esperance' in 1909. There followed the double yellow 'Chromatella' (1928), the bright yellow 'Alice Harding' (1935) and crimson-red 'Sang Lorrain' (1939), which was raised by crossing *P. delavayi* with a *Moutan* tree peony.

The next major development took place in the 1930s when Arthur Saunders started to introduce his own hybrid tree peonies. The majority of the plants have single or semi-double flowers, which range in colour from the bright yellow 'Argosy' to the mahogany-red 'Black Pirate' and purplish red 'Chinese Dragon'. The flowers tend to be smaller than those of the *Moutan* tree peonies.

'Souvenir de Maxime Cornu' is a rather tongue-in-cheek reference to a famous French horticulturist; who said that *Paeonia lutea* would never come to anything as a garden plant.

Hybrid tree peonies eventually form dense multi-stemmed bushes measuring up to 1.8 M (6 FT.) high and the same across. They are very vigorous and grow best when they are planted in an open situation. Some cultivars, such as 'High Noon' and the Daphnis hybrids, will grow larger than this and need to be provided with plenty of space. They make good garden plants, but 'Alice Harding' and some other cultivars have nodding flowers, which are obscured among the foliage. They flower towards the end of the spring, a week or two after the Japanese and Chinese tree peonies, and have good resistance to peony blight.

Catalogue of Hybrids

'Alice Harding' (Lemoine, 1935; syn. 'Kinko')

A genetic abnormality in this plant has made it invaluable for breeding; for reasons that are still unclear the pollen of this tree peony is compatible with a number of cultivars of *Paeonia lactiflora* and it has been widely used to produce intersectional hybrid peonies. The flowers are double, bright yellow, but have the unfortunate characteristic of being hidden by the foliage. It was produced by crossing *P. lutea* with the Japanese tree peony 'Yaso-okima'. Height 1.5 M (5 FT.) after ten years.

'Chromatella' has rather heavy flowers, which dangle among the foliage.

above right: 'L'Esperance' was the first hybrid tree peony and created a terrific stir in the horticultural world when it was introduced.

right: The hybrid tree peony 'Souvenir de Maxime Cornu' has very heavy flowers, which tend to hang down among the foliage. The plant needs to be supported from early in the year.

'Chromatella' (Lemoine, 1928)

This hybrid tree peony is readily available and bears lots of very double, bright yellow flowers. The petals are edged with carmine-pink. It is cheap to buy, but badly let down by the heavy flowers, which dangle among the foliage. It is known in Japan as 'Kinshi' and is sometimes offered under this name in the West. Height 2 M (6.5 FT.) after ten years.

'L'Esperance' (Lemoine, 1909; syn. 'Kintei')

One of the main problems of this and many other *lutea* hybrid peonies is that the double forms have very heavy flowers, which tend to droop among the leaves. 'L'Esperance' has single or semi-double, primrose yellow flowers with a conspicuous reddish pink rim around the petals. It has yellow anthers and red filaments. Height 1.5 M (5 FT.).

'Sang Lorrain' (Lemoine, 1939)

The flowers of this unusual-coloured peony are semi-double with glossy dark red petals, marked by reddish black flares, and very fragrant. It is a hybrid between a Japanese tree peony and *P. delavayi*.

Louis Henry

Louis Henry raised few hybrids but 'Souvenir de Maxime Cornu' was one of the first and has stood the test of time.

'Souvenir de Maxime Cornu' (Henry, 1897)

The very large, slightly fragrant, double flowers have deep yellow petals, edged cerise-pink and buff. They are heavily flushed with magenta pigment when young, but this colour fades as the flower matures while the orange and red tints intensify. This hybrid is readily available, but the flowers are very heavy and tend to hang among the foliage.

Arthur Saunders

In addition to producing hundreds of herbaceous hybrids, Professor Arthur Saunders also turned his hand to breeding hybrid tree peonies. It is uncertain how many were produced, but according to the APS checklist *Peonies 1976-1986* he and his daughter Silvia registered seventy-eight cultivars with the American Peony Society between 1928 and 1960. The plants were divided into six groups:

Group	Description
Roman Gold Group	Mainly single, with clear yellow flowers.
Golden Hind Group	Mainly semi-double or double with clear yellow flowers.
Tea Rose Group	Single to double, with yellow flowers, flushed with reddish tints.
Banquet Group	Single to double with reddish coloured flowers with yellow undertones.
Black Pirate Group	Single to double with crimson to blackish red flowers.
Mystery Group	Single to double, with ivory flowers and suffused shades of mauve.

Saunders' hybrid peonies have been very successful commercially and are widely grown around the world. The plants are very vigorous and have good disease resistance.

'Amber Moon' (Saunders, 1948)
Roman Gold Group. The single, primrose yellow flowers have small raspberry red flares and golden yellow anthers, supported by short red filaments. The green carpels have yellow styles and are surrounded by an ivory white sheath. Its leaves look rather similar to those of *Paeonia ludlowii*.

'Black Pirate' has very dark red petals, but they come to life when they are backlit by late evening sunshine.

The hybrid tree peony 'Chinese Dragon' has unusual purplish red flowers.

'Black Pirate' (Saunders, 1941)
Black Pirate Group. One of the most readily available of Saunders' hybrids. The slightly nodding single or semi-double flowers have 15 satin-textured petals. The colour is dark maroon-red (187B) and it intensifies as the flower matures. The green carpels have pink styles and are surrounded by a rudimentary, pinkish red sheath. It has golden yellow anthers supported by dark red filaments. The foliage is deeply dissected, bright green along the veins and purplish reddish towards the margins.

'Chinese Dragon' (Saunders, 1950)
Banquet Group. A very vigorous hybrid tree peony with bold upright stems and highly fragrant reddish purple flowers, which have a distinct blue tint as they catch the light. The petals are stiff and waxy in texture, with notched margins, dark magenta (57A) at the edges becoming darker towards the centre and with dark red flares. The golden yellow anthers have long filaments, which become purple towards the base. A short, sometimes rudimentary deep red sheath encloses pale green carpels topped by pink styles. Plants have orange-brown stems and attractive purplish brown, deeply dissected foliage with triangular lobes. It is one of the first hybrid tree peonies to flower in the spring.

'Golden Bowl' (Saunders, 1948)

Roman Gold Group. The single, bowl-shaped flowers are bright canary yellow with bright scarlet flares on the petals. The green carpels have greenish yellow styles and light yellow filaments support the golden yellow anthers. The blooms are held on strong stems well above the very dissected leaves. Vigorous.

'Golden Isles' (Saunders, 1948)

Golden Hind Group. A very vigorous hybrid with deeply dissected, purple-tinged foliage, it holds its flowers upright on strong stems. The semi-double to double, bright yellow flowers (3c) have notched petals, each marked with a deep reddish brown flare, and a sweet, rather spicy fragrance. The flowers have very long anthers, measuring 0.8–1.0 cm (0.32–0.4 in.) and relatively short yellow filaments. A rudimentary white sheath surrounds tomentose, mint green carpels, which have similarly coloured styles. The foliage is quite distinctive with narrowly elliptic leaflets.

'Golden Mandarin' (Saunders, 1952)

Tea Rose Group. This hybrid holds its yellow flowers well above the foliage. They are double, rosette-shaped, with a pink edge and raspberry red flares. Some of the stamens develop into petaloids, while the others have yellow anthers and red filaments. The pale green carpels have pink styles and are surrounded by a striking dark red sheath.

'Golden Vanitie' (Saunders, 1960)

Roman Gold Group. Single, pale yellow flowers with pink-edged petals and small purple flares. The pale green carpels have pink styles and are surrounded by a mauve sheath. The filaments are pink at the base and yellow towards the top.

'Goldfinch' (Saunders, 1949)

Roman Gold Group. Single, pure yellow (2b) flowers have no flares, but the large yellow anthers have bright red filaments. The centre is occupied by greyish green carpels with pale yellow styles.

'High Noon' (Saunders, 1952)

Golden Hind Group. Semi-double, cup-shaped, bright lemon-yellow flowers have dark red flares. In the centre are golden yellow anthers on yellow filaments and a rudimentary, ivory white sheath surrounds pale green carpels with pale yellow styles. It blooms in late spring and may produce a second flush in the summer. The flowers have a slight scent. It is a very vigorous plant that can grow to a height of 1.8 m (6 ft.).

'High Noon' is one of the few tree peonies to have received a Gold Medal from the American Peony Society.

'Renown' is one of Arthur Saunders' lesser-known hybrid tree peonies.

The flowers of the hybrid tree peony 'Roman Gold' are a richer yellow than many of its siblings. The petals have small red flares.

'Renown' (Saunders, 1949)

Banquet Group. The bright copper-red, single flowers have 10–12, slightly crinkled petals. They are quite red when they first open and have small purplish red flares. The reverse of the outer petals has a violet flare and is often marked with white stripes. The green carpels have cream-coloured styles and a lilac sheath, surrounded by golden yellow anthers with orange-flushed filaments. It normally flowers in the spring, but often produces a second flush in the middle of the summer.

'Roman Gold' (Saunders, 1941)

Roman Gold Group. This is one of the best of the yellow hybrids, with vivid, deep bronze yellow (4A), single flowers. Petals are slightly wavy, with angular tips and bold, triangular, deep red flares. The stamens have long yellow filaments, which become slightly orange towards the base. The greyish green carpels have bright yellow styles and are enclosed by a deep yellow sheath, of a shade similar to the petals. The saucer-shaped flowers are highly fragrant and held well above the foliage on strong upright stems.

'Spring Carnival' (Saunders, 1944)

Tea Rose Group. Single, golden yellow flowers have large deep red flares and petals rimmed with cerise-pink and suffused with red and pink veins. The carpels have deep red styles and are surrounded by long yellow anthers with deep red filaments. A very attractive plant.

'Thunderbolt' (Saunders, 1948)

Black Pirate Group. Young buds are conical and reddish brown and they open to display glossy reddish brown, single flowers, slightly redder than those of the more readily available 'Black Pirate'. The slightly wrinkled petals have a white flare on the outside and a violet margin. The carpels are pale green with reddish purple styles, enclosed by a dark red sheath, and the golden yellow anthers have dark red filaments. The leaflets have lanceolate lobes.

'Vesuvian' (Saunders, 1948)

Black Pirate Group. Aptly named, this has double, bright cardinal red flowers and looks remarkably like a giant form of *Paeonia delavayi* with numerous petals. It has few stamens, but those that are present have pale yellow anthers with short red filaments. The carpels are pale green with crosier-shaped purple styles. Very late flowering.

Nassos Daphnis

Most of Daphnis's tree peonies are named after characters in Greek mythology; the number in brackets (prefixed by the letter D) is his seedling number. His plants are highly regarded by peony breeders and several have been used to produce intersectional hybrids. Nassos Daphnis, a famous American artist, has taken tree peony breeding to new heights. The great majority of Arthur Saunders' F1 hybrid tree peonies are highly infertile, but a tiny number have subsequently proved to be fertile and have produced F2 seedlings. Daphnis has used pollen from his own F2 hybrid tree peonies, which are fertile, to pollinate the fertile Saunders plants. He has also tried to backcross the F2 hybrids by pollinating them with pollen from *Moutan* tree peonies to increase the amount of their genetic material in his plants. This has not been completely successful because the *Moutan* genes appear to be dominant. While some of his peonies have vivid scarlet flowers, others have more subtle colours, with layers of violet, yellow and magenta pigment. Daphnis' plants are currently more expensive than those produced by Arthur Saunders, but the price should decline as micropropagation becomes a viable means of propagation.

'Ariadne' (Daphnis, D-304-1977)

Named after the daughter of King Minos, who helped Theseus defeat the Minotaur. It is a stunning plant whose flowers present a veritable kaleidoscope of colours. They are semi-double with deep peach-coloured petals edged with magenta and suffused with dark red veins, and there are dark red flares. A peach-coloured sheath encloses green carpels with salmon pink styles. An excellent plant. Backcross.

'Demetra' (Daphnis, D-19-1965)

Named after the Greek goddess of the earth, Demeter. Semi-double, yellow flowers with pink edges and deep maroon flares, the petals become progressively smaller towards the centre. The green carpels have pink styles and are surrounded by a maroon-coloured sheath. The stamens have red-flushed filaments. F1 hybrid.

The flowers of 'Gauguin' consist of a complex medley of colours, which almost defies description. It was named after the French Post-Impressionist painter Paul Gauguin, who used bright colours in his work.

below: 'Hephestos' has deep brick red flowers with darker flares.
(Credit: Roy Klehm)

'Gauguin' (Daphnis, D-22-1965)

I struggled for a long time to describe this flower because there are so many layers of colour. The single amber flowers are overlaid with raspberry red and have deeper raspberry red veins. The petals, yellow on the reverse, are tinted magenta at the tips, while at the base there are bold, very dark red flares. The large yellow anthers have dark red filaments. F1 hybrid.

'Hephestos' (Daphnis, D-240-1968)

Named after the Greek god of fire. Very large, double flowers are a deep brick red and marked with darker flares. There are very few stamens with yellow anthers and dark red filaments, surrounding pale green carpels with salmon pink styles. A pink sheath encloses the carpels. Backcross.

'Iphigenia' (Daphnis, D-303-1977)

Iphigenia was the daughter of Agamemnon. An extremely pretty tree peony with ruby red petals marked with very dark reddish black flares, and on the reverse a distinct white line. A pinkish magenta sheath surrounds the pale green, pilose carpels with magenta-pink styles. Backcross.

'Kronos' (Daphnis, D-23-1966)

Kronos was the Greek god of time. A vigorous plant with single, burgundy red flowers and darker flares. The pale green carpels have salmon pink styles and are surrounded by a pink sheath. It has pale yellow anthers, supported by dark red filaments. F1 hybrid.

'Leda' (Daphnis, D-308-1977)

Named after the mother of Castor and Pollux, a Queen of Sparta. The stunning semi-double, pinkish mauve flowers have conspicuous purple veins and maroon flares. In the centre a cream-coloured sheath surrounds the pale green carpels with cream styles. The yellow anthers have dark red filaments. A wonderful plant with rather wavy petals and fragrant flowers. 'Leda' was raised by crossing a *Moutan* tree peony with an unknown

above: 'Leda' was originally registered as a single tree peony, but mature plants usually have semi-double flowers. The plant was produced by backcrossing a hybrid tree peony with 'Kokamon', a Japanese tree peony, and has very large, pinkish-mauve flowers. It is 75 percent *Moutan* tree peony and 25 percent lutea hybrid.

left: 'Nike' has pale yellow flowers with maroon flares.
(Credit: Roy Klehm)

hybrid. The plant was originally registered as a single-flowered tree peony, but in ideal conditions the flowers can be quite double. Backcross.

'Nike' (Daphnis, D-368)

Named after Nike, the personification of victory. A single hybrid tree peony with pale yellow flowers, which are flushed at the edges with peach-coloured veins. The petals are marked with large maroon flares. In the centre green carpels are surrounded by a cream-coloured sheath and have pale green styles. BC2 (backcross 2) × 'Guardian of the Monastery'; BC2 was produced by backcrossing a *Moutan* tree peony with F2 pollen.

'Persephone' (Daphnis, D-26-1966)

Persephone was Demeter's daughter. The buds look rather like those of a rose when they are opening. The flowers are semi-double with deeply notched, pale yellow petals and small raspberry red flares. It has pale green carpels and cream styles, surrounded by golden yellow anthers on yellow filaments. F1 hybrid.

The hybrid tree peony 'Tria' has three flowers to each stem, which open in succession.

'Golden Era' is one the best hybrid tree peonies, with golden yellow petals and maroon flares.

'Tria' (Daphnis, D-3-1965)

The three Roman goddesses of fate are referred to as the Tria Fata. Aptly named because there are three flowers to each stem, which open in succession. This enables 'Tria' to have a very long flowering period. The single flowers open deep yellow with raspberry red flares and fade slightly after a couple of days. The pale green carpels have cream-coloured styles and are surrounded by a pink sheath. The long yellow anthers have short red filaments.

David Reath

David Reath's tree peonies are less well known than those of Arthur Saunders and Nassos Daphnis, but this is partly because he registered so few. The best known is 'Golden Era', which is a seedling of Arthur Saunders' 'Golden Isles'. 'Golden Era' has been widely used for breeding inter-sectional hybrid peonies and is a superb plant in its own right. The plant produces fertile pollen and viable seed. Among the most recent posthumous introductions is 'Center Stage', a *lutea* hybrid with creamy white flowers and burgundy-coloured flares.

'Golden Era' (Reath, 1984)

One of the most popular hybrid tree peonies, it has pale yellow, single flowers with nicely rounded petals, maroon flares and a yellow sheath. The pilose carpels have yellow styles and are surrounded by yellow anthers, supported by purple filaments. This is a reliable tree peony with plenty of flowers.

Chapter 10
Intersectional Hybrid or "Itoh" Peonies

American peony breeders have always dreamt of producing an herbaceous peony with double deep yellow flowers and several people spent much of their lives pollinating thousands of plants in the hope of achieving this elusive goal. The obvious candidate for the work was the Caucasian peony *Paeonia mlokosewitschii*, which has butter yellow flowers. Unfortunately this species is difficult to grow in the United States and most attempts at pollination proved unsuccessful. A handful of yellow hybrids were produced, but few of the flowers were significantly deeper in colour than those of *P. mlokosewitschii*. The solution to the problem came from an unexpected quarter and was achieved by a breeder who lived on the opposite side of the world.

For many years it had been assumed that it would be impossible to cross an herbaceous peony with a tree peony. Success in this arena would create the prospect of introducing a new palette of colours for herbaceous peonies. In 1948 Toichi Itoh (pronounced *ee-toe*), a Japanese nurseryman, succeeded in crossing the yellow hybrid tree peony 'Alice Harding' with a double white herbaceous lactiflora called 'Kakoden'. While this may sound a simple task it was the result of pollinating twelve hundred peonies.

Nine of the resulting thirty-six seedlings had the appearance of tree peonies, while the rest were herbaceous in character. Toichi Itoh died in 1956 before any of his seedlings had flowered, but his son-in-law Shigao-Oshida looked after them and in 1963 the first of the plants started to flower. Four of the seedlings were considered to have the potential to be particularly good garden plants and were named 'Yellow Crown', 'Yellow Emperor', 'Yellow Dream' and 'Yellow Heaven'. In 1949 Mr. Itoh had also experimented with a pink tree peony, called 'Kagura Jishi'. This also produced hybrids with 'Kakoden' and the plants were subsequently named 'Pink Heaven' and 'Pink Purity'. These were grown in the nursery for several years and, if they had survived, would have had great commercial potential. Unfortunately both plants were destroyed when a large Japanese railway company drove a new line through the old nursery. Itoh's original plants grow to a height of approximately 90 CM (3 FT.) and form a nicely rounded bush, measuring about 90 CM (3 FT.) across. All four varieties have semi-double, bright yellow flowers with red flares at the base of the petals. The plants show their tree peony ancestry by having a creamy white sheath surrounding the carpels; this sheath is absent in all other herbaceous peonies.

For over a decade the rest of the world was ignorant of Itoh's achievement. It may have remained unnoticed if it had not been for the interest of Louis Smirnow, an American peony grower. Smirnow asked Mr. Itoh's widow whether he could have permission to register the plants and offer them for sale in the United States. The peonies were registered with the American Peony Society in 1974 as 'Itoh-Smirnow' hybrids and immediately caused a stir among peony growers in the U.S.A. Itoh's main achievement was not in producing the first hybrids between tree and herbaceous peonies, but showing that it could be done. This acted as a stimulus for American peony breeders, who attempted to repeat Itoh's success by pollinating their own plants, and much to their amazement, they succeeded.

The American Peony Society has created a new category for these peonies and has called it the "Itoh Hybrids Group", in recognition of Itoh's achievement. This has proved to be contentious because in some people's eyes it suggested that Itoh was the sole originator of all hybrids between tree and herbaceous peonies; which is not the case. Some breeders have consequently insisted that they should be referred to as "intersectional hybrids", between the botanical sections *Moutan* and *Paeon*. This caused a lot of upset within the American Peony Society, the repercussions of which are still with us.

These intersectional hybrids combine the characteristics of both parents. At first sight they appear to be tree peonies, but the shoots are usually herbaceous and die back in autumn. The flowers are held erect on long stems, well above the leaves. The plants have a neater habit than most herbaceous peonies, retaining their shape throughout the year regardless of the weather. Cultivars with single flowers have five petals, and functional stamens and carpels. The carpels are enclosed by a sheath, which has been inherited from the tree peony parent. The flowers are ideal for cutting because the stems are very strong and the blooms can be expected to last for a minimum of five days at normal room temperature. Intersectional hybrids are very vigorous and divisions produce plenty of feeding roots within a few weeks of planting out.

"Itoh" or intersectional hybrids, such as 'Yellow Heaven', have a rudimentary sheath, which partially encloses the carpels.

In recent years a number of American breeders have succeeded in raising new intersectional hybrids, but at the time of writing only fifty or so had been registered. The three leading breeders are Don Hollingsworth, Roger Anderson and Donald Smith. Don Hollingsworth is best known for 'Garden Treasure', the first Itoh hybrid to be awarded a Gold Medal by the American Peony Society in 1996. 'Garden Treasure' is a more vigorous plant than the original Itoh hybrids, with large semi-double, deep yellow flowers and slightly glossy dark green leaves. 'Garden Treasure' is an outstanding garden plant with 50–60 deep golden yellow, semi-double flowers on a mature plant.

The main competitor of 'Garden Treasure's is Roger Anderson's 'Bartzella', which was registered two years later and has double, bright yellow flowers. The demand for

'Bartzella' was so great in the late 1990s that divisions were being sold for $1000 each. Much of this demand appears to have been created by the wholesale market, which could see the plant's potential as a cut flower. Anderson was the first person to produce the complete range of colours and he is now concentrating on trying to create the first herbaceous peony with pure orange flowers. Roger's intersectional hybrid 'Kopper Kettle' has bright orange flowers, but close inspection reveals that the colour is created by a combination of red and yellow pigments. While he has had considerable success in producing F1 hybrids they are almost entirely sterile and he hopes to produce a fertile F2 hybrid. In recent years he has succeeded in using *Paeonia potaninii* as a pollen parent, producing 'Unique', a stunning intersectional hybrid with deep red flowers. To date he has raised approximately four hundred different intersectional hybrids, but only forty or so of these have been named.

The number of intersectional hybrids is likely to increase dramatically during the next few years because several other breeders have started to experiment with the known pollen and pod parents. The majority of the plants that have been registered to date have semi-double or double yellow flowers, satisfying the demand for the elusive double yellow peony.

Characteristics

The range of colours produced in the intersectional hybrids is quite astonishing, including lavender, orange, copper red, pink, various shades of red, white and the original yellow; indeed the only colour missing is blue. Many of the plants have striking flares, a character inherited from the tree peony parent. While there is considerable variation between cultivars they share several desirable features, namely they are very vigorous; they hold their blooms on strong upright stems; they flower over an extended period; and they appear to have good resistance to fungal diseases. The herbaceous and tree peony parents donate an equal number of characteristics to their offspring, but on the surface they look more like tree peonies, although they are cultivated in much the same way as the herbaceous peonies because the shoots die back in autumn. However, because their buds are produced on short woody shoots, it is important not to damage them when you are weeding the garden in the winter. The shoots can also be quite brittle when they are young and you must take care to avoid knocking them off when you walk past. Intersectional hybrids flower for a much longer period than most peonies, but are more likely to produce double flowers towards the end of the season. The flowering period lasts for a minimum of two weeks in a hot year and three weeks in a cool one. Most will flower successfully in partial shade.

One of the most interesting features about intersectional hybrids is that they appear to be capable of repeat flowering. According to Roger Anderson the plants will re-bloom if they are cut back after the first flowering. The second flush will be smaller, possibly only two or three flowers, but these are more double and better formed than those that appeared earlier in the season. The cutting back does not appear to affect the plants, but you would be advised to give them an additional dose of fertilizer to ensure they grow well during the forthcoming year. Peonies are often criticized for having a short flowering period, but the development of repeat-flowering cultivars would go a long way to refuting this.

Another characteristic of intersectional hybrid peonies is that the flowers often exhibit colour streaking on the petals. Don Smith (2002) says that this occurs in 10–15 percent of all his intersectional hybrid seedlings. Large amounts of streaking can be unattractive, but a limited amount can add to the beauty of the flower. Streaking tends to be most prominent in young plants; on older plants the petals are more likely to display pure colour.

Anderson regularly grafts his plants, but he is wary about revealing his methods. When I met him in 2002 he had serious doubts as to whether anyone would ever succeed in micropropagating intersectional hybrids because in his opinion they are genetically unstable. He cites the example of 'Joanne Marlene', a new intersectional hybrid seedling he registered in 1999. The plant had single flowers with magenta flares before it was divided, but after division the plant produced double flowers with mixed colours and the flares could no longer be seen. Roger says that you cannot judge an intersectional hybrid by the first flowers and plants need to be grown for four or five years before they can be appraised. In most cases divisions have smaller flowers than the original plant, but in other ways they are identical. However, Don Hollingsworth believes the colour variation in intersectional hybrids is probably the result of differing temperatures when the flowers develop in the spring.

Itoh's original hybrids are relatively easy to obtain and, because they have been in commerce for some time, they are reasonably cheap to purchase. However, they are inferior to the more recent cultivars, such as 'Bartzella' and 'Garden Treasure', and appear to have been mixed up when they have been passed from one nursery to another. 'Yellow Crown' and 'Yellow Heaven' seem to be the most widespread, but it is quite possible that when you buy either of these plants you are actually purchasing one of the siblings. Most modern intersectional hybrid peonies are very expensive because they have to be propagated by division and demand always exceeds supply. 'Bartzella' has never been patented and this has allowed several nurseries to propagate the plant. As supplies increase, the price of 'Bartzella' is likely to fall and it may be destined to become of one of the world's most sought-after garden plants.

There is likely to be an increasing number of new introductions in the future. In 2002 Donald Smith registered twelve new intersectional hybrids, mainly the result of crossing *Paeonia lactiflora* 'Martha W.' with the *lutea* hybrid 'Golden Era'. A couple of years later he introduced 'Impossible Dream', a double intersectional hybrid with double pink flowers.

Catalogue of Hybrids

Intersectional hybrids normally flower from the late spring to early summer. Mature plants can often flower for as much as four weeks and occasional blooms may appear later in the season. They perform best when planted in full sunshine and when there is no competition from other plants. Intersectional hybrids reach maturity after four or five

'Yellow Heaven' was one of the first intersectional hybrids. It forms a neat, compact bush with plenty of double yellow flowers.

years and will eventually form a substantial bush. In the following descriptions the seed parent is given and then the pollen parent.

The original Itoh hybrids

These are quite similar to one another. All four have large semi-double, bright yellow flowers with small red flares and 5–7 pale green carpels enclosed by a vestigial ivory white sheath. 'Yellow Heaven' and 'Yellow Emperor' are very similar with elongated flower buds and red sepals (Langhammer, 2004). 'Yellow Crown' and 'Yellow Dream' both have round flower buds, but the sepals of the former are green and those of the latter red. 'Yellow Crown' has a more upright habit and grows to a height of 90 CM (3 FT.), while the others achieve 75 CM (30 IN.). They are all good garden plants and somewhat cheaper to buy than more recent intersectional hybrids.

The intersectional hybrid 'Bartzella' quickly gained the world's attention when the asking price rose to $1,000. *(Credit: Roy Klehm).*

'Bartzella' (Anderson, 1986)

This is one of the most famous of all intersectional hybrids, partly because of the astronomical prices that it commanded in the late 1990s. 'Bartzella' is very similar to 'Garden Treasure' but its flowers are slightly more double, it has an erect habit and more dissected, dark green leaves. The flowers are bright yellow (2B fading to 2C) and on mature plants can measure as much as 24 CM (9.5 IN.) across. The pale green carpels are slightly sericeous, with pale yellow styles and surrounded by a rudimentary pale yellow sheath. The anthers and filaments are also pale yellow. It is very vigorous and free flowering, with the blooms held erect and well above the leaves. The flowers have an attractive, slightly spicy fragrance. It flowers in the middle of summer. Height 75 CM (30 IN.).

'Border Charm' (Hollingsworth, 1984)

The single, or slightly semi-double, flowers have large pinkish red flares and a sweet fragrance. The green carpels have yellow styles and are surrounded by a rudimentary pale yellow sheath that partly encloses them. Only a few of the stamens are functional, the remainder being reduced to a short filament, without any anthers. It is very hardy and forms a low spreading plant with stems up to 60 CM (24 IN.) long. (*P. lactiflora* 'Carr East #2' × *P. ×lemoinei* 'Alice Harding'). Height 45 CM (18 IN.).

'Callie's Memory' (Anderson, 1999)

This beautiful peony has semi-double or double flowers with creamy yellow petals (2C becoming 2D) and orange-red flares. The flowers have slightly wavy petals with notched tips and a rudimentary ivory white sheath surrounds the sericeous, pale green carpels, which have pale yellow sickle-shaped styles. The stamens are not functional, pale yellow, with slightly darker filaments. The flowers have a rather piquant fragrance and have plenty of side buds. Roger Anderson named this peony after Callie, a pit bull terrier and his last dog. (*P. lactiflora* 'Martha W.' seedling SD19 × *P. ×lemoinei* Daphnis, D-74 tree peony). Height 75 CM (30 IN.), spread 1 M (3.3 FT.).

The apricot-coloured flowers of 'Canary Brilliants' turn deep yellow as they age.

'Canary Brilliants' (Anderson, 1999)

According to the breeder, this plant had canary yellow, bomb-shaped flowers when it was very young, but with age it has started to produce semi-double blooms. They are bright apricot (16C) with red-tinged edges, fading to deep yellow with red flares, and measure about 10 CM (4 IN.) across. The flowers are multi-carpelled, with fragments of ivory white sheath around the pale green carpels, which have ivory white styles. A few yellow anthers on yellow filaments surround the carpels. 'Canary Brilliants' is a vigorous plant, with deeply cut, dark green leaves. It forms a spreading bush 1 M (3.3 FT.) across. (*P. lactiflora* 'Martha W.' seedling × *P. ×lemoinei* Daphnis, D-75 tree peony). Height 70 CM (28 IN.).

'Cora Louise' (Anderson, 1986)

The great majority of intersectional hybrids have yellow flowers, but Roger Anderson has produced 'Cora Louise', which has large semi-double white flowers and dark lavender flares. The flowers open pale pink, but quickly fade to white in bright sunshine, and they have a slight fragrance. It was named after Roger's grandmother. (Unknown *lactiflora* × *P.* ×*lemoinei* 'Golden Era'). Height 60 CM (24 IN.).

'Court Jester' has dramatic yellow flowers with bright red flares.

'Court Jester' (Anderson, 1999)

This is a showy extrovert of a plant and one of the most dramatic of the intersectional hybrids. The single flowers open to a star shape, with orange outer petals and apricot inners, all marked with bold red flares. As the flower ages the orange tints disappear to leave a bright yellow flower with deep red flares, fading to violet-red. The petals can occasionally have a purple stripe along their length. The flowers have a bold centre of large, sericeous green carpels with bright red styles and a violet sheath, surrounded by a neat ring of yellow anthers, held on long yellow filaments. The sepals are tinged with purple pigment and there are plenty of side buds. It is an amazing plant that has few peers, but is difficult to photograph and needs to be seen "in the flesh". Young flowers have rather small petals and can be disappointing, but by the time that the plant is two or three years old they will be more typical. The upright plants grow to a height of 80 CM (32 IN.) and spread 1 M (3.3 FT.) across. (*P. lactiflora* 'Martha W.' × *P.* ×*lemoinei* Daphnis, D-256 'Tria' seedling).

'First Arrival' was Roger Anderson's first intersectional hybrid; it has lavender-pink flowers with reddish purple flares.

Intersectional hybrids, such as 'First Arrival', form a compact bush and are very free flowering.

'First Arrival' (Anderson, 1986)

Roger Anderson was, to say the least, surprised when this, his first intersectional hybrid seedling, flowered. The rose-scented flowers are semi-double and large, measuring 15–20 CM (6–8 IN.) across, with lavender-pink (75C) petals marked with vivid reddish purple flares. The yellow stamens have purple filaments, and the carpels are mid green with pink styles and surrounded by a reddish purple sheath. Young flowers are heavily flushed with magenta, but this fades as the flower opens. The colour of the flowers can vary in different places and in some years they are pinker and in others more lavender. 'First Arrival' makes a vigorous and a free-flowering plant, with 30–40, flowers, strong upright stems and deeply cut, dark green leaves. A five-year-old plant measures 70 CM (28 IN.) high by 1 M (3.3 FT.) across. (*P. lactiflora* 'Martha W.' × *P. ×lemoinei* 'Golden Era').

'Garden Treasure' (Hollingsworth, 1984)

This is a vigorous plant with numerous erect stems clothed with dark purplish green leaves, which become mid green as they mature. Young plants have semi-double, bright golden yellow flowers (2B becoming 2C) with rather diffused scarlet-red flares, but they become more double as the plant matures. The flowers have 10 sericeous pinkish green carpels with pink styles partially enclosed by a rudimentary pale yellow sheath. Anthers are pale yellow on greenish yellow filaments, and a few stamens are converted into pale yellow staminodes. Plants can be in bloom for up to a month, because the flowers do not all mature at the same time. A young plant forms a short spreading clump, but with maturity it develops into a nicely rounded bush up to 90 CM (3 FT.) high with a spread of as much as 1.5 M (5 FT.). At the time of writing 'Garden Treasure' is the only intersectional hybrid to have won a Gold Medal from the American Peony Society. (*P. lactiflora* 'Carr East #2' × *P. ×lemoinei* 'Alice Harding'). The plant is patented and cannot be propagated without the permission of the breeder.

'Garden Treasure' is the only intersectional hybrid to have received a Gold Medal from the American Peony Society.

'Hillary' (Anderson, 1999)

Semi-double or double, saucer-shaped flowers are apricot coloured and have a spicy fragrance. The petals are strongly overlaid with magenta and have the general appearance of 51A, with apricot centres. The outer petals are large and rounded, with large deep red flares at the base. In the centre are slightly wavy, lanceolate or spoon-shaped staminodes and mint green carpels with ivory styles. If present the sheath is ivory coloured. The very few stamens are pale yellow with yellow filaments. Overall it forms a vigorous bush with dark green leaves, 60–65 CM (24–26 IN.) high and a spread of 90 CM (3 FT.). Roger Anderson believes this may be an F2 hybrid from 'Bartzella', but it has no fertility.

'Impossible Dream' (Smith, 2004)

The double flowers are deep lavender-pink when they open from their rose-shaped buds, becoming deep pink with silvered edges and have white flares. The 3–4 pale green carpels with cream-coloured styles are surrounded by a cream-coloured sheath. The flowers, which open early in the season, have 45–50 petals and are held well above the foliage. 'Impossible Dream' forms an upright bush, up to 90 CM (3 FT.) high, with glabrous dark red stems and dark green leaves with yellow tips. (*P. lactiflora* 'Martha W.' × *P.* ×*suffruticosa* 'Stolen Heaven').

'Julia Rose' (Anderson, 1991)

The flowers almost defy description; red in bud, they open to orange and apricot, with purple-flushed edges (39B with 51A edges), and measure 10–15 CM (4–6 IN.) across. A five-year old plant can bear up to 30 flowers, which have a spicy scent and are borne on strong stems. It has deeply toothed, dark green leaves and makes a vigorous barrel-shaped bush up to 70 CM (28 IN.) high and 1 M (3.3 FT.) across. (unknown *P. lactiflora* seedling × *P.* ×*lemoinei* 'Renown').

'Kopper Kettle' (Anderson, 1999)

The semi-double, spicily fragrant flowers have large apricot guard petals, suffused with buff and purple pigment. The petals are unusual because they are covered with dark flecks of pigment and have deep red flares. The carpels are pale green with ivory styles and an ivory-coloured sheath. In the centre of the flower are a few narrow, copper-coloured staminodes and yellow anthers on copper-coloured filaments. The overall impression is of a copper-coloured flower with occasional yellow streaks. A mature bush has 20–30 flowers and measures 66–70 CM (26–28 IN.) high and 90 CM (3 FT.) across. (*P. lactiflora* 'Martha W.' × *P. ×lemoinei* 'Golden Era').

'Pastel Splendor' (Anderson-Seidl, 1996)

When Roger Anderson divided this plant when it was young, half the divisions had flowers with a yellow flush, while the remainder were pink. The flowers of 'Pastel Splendor' are single, yellow in colour with deep magenta-pink edges and deep red flares. It has an interesting centre of mint green carpels with ivory white styles, surrounded by a cream-coloured sheath. The strongly scented flowers are sometimes multi-carpelled, with the carpels filling the centre of the flower. Most of the ivory white stamens are only partly

above: The aptly named 'Kopper Kettle' has copper-coloured flowers.

above right: Peonies such as 'Scarlet Heaven' make a good substitute for roses, because they have a compact habit and no thorns.

right: The flowers of 'Sequestered Sunshine' are often multi-carpelled.

functional, reduced to small dagger-like staminodes, but a few are functional and have bright red filaments. Plants are very vigorous, with dark green, deeply cut foliage. (*P. lactiflora* 'Martha W.' × Saunders F2 A).

'Prairie Charm' (Hollingsworth, 1992)

Semi-double blooms of greenish yellow have contrasting reddish purple flares and, occasionally, slightly toothed petal tips. The carpels are green with creamy white styles and a similarly coloured sheath. Yellow anthers have creamy white filaments. It is a free-flowering plant up to 75 CM (30 IN.) high, and 90 CM (3 FT.) across. (*P. lactiflora* 'Miss America' × *P. ×lemoinei* 'Alice Harding').

'Scarlet Heaven' (Anderson, 1999)

This is one of the brightest red intersectional hybrids with single flowers. The heart-shaped petals are scarlet-red with slightly darker red edges (53B with 53A edges). The emerald green carpels have large bright red styles, surrounded by a violet sheath and yellow stamens with orange filaments. It is free flowering with at least 20 spice-scented flowers to a bush. A mature specimen measures 90 CM (3 FT.) high and has a spread of 1 M (3.3 FT.). (*P. lactiflora* 'Martha W.' × *P. ×lemoinei* 'Thunderbolt').

'Sequestered Sunshine' (Anderson, 1999)

Single or occasionally semi-double flowers have a spicy fragrance and are bright canary yellow (4A), highlighted by reddish pink flares. The sericeous, greyish green carpels have red styles, enclosed by an ivory white sheath and small yellow stamens, supported by yellow filaments. The foliage is coarser than in other intersectional hybrids, mid green and slightly waxy in texture. A very strong-stemmed, erect-growing plant, which measures approximately 80 CM (32 IN.) high and 90 CM (3 FT.) across. (*P. lactiflora* 'Miss America' × *P. ×lemoinei* D-74).

'Smith Family Yellow' (Smith, 2002)

The cross between the lactiflora cultivar 'Martha W.' and the tree peony *P. ×lemoinei* 'Golden Era' seems to be particularly fertile and Donald Smith has raised several intersectional hybrids from it. 'Smith Family Yellow' is a vigorous example, with semi-double or double deep yellow flowers, small red flares and 4 light green carpels with yellow styles. The plant has 2–3 buds to a stem and fragrant flowers. The flowers measure up to 20 CM (8 IN.) across and are held well above the dark green foliage. Height 70 CM (20 IN.).

'Unique' (Anderson, 1999)

'Unique' is descended from *Paeonia potaninii* and produces a nicely shaped bush, covered with deep purplish red (61A) flowers, measuring up to 10 CM (4 IN.) across. It is much taller than most intersectional hybrids, with finer foliage. The single flowers have sericeous, pale green carpels with bright reddish purple styles, surrounded by a vivid reddish purple, star-shaped sheath. The yellow anthers are held on orange filaments. The flowers have a

'Unique' inherits its bright red colour from *P. potaninii.*

strong, spicy fragrance. The stems of this plant are quite brittle and care should be taken when weeding in the spring. (*P. lactiflora* 'Martha W.' × *P. potaninii* var. *trollioides*, a distinctive plant with yellow flowers). Height 75–85 CM (30–34 IN.).

'Viking Full Moon' (Pehrson/Seidl, 1989)

This is an attractive plant with single, light greenish yellow flowers measuring up to 15 CM (6 IN.) across and rounded petals with small red flares. A pale yellow sheath surrounds the greyish green carpels, which have pale yellow styles. It forms a rounded bush up to 85 CM (34 IN.) high and has side buds, which extend the flowering period. Its parents are unknown, but were presumably a cultivar of *P. lactiflora* and *P.* ×*lemoinei.*

Chapter 11
Growing Peonies

The secret to growing most plants is to understand how they grow in the wild. If you can imitate a plant's natural environment it will grow well, but if the conditions in your garden diverge too much from its normal habitat, it will invariably languish. This maxim applies to all species and there is little point in trying to grow a plant that needs moist acid conditions, such as a blueberry, if your soil is calcareous and dry. The most successful garden plants are able to grow in a wide range of soil types and in most situations.

While tree peonies have a complex ancestry, the majority of the ancestral species grew in upland areas of China where winter temperatures could fall to as low as -29ºC (-20ºF). The soil in these parts of China is often stony, but well drained and covered with scrub. This is the key to growing tree peonies. They are not as tender as they appear and will usually tolerate very low temperatures when they are dormant. Occasionally North America will experience temperatures as low as -37ºC (-35ºF). This may well kill some of the aerial branches of a tree peony, but in most cases it will produce new shoots from below the ground in the spring.

If you live in area prone to late frosts it is a good idea to plant tree peonies where they will receive some shade from early morning sunshine. This will allow the frozen tissues to thaw slowly, whereas immediate exposure to strong sun can cause serious damage to the young shoots. Nevertheless tree peonies need fresh air circulating around them and plenty of sunshine; they should not be planted in heavy shade.

Herbaceous peonies on the other hand occupy a wider range of habitats including the margins of deciduous woodland, meadows, among scrub on limestone cliffs and steppe grassland. The majority of herbaceous species, such as *Paeonia mascula*, *P. officinalis* and *P. peregrina*, grow best on well-drained, calcareous soils with some protection from the full strength of summer sunshine. A few species such as *P. californica*, *P. clusii*, *P. brownii* and *P. rhodia* occupy a very narrow environmental niche and they will rarely survive unless they are provided with ideal growing conditions. However, all peonies have one thing in common—they cannot tolerate waterlogging and will die if the roots are deprived of oxygen for more than a day or so. The damage is more likely to occur during the summer, when the plants are growing and transpiration is taking place in the cells. It is therefore inadvisable to plant peonies in low-lying areas, particularly those that may be flooded during the growing season.

Peonies are remarkably easy to grow as long as you follow a few simple guidelines. One of the most common fallacies is that they do not like to be moved. This is an old wives' tale, because if a peony is moved at the correct time of the year and without disturbing its root system, it will often recover very quickly. Most peonies are divided before they are replanted and this is bound to have an adverse effect on the plant. If a plant is heavily divided and split into many small pieces, it should come as no surprise if it takes a long time to recover.

Peonies can be moved in the summer, but the foliage is likely to die and it may take some time for the plant to recover. The best time to move a peony is during the autumn, when the foliage has started to die, but the roots are still actively growing. It is important to keep the plant well watered during the following summer, but avoid excessive watering because this can result in crown rot.

On the whole, peonies should be grown in an open situation, in well-drained soil. Few species will grow successfully under shade and while they may not die immediately, the plant will gradually decline, becoming smaller and eventually disappearing. Specimens of *Paeonia lactiflora* can survive for many years in shade as long as they receive sufficient moisture, but they will not flower, producing short stems with one or two leaves. These plants can spread to form quite a large clump, which may be split and replanted in the open, where they will eventually recover and thrive as normal. Tree peonies will tolerate a degree of shade, as long as they receive full sunshine for at least part of the day. If you plant peonies in the shade and they show poor growth, you have two choices: either cut back the trees and shrubs that are creating the shaded conditions or move the peonies to a sunnier position. A few species will grow happily in dappled shade; they include *P. mascula* subsp. *mascula*, *P. japonica* and *P. obovata*. They will not, however, tolerate heavy shade or being planted in dry soil beneath conifers.

With the exception of species such as *P. clusii*, *P. sterniana*, *P. rhodia* and *P. cambessedesii*, herbaceous peonies should not be planted beside walls. However the aforementioned species do quite well against a wall, which radiates heat on a sunny day and prevents the roots from becoming too wet during the winter. The best artificial habitat for many species peonies is very well-drained soil on an artificial rock garden: this comes closest to mimicking its natural habitat.

Buying Plants

When you are buying peonies it is a good idea to remember the old maxim: "you get what you pay for". Peonies may appear expensive when they are compared with other perennials, but there is a very good reason for this. Commercial nurseries usually propagate named cultivars of herbaceous perennials by using root cuttings or micropropagation. These are very quick and efficient methods of propagating plants, which enable the nurseries to sell them at relatively low prices. However, with the possible exception of a few hybrids, peonies cannot be propagated from root cuttings and it is only recently that micropropagation has been applied successfully to the genus. As a consequence growers have to rely upon dividing their plants every three to four years before they have enough stock to sell. The demand for some recently introduced cultivars can be so high that prices have attained astronomical levels, as occurred with the intersectional hybrid 'Bartzella' in the late 1990s. However, while peonies can be quite expensive to buy initially, few perennials will live as long and it is quite common to hear of peonies that have lived for more than a hundred years. Indeed if you visit a garden that has become derelict you will find that most of the herbaceous perennials will have disappeared, but the peonies will still be going strong.

We live in a competitive world and there is a lot of pressure on retailers to keep the price of peonies as low as possible. There are only two ways that this can be achieved; by keeping divisions as small as possible and only selling the cheapest plants. However, these small divisions will turn out to be a false economy because they take a long time to become established and may not flower successfully for several years. The cheapest peonies are those that are in plentiful supply, such as *Paeonia* 'Festiva Maxima', 'Sarah Bernhardt' and 'Felix Crousse'. All of these cultivars were first bred in the nineteenth century and nurseries have had plenty of time to build up their stocks. They are not necessarily the best, nor the most popular; they just happen to be the cheapest and most readily available. Peonies will usually outlive the majority of the other herbaceous perennials in your garden and for this reason alone it makes sense to choose them carefully.

When it comes to actually buying peonies I would strongly recommend that you purchase them as bare roots in the autumn. Most gardeners buy peonies from their local garden centre and are disappointed when the new plant takes a long time to become established. This is because most potted peonies have two to three buds per division, rather than the four or five that a specialist nursery will supply. Bare-root plants are considerably larger and should produce a good-sized flowering plant within a couple of years, compared to three to four years for a potted specimen with only two or three buds. Pot-grown plants should certainly be avoided if they have been in the pot for more than one season. They are often less vigorous and there is a strong chance that the roots will have girdled the inside of the pot. The roots are almost impossible to straighten out because they are very brittle and are likely to break.

Wherever possible try to buy the plants from a specialist peony nursery, where you can see the peonies in flower during the spring and early summer. Most of these nurseries welcome visitors when the peonies are flowering and will have a couple of hundred cultivars available for you to see. The nurseries accept orders throughout the summer and will then deliver the plants in the autumn. Some cultivars may be in short supply and it is therefore advisable to place your order as soon as possible. The divisions are shipped to the customer before the ground freezes in the winter. A few nurseries will also dig roots up in the spring if they have sufficient stock, but the plants will need to be watered during hot weather because they will not have had time to develop a good root system.

Buying tree peonies

The cheapest tree peonies are sold with a large plastic label, illustrated with a colour photograph of a tree peony flower. While these may appear very inviting you are unlikely to obtain a named cultivar and the plant could be a disappointment. Tree peonies are also found in chain stores, packed in attractive looking cardboard boxes. I would strongly advise you to avoid these plants because they often sprout prematurely in the boxes and are rarely true to the photograph shown on the outside of the box. It is much better to buy a plant that is in flower and most specialist nurseries allow their plants to produce flowers before they offer them for sale. These plants may be more expensive than those purchased from a chain store, but they are likely to be of better quality and if they turn out to be different from the name on the label the nursery will usually exchange the plant without question.

Buying species peonies

The most common way of building up a collection of species peonies is to raise them from seed. While this may be the cheapest method, the species grow comparatively slowly and it may be at least four or five years before they are mature enough to flower. Peony seed is available from two sources, from a nursery or as wild-collected seed. Nursery-raised seed is the cheapest source, but because the great majority of species will hybridize given the opportunity, most of the peonies from this source are likely be of hybrid character. Hybrid seedlings will usually take on the appearance of one of the parents and most gardeners will be more than happy with the results. Some species, such as *Paeonia cambessedesii* and *P. mascula* subsp. *russoi*, flower early in the year and in the absence of a suitable suitor the seed is normally genetically pure. Some peony species are almost impossible to obtain, but you may be able to negotiate a swap with someone who has the plant you desire. While some gardeners may be very protective about their plants it is always a good idea to exchange your rarest specimens with a friend, then if your plant dies you can ask for a piece of it back.

The best plants are those grown from wild-collected seed and the seedlings are usually identical to the parent. However you should be aware that the regular collection of seed from wild populations of peonies could ultimately limit the ability of a plant to propagate itself and may eventually lead to its local extinction. In reality very little of the seeds produced by wild peonies actually gives rise to a new plant, but seed collectors have a moral responsibility to ensure that they always leave a few to ensure the long-term survival of the population. Another issue that needs be borne in mind is that some species, such as *Paeonia clusii*, are extremely difficult to grow in the long term unless you have an alpine house. The chance of the species surviving for more than a year or two in a normal garden may be so slim that you should question whether you should attempt to grow them in the first place. Most are grown from wild-collected seed and there is little point in buying the plants if they succumb to the first hard frost.

Importing peonies

Few American buyers will ever need to import plants, because most cultivated varieties of peony are already readily available in the United States. However, readers who live in other parts of the world may find that the less common cultivars are unavailable in their own country and the only way to obtain them is to import them from abroad. American nurseries have the widest range of plants, but a large number of cultivars are also becoming available from New Zealand. American nurseries will usually ship their plants from the beginning of September to the beginning of October, while those in New Zealand export peonies in April. The range of plants available from European nurseries continues to grow and they can be exported to other parts of Europe without phytosanitary inspection.

The importation of plants may appear a daunting undertaking, but the nursery does the important paperwork. By far the most important piece of paper is the phytosanitary certificate, which must accompany exported plant material. Plants cannot be imported into another country without this essential certificate, which confirms the plants are free from any prohibited disease. If the peonies arrive without a certificate they are likely to be destroyed by the national Department of Agriculture. The situation within the European Union is slightly different because plants can be transferred between member countries as long as they have a plant passport, which performs a similar function to the phytosanitary certificate but the inspection regime is less rigorous.

Plants are usually sent by airmail, because they can deteriorate if they are in transit for more than seven to ten days. If your plants have not arrived after this period it is a good idea to inform the supplier. The most likely reason for a hold up is that the plants have been placed in quarantine by customs and in this case it is worth finding out to which airport the plants have been delivered. Telephone the airport as soon as possible because the plants will deteriorate if they are left in a hot warehouse for any length of time. If the plants fail to arrive contact the nursery again, so that they can claim on their insurance. The nursery will either send you another consignment or, if they are out of stock, offer to supply the missing plants the following year.

When the plants arrive at your home remove them from their packaging as soon as possible and check them against the consignment note. If anything is missing advise the supplier at the earliest opportunity. The plants will have been carefully washed to remove any soil, which could harbour dangerous diseases, and the feeding roots stripped off because they might be infected by eelworm. The feeding roots will quickly grow back when the peonies have been planted out. If the plants arrive early and you are unable to plant them immediately in their permanent home, heel them in in a temporary site.

Cultivation of Species Peonies

The demand for species peonies has grown considerably during the past few years and a few specialist nurseries can now supply them as young plants. Divisions are occasionally available and this method is the most reliable, but also the most expensive way of obtaining a species peony. Take care when purchasing young species peonies from nurseries in the spring. Many are grown in polytunnels during the winter and may not have been hardened off prior to sale. Considerable care should be taken before the young peonies are planted outside because they can be easily damaged by frost. The foliage can also be damaged by strong winds and although the plant will probably reappear the following spring, the damage can weaken it. If in doubt, leave new acquisitions in a cold-frame until the risk of frost and high winds has passed.

Species peonies are less vigorous than their hybrid cousins and should be planted so that their buds are just below the level of the soil. If they are planted deeper they will adjust and new buds will be produced at ground level. If the peony has been purchased in a pot it should be planted at the same depth as it is in the pot.

The choice of planting location is very important if your peonies are to thrive. The majority of herbaceous peonies grow best in full sun, although a few species, such as *Paeonia japonica* and *P. obovata*, will grow happily under deciduous trees. Species peonies will grow best when they are planted in a sunny, well-drained position, in good-quality soil.

Most peonies look best when they are growing alongside plants that have blue flowers, such as hardy geraniums and irises. Plants with brightly coloured flowers, such as Oriental poppies, should be avoided.

Herbaceous peonies look best when they are planted by themselves or with other species that do not compete with, but rather complement the colour of their flowers. Oriental poppies should be avoided because they have rather brash, brightly coloured flowers that rather overwhelm the more subtle shades of hybrid peonies. Peonies with pink flowers look absolutely wonderful when planted with blue tall bearded irises, such as *Iris* 'Jane Phillips' and 'Sapphire Hills' (for further information about suitable irises see Austin, 2001). Other suitable companions includes blue-flowered hardy geraniums, such as *Geranium pratense* 'Mrs. Kendall Clark' and *G. sylvaticum* 'Mayflower'.

Planting and Cultivating Herbaceous Peonies

Cultivars of *Paeonia lactiflora*, most hybrid peonies and intersectional hybrids will grow in most countries with a temperate climate, including the United Kingdom, as long as the winter is cold enough to initiate flower buds. In New Zealand peonies can be grown on

South Island and the central and southern parts of North Island. Peonies cannot be grown in the vicinity of Auckland because the winter is too mild and the humidity too great. In the United States they will grow successfully in U.S.D.A. hardiness zones 2–7, but may not flower successfully in zone 8. They will not grow successfully south of Birmingham, Alabama, U.S.A. and in California the plants should be watered every few days during the summer months. The plants may also need to be provided with shade to protect them from the full strength of the sun. The coral hybrids, such as 'Coral Supreme' and 'Pink Hawaiian Coral', grow well in the American Midwest, but are less successful in the United Kingdom.

Cultivars of *Paeonia lactiflora* should be planted in the autumn. If they have been bought in a pot the plant should be removed and the compost carefully teased away from the roots. Dig a large hole measuring approximately 45 CM (18 IN.) deep and across, sufficient to accommodate the roots. Break up the soil thoroughly, using a garden fork, to allow the roots to penetrate the ground; this is particularly important if you have purchased a new house. It is a fact of life that most contractors will clear the topsoil from

'Coral Supreme' was raised by the American breeder Samuel Wissing.

a site when they are building a new housing development and when they have finished deposit 25 CM (10 IN.) or so of topsoil over the heavily compacted subsoil. This is almost impossible for plant roots to penetrate, so you need to break up the subsoil with a garden fork and remove any rubble before you plant your peonies.

Mix the compost from the pot with the soil and add a handful of organic fertilizer, such as blood, fish and bone. Bare-root peonies can be placed directly into the soil without any compost being added, but the soil should be fortified with additional organic fertilizer. If you prefer to use a controlled-release plant food (14:13:13) sprinkle a small handful on the surface of the soil in autumn and again in spring before the plants start to grow, approximately 60 G/SQ. M (2 OZ./SQ. YD.).

Place the peony in the hole with the crown approximately 5 CM (2 IN.) below the surface of the surrounding soil and gently spread out the roots. Be careful not to pull them too hard because they are very brittle and easily break. Clods of soil that have been removed from the excavation should be broken up before you backfill the hole, taking care to work the soil into any gaps around the roots. Firm the soil around the peony, taking care not to damage the young buds. The depth of planting is critical, because if a peony is planted with the crown too close to the surface it may not flower and the buds could be damaged when the ground is cultivated during autumn. However, peonies require a period of chilling during the winter to initiate the production of flower buds. In the warmer parts of the United States, such as Texas, peonies should be planted so that the crown is approximately 2.5 CM (1 IN.) below the surface of the soil. This shallow planting should ensure that the plants receive sufficient chilling to produce flowers during the summer.

Once planted, carefully mark the position of the peony with a permanent label. Most bare-root peonies will have a plastic identification tag attached to them; remove this and bury it among the roots. Thoroughly water the plant so that the soil settles and fills all of the gaps around the roots. If necessary add some more soil so that the ground is level, but ensure the peony is not planted too deeply. In very cold areas, where there is little snowfall during the winter (such as the American Midwest) the peonies should be covered with a thick layer of hay or straw mulch, which will protect the feeding roots during the winter. Remove this mulch in spring before the leaves start to grow.

It is very important to label peonies because they are so long lived. This tree peony at Highdown House in West Sussex, England, lost its name many years ago.

Labelling is important because peonies can live for a considerable period of time and this is why it is advisable to bury a second label below the surface of the soil so that the plant can be identified if the original one is lost; birds seem attracted to shiny labels and children think it is great fun to move labels around. Commercial peony growers often use a sharpened hardwood stake, which has been immersed in white paint and then written on with black gloss paint. These have the advantage of lasting for a considerable time, but are too large for most private gardens. Plastic labels are not really suitable because they become brittle after exposure to the sun. Aluminium labels are preferable as they can be written on in soft pencil and remain legible for several years. It is also advisable to draw a plan of your border to record the location of the peonies. If you decide against this, do at least keep a list of the peonies that you have bought, so that you can identity them later if you lose a label.

To get the best from your peonies it is important to feed them. Give each plant a balanced NPK fertilizer in the spring before the leaves appear, another application shortly before the plant blooms and finally a low-nitrogen fertilizer a couple of weeks after flowering. If you prefer to use an organic fertilizer use sterilized bone meal, but remember to mix it well with the soil and ensure that you wash your hands thoroughly afterwards. Fertilizer should be applied away from the crown and carefully mixed with the soil. In the first year after planting apply fertilizer at the rate of 60 G/SQ. M (2 OZ./SQ YD.)

When you have planted your peony it is worth remembering the following old adage: "In the first year it sleeps, in the second it creeps and in the third it leaps." During the first growing season very little seems to be happening, but there is action taking place underground and the plant is producing new feeding roots and creating buds for the following year. In the second growing season the peony produces a few new shoots and a better crop of flowers, but under ground the root system is spreading outwards. The third year is worth waiting for, because after all the subterranean activity the peony suddenly bursts into life, producing a substantial clump of new foliage, crowned by a splendid display of flowers. After this dramatic event the plant settles down to a more leisurely life style, gradually expanding and producing more and more flowers. After ten or more years the plant may show a slight decline in vitality, particularly if it has not been regularly fed. The plant can be left for another fifty or so years, or it can be divided and replanted. In either case your peony will remain a wise investment and will probably be inherited by several other families. Some peonies are so productive that gardeners wonder what they should do with the divisions. This is one of the reasons why *Paeonia officinalis* 'Rubra Plena' is such a common plant.

Peonies are such long-lived plants that they have had to adapt to cope with the changes in soil level that can occur during their lifetime. This can be a serious problem in some countries where torrential rain can cover a plant with soil or wash it away from the crown, exposing the roots to potential damage. If this happens the cultivars of *Paeonia lactiflora* have the ability to adapt to the changed circumstances. If the crown becomes exposed the upper part of the roots may die, but secondary buds usually develop below the new soil level.

Herbaceous peonies in containers

Herbaceous peonies are not suitable for growing in containers, but if you move house and are unable to replant your peonies immediately they grow remarkably well in large baskets, filled with organic soil-less compost (soil-based compost washes out too easily). The most suitable baskets are the rectangular black plastic crates that are used by the horticultural trade for shipping plants. These have perforated sides, which allow the roots to spread out and develop as they would in the open ground, rather than being confined in an impenetrable pot. The baskets measure approximately 60 × 38 × 20 CM (24 × 15 × 8 IN.) and are suitable for growing one mature peony. If the plants are kept in the baskets for any length of time the compost will need to be topped up as it decomposes or is washed out by the rain. As long as you feed them and keep them watered in dry weather, peonies will grow almost as well in these baskets as they would in open ground and should develop a normal root system.

If for some reason you cannot plant a peony immediately, it will grow extremely well in a plastic crate and produce a large root system.

If you cannot obtain these crates and are forced to use plastic pots, make sure that they are large enough—there must be plenty of room for the roots to spread out and also sufficient growing space—and fill them with soil-based (John Innes) compost. It has to be accepted that the plants will deteriorate over time and it is not advisable to keep peonies in pots for more than a year or two. It is also important to realize that potted plants can be badly damaged by frost, particularly if they are in pots that are less than 15 cm (6 in.) in diameter. Good drainage is absolutely essential when peonies are planted in pots, because the plant will die if the soil becomes waterlogged.

Potted peonies seem to be particularly vulnerable to attack by swift moth larvae (*Hepialus humuli* and *H. lupulinus*) and it is advisable to check the roots every year to see if they are present. The larvae can cause severe damage to the smaller feeding roots, which greatly impairs the vitality of the peony. In the case of less vigorous plants, such as species peonies, the larvae can kill the plant outright. In the normal garden situation swift moth larvae are rarely a problem.

Planting and Cultivating Tree Peonies

Tree peonies will grow successfully in most temperate countries, but seem to do particularly well in those that have a continental climate, such as China and the United States. They will tolerate similar levels of cold to the herbaceous peonies, but severe cold can damage the aerial shoots. In the United States they grow successfully in U.S.D.A. hardiness zones 3–8.

The correct way to plant tree peonies will depend upon whether or not they have been grafted. The Chinese have been growing tree peonies as ornamental plants for many hundreds of years and during this time they have discovered several different ways of propagating them.

While some tree peonies have a very strong central root, which cannot be divided, others have a more diffuse root system, which allows the individual stems to be separated. These plants are dug up in autumn and the stems literally fall apart, allowing them to be replanted as new specimens. Among the many misunderstandings about tree peonies is the belief that they cannot be propagated by layering, which the Chinese have been doing for centuries. This is a common method of propagating rhododendrons, but it can also be used to multiply tree peonies. Layering should be carried out when the tree peony has finished flowering, from the end of May to the beginning of June. At the junction between the current year's growth and the previous year's wood you cut a notch and place the branch on the ground and cover it with a layer of soil. Hold the branch down with stones so the notched area remains in contact with soil and water regularly to ensure good root development. When enough roots have developed to support the new plant, it is separated from the parent.

One of the biggest problems with potted tree peonies occurs when the nursery has used too small a pot. Tree peonies can only realistically be grown in a pot that has a capacity of at least 4 litres (1 gallon) and is deeper than it is wide. Occasionally tree peonies are offered for sale in smaller pots, but to get the tree peony into the pot nurseries often resort to cutting off the majority of the roots. The plants can be weakened by this drastic action and may die when they are planted out in your garden. If this happens you should take the remains of the plant back to the nursery and ask for your money to be refunded—it helps if you also return the original pot and its label.

If you purchase a tree peony in a pot during the spring you must wait until autumn before you plant it in your garden. This will enable you to spread the roots out properly and allow the plant to develop a reasonable root system during the winter months. Grafted tree peonies will often die if they planted in the spring because their root system will have been heavily pruned in order to fit it into a pot.

Root control bags are very useful for growing tree peonies if you intend to move house soon. They are made from a non-woven fabric and allow the plant's roots to develop naturally.

A few nurseries sell their tree peonies in root-control bags. These are made from non-woven plastic fabric and allow the tree peony to develop a good root system at the nursery. Root-control bags should also be used if you intend to grow a tree peony in a pot. The bags allow the roots to develop normally, but it is essential to use a frost-proof pot (see below).

The final fallacy, which can be laid to rest, is that the Chinese do not use grafting to propagate their peonies. David Furman, of Cricket Hill Garden, says that the Chinese do graft tree peonies, particularly when they want to raise plants quickly. However, while the Japanese leave the scion attached to the rootstock, the Chinese carefully remove the rootstock when the scion has developed its own roots. This is often carried out with such skill that there is little sign that this method of propagation was ever used.

American, European and Japanese growers usually propagate tree peonies by grafting them on to a *lactiflora* rootstock. The graft union can often be seen, but if it is indistinct the large, swollen rootstock will usually give the game away. Grafted tree peonies should be planted so that the graft union is approximately 15 CM (6 IN.) below the surface of the soil. Incorrect planting is the single most common mistake that gardeners make when they grow tree peonies and the reason why so many of these plants disappoint, producing a weak single stem with two or three flowers. If a tree peony is planted correctly the scion will produce its own roots and the rootstock should eventually rot away. However, if it is planted too shallowly the rootstock may produce suckers and eventually the scion will be rejected. Some peony experts say it is a mistake to leave the rootstock on a grafted tree peony, because the rotting rootstock can act as source of infection. They believe that tree peonies grow best on their own roots and that the rootstock should be removed as soon as the scion has developed its own root system. If the tree peony has produced its own roots they will be tapering and yellowish brown in colour, while the old *lactiflora* rootstock is blackish brown. You can remove the old rootstock with a sharp knife.

Tree peonies have a very extensive root system when they are grown from seed (**left**), but this is greatly reduced when they are grafted (**right**). The lactiflora rootstock can be removed when the scion has produced its own roots; tree peonies have pale yellowish brown roots, while those of the rootstock are blackish brown.

Grafted tree peonies are usually bought in flower from a nursery, but flowering in the first season places a strain on the young plant and it may not flower the following year. To give your plant a chance to establish, it is a good idea to remove any flowers before planting and possibly the following year, then by the third or fourth year it should bear several normal-sized blooms. After planting tree peonies should be watered regularly and, in subsequent years, top-dressed with fertilizer in the autumn.

Japanese tree peonies are often slower growing than their Chinese cousins, having been propagated by grafting. However, when plants have developed their own root system they can grow as quickly as Chinese tree peonies. Japanese tree peonies may need support when they are young, particularly if they have been forced in a polytunnel or glasshouse.

Few people prune tree peonies, but they are like any other shrub and benefit from having a framework of short stout shoots that can support the heavy blooms. Chinese and Japanese tree peonies are vulnerable during stormy weather and heavy rainfall can quickly damage the flowers. The Chinese often use decorated parasols to protect their tree peonies from strong sunlight and heavy rain. The umbrellas can extend the flowering time by as much as four to five days and keep the flowers in good condition.

Root control bags prevent tree peony roots from girdling the inside of a pot.

Tree peonies in pots

Tree peonies can be grown in pots for a few years, but after this time they are best planted out in open ground. To grow them well in pots you will need to use a rich soil-based compost, such as John Innes No. 3, in a pot that measures at least 30 CM (12 IN.) across, and keep the tree peony well watered during the growing season. Earthenware containers are most suitable because the plants are less likely to become waterlogged in them. However the plants will need watering regularly as the compost is likely to dry out more quickly than would be the case with a plastic container. Although they are completely hardy when they are grown in the ground, the roots of potted peonies can be damaged by a hard, penetrating frost. In cold regions the pots should be wrapped in layers of plastic bubble-wrap, hessian, or burlap, to protect them from the worst of the cold.

If you intend to move house in the near future, plant the tree peony in a root-control bag and then dig a large hole in your garden. The tree peony will grow happily until the time comes to move, whereupon the plant can be moved lock, stock and barrel to its new home. The root-control bag can then be cut off, exposing the well-developed root system.

Cultivating Intersectional Hybrids

The cultivation of intersectional hybrids is much the same as for herbaceous peonies. However, intersectional hybrids should be planted so that the first bud above the crown is at ground level, rather than 5 CM (2 IN.) below the surface. This is the view of Roger Anderson, but opinions differ. Don Hollingsworth, on the other hand, believes they do best when they are planted with the buds a couple of inches below the surface of the soil; while he believes this makes a stronger plant, he also points out that the plant will eventually establish its buds at the right level regardless of your intervention. Root systems can vary between cultivars; some should be planted so that the roots are upright, while others need to be laid almost flat to ensure that the buds are correctly orientated.

The best time to plant is in the autumn as young plants are very vigorous and will produce feeding roots in a few weeks. Intersectional hybrids are hardy but they should not be planted on ground that becomes waterlogged in the winter. Although young plants establish quickly, it is not until they are a couple of years old that you will see any of the typical, fully double flowers.

In the spring give them an application of balanced fertilizer (10:10:10), 60 G/SQ. M (2 OZ./ SQ. YD.), when the leaves appear, followed by a further application before they flower and similar quantity of a low-nitrogen fertilizer (6:24:24) when they have finished flowering. The fertilizer should be scattered on the ground at least 15 CM (6 IN.) from the crown and carefully raked in, taking care to avoid any exposed buds.

Plants do not flower very well if they receive high levels of nitrogen feed, and flowering appears to depend more on the level of light than the temperature. On dull days the flowers do not open completely until the sun shines. Intersectional hybrids do not produce typical flowers when they are young and seedlings should not be discarded until they are a few years old; Roger Anderson cites 'Unique' as an example, which produced pink flowers when it was young, but the flowers became red as the plant matured. The appearance of intersectional hybrids varies depending on where they are planted, and the colour of the flowers can be stronger or weaker depending upon the mineral content of the soil. This characteristic has been recognized in peonies before and is not unique to intersectional hybrids.

In autumn cut back plants to a well-developed bud, approximately 2.5 CM (1 IN.) above the surface of the soil; if the bud is damaged it will normally be replaced by a bud below the soil surface. The stems are more brittle than those of tree peonies; if you break one during the growing season it is advisable to cut it back to the bud below to prevent the shoot from becoming infected by pathogenic fungi.

Cut Flowers

At the beginning of the twentieth century peonies were among the most popular of all cut flowers. They were widely portrayed in contemporary paintings and a substantial wholesale industry for the production of cut peony flowers developed in the United States. American growers discovered that flowers could be kept in cold storage for several weeks and this extended the period during which they could be sold. However, the demand for cut peony flowers in the United States has fallen during the past fifty years.

In Europe demand for cut peony flowers declined after the First World War and by the latter part of the twentieth century the flowers were almost unavailable from florists. This situation has now been reversed and in London, England, cut peonies sell for high prices in fashionable florists and department stores.

New Zealand has recently emerged as a major exporter. This has been possible because the summer occurs six months later than in the Northern Hemisphere and so exporters are able to command high prices for cut peony flowers in Europe, Japan and the United States. Exotic-looking peonies, such as those with coral-coloured flowers or the double yellow intersectional hybrids, achieve the highest prices in the wholesale markets.

If you want to grow peonies for cutting it is best to cultivate them in a separate bed, rather then raiding the plants in the herbaceous border. Choose cultivars with strong stems because this will reduce the need for staking. Newly planted peonies should not be harvested until they are four years old. Most cultivars of *Paeonia lactiflora* produce side buds, which should be removed so the terminal bud can develop to its maximum size.

Flowers are ready for cutting when the sepals start to separate and it is just possible to see the colour of the petals. The flowers should be harvested during the early morning or late afternoon, when it is cool and there is no dew on the plants. The buds should be approximately 2.5–3.5 CM (1–1.5 IN) in diameter and have the texture of a marshmallow when they are gently squeezed. It is important to leave at least two thirds of the leaves on the plant after you have harvested the flowers. Cut the flowers with a sharp pair of secateurs and place them to one side; after twenty minutes place them in a tall vase of chilled water for one to two hours.

If there is one Chinese peony that most people know it is 'Sarah Bernhardt', a vigorous cultivar with large, double, pale pink flowers. However, while there is no doubt about its vigour and decorative value, 'Sarah Bernhardt' has weak stems, which are barely capable of supporting the heavy flowerheads. I never fail to be surprised by the popularity of this cultivar, because, while I cannot deny that it has attractive flowers, the stems are so weak they need to be supported with stakes. However, from a commercial point of view 'Sarah Bernhardt' is very cheap and has been propagated for almost a hundred years. Gast (1998) has found that five-year-old plants of 'Sarah Bernhardt' produced 20.2 cut stems per plant, compared with as few as 5.2 for 'Edulis Superba' and 1.8 for 'Monsieur Jules Elie'. These figures should be treated with caution however, because the peonies were only harvested from one location and the yield might be different at other sites.

There are several modern cultivars with double pink flowers which you could grow instead, including 'Chiffon Parfait' and 'Pillow Talk'. Both have strong stems well capable of supporting the flowers in a vase. I would also recommend the following peonies for cutting.

Flower	Name	Flower	Name
Double white	'Charlie's White'	Yellow	'Bartzella'
	'Duchesse de Nemours'		'Garden Treasure'
	'Festiva Maxima'		
	'Gardenia'	Hybrids	'Coral Charm'
			'Cytherea'
Double red	'Kansas'		
	'Paul M. Wild'		
	'Red Charm'		
Double pink	'Chiffon Parfait'		
	'Fairy's Petticoat'		
	'Glory Hallelujah'		
	'Monsieur Jules Elie'		
	'Pillow Talk'		
	'Raspberry Sundae'		
	'Vivid Rose'		

Cut peonies can be left out of water for several days and will still open satisfactorily when they are placed in a filled vase. However, the best results are achieved if the cut flowers are placed in a tall vase filled with chilled water for a couple of hours. They can then be stored for between two and three weeks in a normal domestic refrigerator and up to six or seven weeks in a commercial appliance where the temperature can be maintained at just above the freezing point of water: 0°C (32°F). The flowers will remain open for between five and seven days, depending on the cultivar, but a day less if the flowers have been stored for the maximum time possible.

It may come as a surprise, but there is a large market for dried peony flowers. The process is similar to that used commercially for drying herbs, with the cut flowers suspended from the ceiling of a special room and a constant flow of warm air provided to remove every last drop of moisture. Some companies use freeze-drying to achieve the same result and while the process is much more expensive, the flowers retain most of their original colour and shape.

Propagation
Peonies from seed
The cheapest way to produce new peonies is to grow them from seed, but this takes a long time. However, it is very rewarding to raise a plant from seed and who knows, you may produce a winner. This method is used to raise species peonies but it is not suitable for propagating named herbaceous cultivars, which must be divided (in the manner described below).

Peony seeds should be collected when they are ripe and sown as soon as possible after harvesting. (The seeds of most species are bluish black when ripe, while those of *Paeonia lactiflora* are brownish black; hybrid seed turns black when it is mature.) If the seed is immature it will rot, but if it is collected too late it may enter dormancy and you may have to wait for a further year before it germinates, although it is possible to break the dormancy by seed stratification in a domestic refrigerator.

To sow seeds fill a 13 CM (5 IN.) pot with a soil-based compost, such as John Innes Seed Compost or sterilized loam, and plant the seeds at a depth of approximately 2.5 CM (1 IN.). The plants grow quite slowly and it is therefore advisable to cover the soil with a layer of alpine grit, to prevent weeds from growing. The pot should be thoroughly watered and then placed in a cold-frame.

Fresh seeds will usually germinate in the following spring, when the first roots develop, but the first aerial growth may not occur for another year. If you have purchased wild-collected seeds they may be more than a year old, having passed through several hands before they reach you. This seed is usually fully dormant and may take a further year to germinate. The germination of older seeds can be quite erratic, with one or two germinating in the second autumn, the majority during the following season and the remainder in subsequent years. Seedlings are very vulnerable to attack by slugs during the first year and will not recover if the aerial shoot is damaged. The young peonies can be planted out in the open when they are a couple of years old, but the position should be marked to ensure that they are not damaged when you are weeding the garden.

The majority of peony breeders live in the United States of America and many are members of the American Peony Society. The society organizes a seed distribution service, details of which can be found in the society's bulletin, which is published four times a year.

Division

This is the technique to use to propagate herbaceous peony cultivars and should be done when plants are between three and five years old. The work is best undertaken on a dry, mild day in autumn when the soil can be easily removed from around the roots.

Use a large fork to loosen the soil around the plant, taking great care not to damage the roots that radiate out from the crown. Dig carefully underneath the peony with a spade so the whole rootball can be removed intact. If the plant is growing in sandy soil it is often possible to brush the soil away from the crown, but in most cases the earth must be washed off the roots with a hosepipe. Peony roots are very turgid when they are first removed from the ground and will snap off if they are handled carelessly. If time is available it is preferable to leave the roots in the sun for an hour or two, so they become less brittle. Then use a sharp knife to cut the crown into sections, making sure that each section has at least four or five buds, or eyes. Leave the cut sections to dry in the air for a few hours to form a protective callous. Damaged pieces or areas infected with crown rot should be removed with a sharp knife and the areas liberally sprinkled with green sulphur dust (see later in this chapter). The infected tissue should either be burnt or bagged and placed in the refuse bin. Very old lactifloras can form a large clump measuring up to a metre (3.3 ft.) across. The centre of the clump will consist of a substantial mass of large interwoven roots with a few buds, while the roots on the perimeter will be more active and producing feeding roots and aerial buds.

Older plants are more difficult to divide and the process can be a challenge. The roots are divided in the same way, but they yield less usable material. A very old plant is likely to disintegrate when you dig it up and you should choose the actively growing roots from the edge of the clump. These will probably have a piece of old root attached, which should be removed before the division is replanted. The divisions are likely to be smaller than those from a younger plant, but they will quickly bulk up and produce a healthy peony. It is sometimes impractical to dig up a peony, but it is possible to obtain a viable piece of the plant by removing the soil from the edge of the clump and removing a suitable piece of root with a sharp knife. Herbaceous hybrids are often very vigorous and produce extremely thick roots, which may have to be cut with a saw. If you are in any doubt about dividing such plants it is worth asking someone who has some previous experience.

Grafting

Grafting is by far the most common way of propagating tree peonies. Experienced grafters can achieve a very high level of success and with a bit of practice it should be possible to achieve a success rate of 50 percent or more. Grafting is best carried out towards the end of the summer, in August or September.

In commercial nurseries rootstocks are often raised from seed and harvested when they are four to five years old. These plants are thought to be more vigorous than divisions and have a higher resistance to disease. The soil is washed off the roots and they are then stored in a cool place while the scions are prepared. When the time comes the rootstocks are removed with a sharp knife, which has been previously sterilized to prevent infection with pathogenic fungi. They should measure 10–15 cm (4–6 in.) long.

The best scions are prepared from the terminal bud and should measure approximately 6–8 cm (2.5–3.1 in.) long. These will usually have a flower bud, which is important for commercial nurseries because the grafted peony will usually flower during its first year. The scions can be stored in a polythene bag to stop them from drying out, but it is advisable to use them on the same day that they were cut.

There are several types of graft, but the most frequently used is the wedge, or saddle, graft. The best tool for preparing the graft is a single-sided razor blade or a surgical scalpel, both of which can be obtained from suppliers of laboratory equipment. A sharp angled cut is made along one side at the severed end of the scion and another on the opposite side to create a triangular-shaped point, which will fit into the rootstock. A V-shaped cut is then made in the severed end of the rootstock. It is absolutely essential that the cut ends of the rootstock and scion match, because if they do not the scion will die and the graft will fail. The top of the rootstock, opposite to the graft, is cut away in a downward direction to allow rain to drain away, rather than settling in the graft union. The prepared scion and rootstock are slotted together and tied in place using grafting tape. If you can obtain it the graft can also be sealed with grafting wax; this keeps the graft in place and reduces the risk of infection by pathogenic fungi.

Grafted plants are best planted in a prepared nursery bed, where the ground has been well dug several weeks beforehand and a slow-release fertilizer, like blood, fish and bone, added to the soil. Insert the grafted plants upright, approximately 20 CM (8 IN.) apart and 5 CM (2 IN.) deep. Cover the grafts with a 5 CM (2 IN.) thick layer of bark chips and a sheet of polythene or black woven polypropylene (the material used to control weeds in commercial nurseries is ideal for this purpose). Remove the plastic sheet in spring.

An alternative method for home gardeners is to place the grafted plants in the large plastic baskets that are widely used in the horticultural trade, filled with equal amounts of compost and peat. (Peonies do not do well in many peat-free composts.) The baskets may need to be lined with woven polypropylene fabric to prevent the compost from falling through the holes in its sides. Keep the baskets in a shaded glasshouse or cold-frame until autumn, when the graft should have calloused over. You can then remove the young plants and pot them up individually in 13 CM (5 IN.) pots filled with soil-based compost, taking care to ensure that the graft union is at least 5 CM (2 IN.) below the surface of the compost. Spray them with a copper fungicide, such as Bordeaux mixture, to prevent infection by pathogenic fungi. Return the pots to the glasshouse or cold-frame for winter and lightly water the plants if the soil starts to dry out.

Cuttings

It has always been assumed that it is impossible to propagate tree peonies by growing them from cuttings. However, the late Collingwood Ingram (Ingram, 1963) claims that he achieved 98–99 percent success by growing tree peony cuttings in a "Moraine" pot. This consisted of a double-walled terracotta pot, part filled with charcoal and broken crocks, while the gap between the two walls was filled with water.

> Since I have succeeded during the past twenty years in annually rooting 98 or 99 per cent of all the Tree Paeony [sic] cuttings I have inserted, I think it may be fairly claimed that I have personally experienced no difficulty in their propagation. I described, and illustrated, my method of striking them in the Gardener's Chronicle for Oct. 26, 1946. Nowadays I employ for the purpose a specially constructed "Moraine" pot, which I plunge in a heap of half decayed leaves... The chief advantage of this pot is that it combines uniform moisture with perfect drainage. That these conditions are very desirable cannot be denied, but I attribute the main secret of my success to the time at which the cuttings are taken. I consider it of the utmost importance to insert them not later than mid-summer—preferably immediately after blooming, i.e. towards the end of May or the beginning of June. This gives the cuttings a chance of forming an adequate root system to enable them to over-winter. The cuttings are made from the current year's growth so cut as to leave a butt or disk of the old wood at the base of the cutting. The rooting medium is composed of two parts pure leaf soil and one part of coarse silver sand. Fibrous peat moss, provided it

is not too fine nor, on the contrary, too coarse, may be used in the place of leaf soil. Among the varieties I have rooted and established successfully are 'Souvenir de Maxime Cornu', 'L'Esperance', 'Alice Harding' and ROCK'S Paeonia suffruticosa.

The cuttings were then covered with a large glass dome, which maintained a high level of humidity while the cuttings rooted. I cannot vouch for this method of propagation, but it is highly unlikely that someone as well respected as Collingwood Ingram would have written this story unless it was true.

Propagating intersectional hybrids

Although they are usually propagated by division, the crowns of some intersectional hybrids are so thick that it takes a reciprocating saw to cut through them. The plants are extremely vigorous and if you intend to divide them, do it before they are more than three years old. An alternate method is to plant the intersectional hybrid with its main shoot on one side and rather deeper than usual. If you do this the plant will produce several independent shoots, which can eventually be separated from the old stem.

It is misleading to believe that all tree peonies can be used to create intersectional hybrids. To date all of the pollen parents have been *lutea* hybrids, such as 'Golden Era', 'Alice Harding', 'Thunderbolt' and 'Roman Gold'. While Toichi Itoh had used the herbaceous peony 'Kakoden' as the pollen parent, this was not readily available in the U.S.A. and breeders have used other lactifloras as successful seed parents, including *P. lactiflora* 'Martha W.' (Roger Anderson's favourite), 'Miss America', 'Gay Paree' and 'Carr East #2' (popular with Don Hollingsworth). It is usually possible to make the cross in either direction, but it is more difficult to use pollen from an herbaceous on a tree peony, than the other way around because the herbaceous peonies usually flower after the tree peonies. Earlier I mentioned that Itoh had reportedly succeeded in crossing the Japanese tree peony 'Kagura-jishi' with *P. lactiflora* 'Kakoden' and had produced two viable seedlings. This is interesting because, to date, no one has succeeded in repeating the cross. It may be that 'Kagura-jishi' has a genetic abnormality, which breeders could use to produce a series of herbaceous intersectional hybrids with deep pink flowers.

Micropropagation

Peonies would seem to be ideal candidates for micropropagation because they are slow to raise by conventional means, and consequently expensive to purchase. Over the years several organizations have tried to micropropagate peonies, but it is only now that they seem to be achieving some success. Early attempts demonstrated that the young plants would grow well while they were in a test-tube (*in vitro*), but they quickly succumbed to fungal pathogens when planted in a normal growing medium. In the late 1980s Harris and Mantell (1991) carried out experiments on the tree peony *Paeonia ×suffruticosa* 'Papaveracea'. They discovered that while it was easy to produce micropropagules, mortality was very high when they were planted out, with none of the plants surviving after three and four weeks in culture, and only 27 percent after five weeks. Nevertheless they did succeed in propagating the peony and the young plants flowered after two to three years.

Hansen *et al.* (1995) had reasonable success when they micropropagated the fern-leaf peony (*Paeonia tenuifolia*), but they realized that they had a problem when the stems became damaged. The damaged plant exuded toxic chemicals into the culture medium, which caused browning and may have injured the plant when the chemicals were reabsorbed by the roots. The team succeeded in getting 55 percent of the cuttings to root, but they did not indicate how the plants performed when they were planted outdoors. More recently Habib and Donnelly (2001) have claimed that they have achieved 80 percent success when they transferred young plants to a peat-based potting compost, but this still occurred under controlled laboratory conditions. They also indicated that they have succeeded in growing some of the plants outdoors.

At the time of writing a Canadian company, called Planteck Biotechnologies Inc., appears to have achieved a high success rate with peony micropropagation. The company is concentrating on propagating high-value plants such as tree peonies and intersectional hybrids. If Planteck is as successful as it claims the price of peonies should fall considerably and new cultivars will become available far quicker than was previously the case. The high price of peonies does restrict their popularity, but as micropropagation becomes more widespread we can expect to see prices fall. Planteck have succeeded in micropropagating intersectional hybrids, but they have had less success with *Paeonia tenuifolia* and *P. rockii*. While micropropagation will clearly be an important tool in the mass production of peonies, readers should be aware that the new plants will be very small and they may take several years before they are the same size as one grown from a root division. There are also concerns about the longevity of micropropagated plants and they may not live as long as those that have been propagated by conventional means.

The advent of micropropagation means that in future peony breeders will have to ensure that they have patented their new plants before they are released, or they will lose any right to make money from their time-consuming passion. It takes many years to produce a new peony cultivar and it is only right that the breeder should receive some financial return for all their hard work.

Roger Anderson, one of the world's leading breeders of intersectional hybrids, believes that the genetic instability of these plants will prevent their successful micropropagation. On several occasions he has divided a promising new intersectional hybrid seedling only to find that the divided plants bear little resemblance to the original. Sometimes the divisions are better than the original undivided plant, but in other cases they are worse and are not suitable for sale. If this dramatic transformation can occur with simple physical division, what will happen to a plant when it subjected to the trauma of micropropagation?

Pests, Diseases and Other Problems

Peonies are pretty tough plants and are prone to fewer pests and diseases than most other herbaceous and woody plants. Aphids show no interest in peonies and the majority of insects do not eat the foliage because it contains toxic chemicals. Most diseases occur because of poor growing conditions or after long periods of excessive rainfall.

Most insect pests avoid peonies because of the toxic chemicals in their roots, but swift moth larvae can cause serious damage.

Pests

Swift moth larvae

The toxic chemicals in peonies deter the majority of insect pests, but swift moth larvae (*Hepialus humuli* or *H. lupulinus*) can cause serious damage to their roots. The female moths are attracted to overgrown weedy areas and release their eggs while they are in flight. These eggs hatch after a couple of weeks and the larvae then burrow into the soil where they eat the feeding and storage roots. The caterpillars can be controlled if the soil is regularly cultivated and weeds are removed when they appear.

Peonies growing in pots are particularly vulnerable to swift moth attack, so it is important to ensure that the surface of the compost remains free of weeds. Plants are less likely to be troubled if they are planted in a soil-based compost, such as John Innes No. 2 or 3, rather than one with a high organic content. The pest may only be a problem in Europe.

Nematodes

Both herbaceous and tree peonies can be affected by nematodes. The damage is most obvious when the peony is dug up, but above-ground symptoms include stunted growth and the leaves dropping off shortly after flowering. The nematodes damage the feeding roots and form pale yellow globular structures, measuring 2–4 MM (0.07–0.16 IN.) across. The nematodes are spread with soil, on new plants and garden tools. On commercial nurseries they are controlled by using powerful chemicals unavailable to the amateur. New plants should be isolated for a few weeks after purchase and inspected carefully before they are planted.

Ants

Peonies are very attractive to ants because the young flowers produce profuse quantities of nectar in the spring. They rarely cause a serious problem, but in sandy soil they can undermine the roots and deprive the plant of water. They have also been implicated in the transmission of disease and may transmit fungal spores from one plant to another.

Other pests

In the United States there are several insects that eat the leaves of peonies. These are black vine weevil (*Otiorhynchus sulcatus*), Japanese beetle (*Popillia japonica*) and the rose chafer (*Macrodactylus subspinosus*). Insects rarely eat peony leaves in Europe, although vine weevils will eat them if there is no other suitable food available. Vine weevils can be controlled by using the systemic insecticide based on imidacloprid. Effective biological control can also be achieved by using the pathogenic nematode *Heterorhabditis megidis*.

Diseases

Crown rot

This is one of the most difficult diseases to control because it is caused by soil-borne fungi (*Botrytis* and *Rhizoctonia* sp.) and bacteria (*Erwinia carotovora*). It usually occurs because the soil is too wet or mulch has been placed too close to the crown.

The damage takes place below the surface of the soil and by the time that the aerial stems have collapsed it is usually too late to do anything about it. If the disease hasn't progressed too far it may be possible to rescue part of the plant. Remove all the soil from around the infected roots and cut away any rotting tissue. Dust the roots liberally with green sulphur and replant the peony in a new position, where the soil is well drained. It is advisable not to plant another peony in the original location.

Peony blight

Peony blight is caused by *Botrytis paeoniae* and is one of the few diseases that can seriously damage peonies. Infected tissues darken in colour and then turn dark brown, eventually wilting and finally collapsing.

Infection is most likely to occur during wet springs and for this reason peonies should be planted in the open, or in situations where the air can circulate. Plants are best watered at the base during the early morning and care should be taken to avoid wetting the leaves. Many gardeners succeed in controlling the disease by removing and burning or burying the infected tissue when it appears. This prevents the disease from spreading to other parts of the plant. However, in very wet springs your peonies should be given a preventative spray as soon as infection is detected. Countries such as the United Kingdom and those parts of the United States with an Atlantic climate are more humid in the spring and plants are therefore more vulnerable to peony blight.

The disease should not be underestimated; in England an entire collection of tree peonies was wiped out by peony blight in the 1960s. If you have a large collection inspect each plant every few days to check it is free of the disease. The easiest way to control

Peony blight (*Botrytis paeoniae*) can cause serious damage to peonies during wet weather.

Infected tissues turn dark brown and a few days later brown conidia appear on the surface. These produce masses of spores, which can infect the other plants in your collection.

botrytis is to remove all of the dead peony leaves in the autumn and burn them. This will greatly reduce the number of spores in the soil and reduce the likelihood of infection during the following spring. Peonies should be treated with extra care in the spring because botrytis infection is more likely to occur when the shoots have been damaged in some way.

Peony blight can be controlled very successfully with a systemic fungicide, but it also responds well to treatment with Bordeaux mixture—a traditional copper-based product. which is particularly effective on tree peonies. In the United States systemic fungicides are available based on the active ingredient thiophanate-methyl or chlorothalonil. Either one should be applied when the young leaves appear in the spring, a couple of applications at seven to fourteen-day intervals and then repeated every few weeks. At the time of writing there was no systemic fungicide approved for use in the United Kingdom.

Verticillium wilt

This pernicious disease is caused by the soil-borne fungus *Verticillium albo-atrum*. Shoots wilt and if a section is taken it is possible to see that the water-conducting tissue of the plant has turned brown. Fungicides are rarely effective and it is best to destroy the peony and avoid planting another in the same location. In the United States thiophanate-methyl is claimed to control *Verticillium* wilt.

Phytophthora cactorum

This fungus can be a major problem in gardens where the drainage is impeded and causes the stems to rot at the base. The infected parts of the plant turn brown and the stem then collapses. The shoot can appear healthy at the apex, but closer inspection will reveal rotting at the base.

The disease can be controlled by removing the soil at the bottom of the stem and cutting away all of the diseased tissue. The cut surface should be left to dry out and then dusted liberally with powdered sulphur. Try to avoid watering unless it is absolutely necessary and only replace the soil when the disease appears to be under control.

Peonies should never be planted in areas that are prone to flooding or where the water table is very high because the fungus is usually transmitted by water. The disease can be avoided by planting peonies where the soil is well-drained and by avoiding excessive watering in the spring and summer.

Spraying is usually ineffective, but in the United States it may be worth using a spray containing fosetyl-Al, which the manufacturer claims will control *Phytophthora* root rot. The fungicide should be sprayed on the foliage at fourteen-day intervals.

Peony replant syndrome

This physiological disorder appears to be similar to rose replant syndrome and like the latter the cause is unknown. It is a serious problem for commercial peony growers, who have to plant their divisions in new soil and cannot reuse the original land for several years. It does not appear to affect garden plants to the same degree, but so little is known about its effects that it should be considered if your peonies are unhealthy. In Holland, French marigolds are used to reduce the effect of rose replant syndrome and they have been used at the Royal Horticultural Society's Garden at Wisley, in England. Some researchers have suggested that replant syndrome is the result of a build up of nematodes, while others have proposed that it could be due to a high level of antagonistic fungi specific to the species that has been growing in the soil.

Viruses

Peonies are prone to several viruses, including mosaic, leaf curl and ring-spot. Plants can grow normally, but they are likely to show reduced vigour. The disease cannot be cured and infected plants should be burnt. Viruses are usually transmitted on contaminated secateurs or scissors: transmission can be prevented by dipping tools in a 10 percent solution of bleach or in concentrated alcohol before you use them.

Other damage
Pêche

Herbaceous peonies are relatively invulnerable to chemical sprays when they are dormant and weeds can be controlled in the winter by spraying them with a contact weedkiller containing glyphosate. However when peonies start to grow, chemical sprays can cause pink, red and green mottling of the leaves. The damage will be restricted to the current season's growth and the plants will usually recover during the following year.

Frost damage

Tree peonies originate from the mountainous areas of western China, where, depending upon the species, they grow at altitudes of up to 3000 M (9800 FT.). They are very hardy when dormant, but the flower buds and young foliage can be damaged by late frost. The damage is minimal if the plants can thaw out slowly, but if they are in full sunshine the foliage may be badly damaged. The risk can be reduced by planting the tree peonies in situations where they are protected from the early morning sunshine, such as against a west-facing wall or between deciduous tree and shrubs. In Japan and China tree peonies are often protected from adverse weather by erecting umbrellas above the plants or creating a protective canopy of bamboo canes and cloth. An extremely hard frost of -30°C (-22°F) can damage tree peonies, but in most cases the plants will produce new shoots from below the ground in the spring.

While the majority of species peonies are fully hardy, those originating from the area of the Mediterranean, such as *Paeonia clusii* and *P. parnasicca*, will be killed by hard frosts unless they are provided with some protection. It does not appear to be the winter cold that does the damage as much as the wet soil, which is always a problem in a damp climate. These species are best grown in a cool glasshouse or a cold-frame. Excessive rainfall during the summer months can also be a problem because in their native habitat these species normally enter dormancy in the summer.

Late frosts can blacken the petals and stamens of peonies.

The flowers of hybrid peonies, which have *Paeonia wittmanniana* as one of their parents, can often be damaged by late frosts. The damage may not appear until the flowers open to reveal blackened stamens. Extreme cold can kill herbaceous peonies unless there is a protective layer of snow. Plants usually die from desiccation, rather than the cold, but the risk can be reduced if they are mulched in autumn with a thick layer of bracken or straw. It is extremely important to remove the mulch in spring, before the shoots emerge, as excessive mulching can increase the risk of peony blight.

Chapter 12
Peony Breeders

Precisely when herbaceous peonies were first hybridized and who performed the first cross is very difficult to determine exactly, but hybridization may have been achieved much earlier than was previously thought. It has even been suggested that the well-known peony 'Rubra Plena' is a hybrid between *Paeonia officinalis* and *P. peregrina*. If this is the case the cross cannot have occurred until the latter part of the sixteenth century, when *P. peregrina* was first introduced into Western Europe. *Paeonia officinalis* 'Rubra Plena' is by far the most widespread peony in cultivation, but it is very different to the wild form of the plant. It is considerably larger, with more rounded leaflets than the wild species and flowers as much as two weeks later. Whether the cross happened by chance or design is impossible to say. However the plant came into existence it certainly shows hybrid vigour and will tolerate all sorts of abuse.

The world would be a poorer place without plant breeders, for although there are many beautiful species of wild peony we must thank these dedicated people for bringing us a kaleidoscope of colour, in the form of intersectional hybrids and brightly coloured hybrids, such as 'America' and 'Coral Charm.' It would be impossible to include all of the people that have bred peonies over the past 150 years. I have therefore concentrated on those who have achieved the key developments in peony breeding during the past century.

Roger Anderson

Roger Anderson was born in Whitewater, Wisconsin in 1938. He grew up in a farming community and spent much of his time on his grandparents' farm, where his grandfather bred Holstein cattle. His grandmother grew a lot of Chinese peonies (*Paeonia lactiflora*) and Roger says that this is where he developed his love for genetics and peonies. Over the years Roger has bred pedigree chickens and dogs, as well as peonies.

He started to breed peonies in 1972, with the aim of producing a yellow herbaceous hybrid peony. He was strongly influenced by Roy Pehrson (1905–1982), who raised some of the earliest intersectional hybrids in the United States. Originally an engineer, Roger spent over ten years trying to find a suitable seed parent that was receptive to tree peony pollen. His first batch produced 150 seedlings, but over 75 percent of them died. The aptly named 'First Arrival' was the first, followed by 'Cora Louise', which had white flowers with lavender flares. His second batch of seedlings produced 'Bartzella'—one of the most famous peonies ever produced. It was six years before a plant flowered, but when it did it produced thirty double yellow blooms.

A trip to Roger Anderson's nursery in Wisconsin is a revelation, because it overturns many of your pre-conceptions about peonies. His nursery is dedicated to the production of intersectional hybrids and most of the other plants, such as tree peonies and herbaceous peonies, have been planted to provide pollen or to act as seed parents for his groundbreaking hybrids. The first thing that you notice is how extremely vigorous the peonies are, being half way between an herbaceous and a tree peony. There are lines of plants with deep yellow, fiery red and even orange flowers.

So far he has raised approximately four hundred intersectional hybrids, but only forty of them will be named. He says that his biggest problem is finding suitable names for them all. Some fascinating new plants are in the pipeline, including a double red, a coral red and an orange-flowered hybrid. The existing intersectional F1 hybrids have low fertility and another of Roger's aims is to produce a fertile F2 hybrid.

Roger sold the commercial part of his business, Callie's Beaux Jardins, to Tim Komder of Belle Plaine, Minnesota in 2004. He is now working on a new range of herbaceous peonies with flowers in pastel shades and also on daylilies, as well as continuing to raise more intersectional hybrids.

Nassos Daphnis

Nassos Daphnis was born near Sparta, Greece in 1914 and immigrated to the United States in 1931. He spent the first eight years of his life in the United States working in his uncle's flower shop, but developed an interest in painting and staged his first exhibition in the Contemporary Art Gallery in New York in 1938. In 1939 he sold a painting to William Gratwick, a well-known peony enthusiast, who lived in the town of Pavilion, New York State. For the next three years he visited Pavilion every spring to paint the tree peonies and after spending four years in the army he returned to America and decided to breed his own plants.

Daphnis was aware of the problems that other breeders had experienced when they had crossed Chinese tree peonies with *Paeonia lutea*. For example Victor Lemoine's 'Souvenir de Maxine Cornu' and 'Chromatella' had been commercially successful, but they had rather disappointing flowers, which hang down among the foliage. Aware of this shortcoming Daphnis selected Japanese cultivars of tree peony, which had lighter, less double flowers and crossed them with selected forms of *P. ×lemoinei* (*lutea* hybrids) with well-coloured flowers and strong stems.

The first successful cross was made in 1946, but after waiting ten years for the first seedling to flower, it died after producing attractive pink flowers. Undeterred, Daphnis continued to produce a series of outstanding F1 hybrids, including the well-known 'Tria', which has three flowers to each stem, the light pink 'Themis' and copper red 'Gauguin'. F1 hybrids are usually infertile, but in 1949 he became aware of a couple of F2 seedlings that William Gratwick was growing in his nursery. These plants had been raised by Arthur Saunders and had been given to Gratwick as a gift. In 1953 Daphnis used pollen from the F2 hybrids to backcross some of Saunders' original F1 tree peonies. The resulting offspring, which had good fertility and were more vigorous than their parents, included the coral pink 'Terpsichore' and burgundy red 'Boreas'.

In 1959 he decided he would try to make the difficult cross of pollinating pure Japanese tree peonies with pollen from the F2 hybrids. The chances of success were slim because the two were genetically very different. After pollinating eight hundred tree peonies he produced only one fertile seed, which grew into 'Zephyrus'. This hybrid has pink flowers overlaid with lavender and dramatic dark maroon flares.

Daphnis has received considerable acclaim for his peonies, because he has set himself such high standards. His tree peonies have symmetrical, beautifully coloured flowers, which are held well above the foliage and make excellent garden plants. That they are so highly regarded is partly due to the fact that he rejected so many plants he considered were inferior. While he has produced in the region of five hundred seedlings, only fifty or so have been registered. There are many who consider the Daphnis hybrids to be at the summit of peony breeding.

Don Hollingsworth

Don Hollingsworth was born in 1928 and is one of America's most highly respected peony breeders. He started breeding the plants when he was forty and it has subsequently become an all-consuming passion. He received his degree in production agriculture and animal breeding from the University of Missouri and worked for cattle-breeding establishments in New York and Texas. He then moved to Missouri, where he worked for the University of Missouri on its agricultural extension programs.

At first he bred irises and daylilies, but then became interested in peonies, which he first crossed in 1968. In order to develop his understanding of the plants he took postgraduate courses in taxonomy and plant ecology. Don is very scientific in his approach to peony breeding and works in a very methodical way and this has enabled him to produce outstanding plants such as 'Cherry Ruffles', a double peony with bright, cherry red flowers, and 'Delaware Chief', which has very large double red flowers. However, Don is best known for his beautiful intersectional hybrid 'Garden Treasure', the only intersectional hybrid so far to have been awarded a Gold Medal by the American Peony Society. Don's nursery in Maryville, Missouri, is fascinating because the majority of his peonies have been collected for their breeding potential, rather than as a commercial crop, and many are not otherwise available.

Toichi Itoh

Toichi Itoh, a Japanese nurseryman, is celebrated for his achievement in crossing an herbaceous Chinese peony with a tree peony for the first time. In 1948 he crossed *Paeonia lactiflora* 'Kakoden' with the *lutea* hybrid 'Alice Harding', but he may not have been aware of the significance of the cross because the seedlings did not flower until after he died in 1956. His son-in-law Shigao-Oshida continued Itoh's work and the plants flowered for the first time in 1963. His father-in-law's achievement could have remained unknown if it were not for the intervention of Louis Smirnow, an American nurseryman. Smirnow approached Itoh's widow and obtained her permission to patent the plants.

The discovery that tree peonies could be crossed with herbaceous stimulated a number of other peony breeders to attempt the cross for themselves. In the past twenty years many other intersectional hybrids have been introduced and they look set to transform the public's perception of peonies. Itoh's success in achieving the first intersectional cross (between the sections *Paeon* and *Moutan*) has been recognized by the American Peony Society who coined the term Itoh hybrid to describe this fascinating group.

Roy Klehm

Born in 1942, Roy is one of America's most influential peony breeders. His family has been growing peonies since the beginning of the twentieth century and his grandfather, Charles Klehm, was one of the founding fathers of the American Peony Society, when it was established in 1903. While many American breeders have concentrated on raising new hybrid peonies, the Klehm family has specialized in introducing improved forms of *Paeonia lactiflora* with strong stems, the lack of which was the main weakness of many of the earlier cultivars. Roy's father, Carl G. Klehm, introduced the superb 'Chiffon Parfait', 'Raspberry Sundae' and 'Cheddar Cheese'. The family's "Estate Peonies" are very robust with strong stems and were the first peonies to receive U.S. patents.

A graduate of the University of Illinois, Roy did much to stimulate interest in peonies when he updated Alice Harding's *Peonies in the Little Garden* and *The Book of the Peony* (Harding, 1993). His superb photographs persuaded many people, including myself, to grow hybrid herbaceous and tree peonies. Roy has introduced many other plants into commercial horticulture, including cultivars of *Hamamelis*, *Tilia*, *Syringa*, *Viburnum* and *Hemerocallis*.

Roy is actively involved in Beaver Creek Nursery in Poplar Grove, Illinois, and Klehm's Song Sparrow Perennial Farm in Avalon, Wisconsin, established in 1996. In recent years he has introduced a number of lactiflora cultivars with extremely narrow or triangular-shaped petals, including the raspberry-striped 'Circus Circus', 'Crazy Daisy', 'Raspberry Rumba' and 'Moon Fritters', which has twisted red and white petals. These are not to everyone's taste, but will certainly appeal to the collector. More conventional plants include the wonderful 'Reine Supreme', the elegant, single white 'Snow Swan' and renowned 'Pink Hawaiian Coral', which received an American Peony Society Gold Medal in 2000.

William Krekler

Bill Krekler (1900–2002) was probably the world's most prolific peony breeder. He registered 383 cultivars (Krekler, 2002) with the American Peony Society and for many years was a Director of the society. He studied landscape architecture at the University of Illinois and owned a conifer nursery at Somerville in Ohio. He had a large collection of peonies, which was sold to Charles Klehm and Son in 1977. The Klehm family has subsequently introduced many of his peonies into commercial horticulture.

Among Krekler's best-known cultivars are 'Cora Stubbs', 'Butch' and 'Lil' Sweetie'. Krekler adopted a rather unusual method for his peony breeding. Every spring he would collect the pollen and mix it together with his finger in a kettle, then dab some on the stigmas of the peonies. While this may not have been a very scientific approach he did succeed in producing some wonderful peonies. Among his interesting observations were that "registering does not signify a perfect peony but only that it is too good to be composted".

Victor and Emile Lemoine

The Lemoines were among France's most influential plant breeders and also introduced lilacs (*Syringa*) and *Philadelphus*. In the early twentieth century Victor (1823–1912) and his son Emile Lemoine (1862–1943) succeeded in crossing a Japanese tree peony with the Tibetan species *Paeonia lutea* and thus produced the first hybrid tree peonies with large yellow flowers.

The Lemoines' achievement was recognized in 1920 when Alfred Rehder coined the species *Paeonia ×lemoinei* to describe the hybrids between section *Moutan* and subsection *Delavayanae*. A large number of hybrid tree peonies have been raised since by other people, the great majority in the U.S.A. There is some dispute as to who produced the first hybrid tree peony. The honour is usually accorded to Victor and Emile Lemoine, but there is a possibility that Louis Henry introduced 'Souvenir de Maxime Cornu' in 1897, predating the Lemoines' achievement by twelve years. The Lemoines' cross was particularly important because it eventually enabled herbaceous tree peonies to be crossed with tree peonies, producing the intersectional hybrids; it is true to say that they achieved a quantum leap in peony breeding.

Victor is best known for raising *Paeonia lactiflora* 'Sarah Bernhardt' in 1906, commercially the most successful peony in existence. Between 1905 and 1909 father and son introduced the first intentional hybrids between two species of herbaceous peony, namely *Paeonia wittmanniana* and *P. lactiflora*; these were 'Le Printemps', 'Mai Fleuri', 'Avant Garde' and 'Messagère'.

David Reath

Dr. David Reath qualified and worked as a vet, but developed an interest in horticulture while he was at Michigan State University. He devoted much of his spare time to peony breeding, but also had an interest in daffodils, day lilies and martagon lilies. In 1977 he acquired the majority of Arthur Saunders' collection of hybrid peonies when Silvia Saunders retired. Silvia did much to ensure that the plants were correctly labelled and so preserved her father's plants for posterity.

David bred his own peonies, including the herbaceous hybrid 'Salmon Dream' (illustrated on the cover of my previous book, *The Gardener's Guide to Growing Peonies*) and the well-known hybrid tree peony 'Golden Era'. He developed the art of grafting, which allowed many of Arthur Saunders' tree peonies to be made more widely available and in 1989 received the Saunders Memorial Medal from the APS for his contribution to peony breeding. He died in 1995, but his son Scott Reath now operates the family nursery. Scott has continued to introduce his father's plants into the trade.

Arthur Saunders

Few people have influenced the development of a group of flowering plants as much as Professor Arthur Saunders. Born in 1869, Saunders made a unique contribution to the development of peonies as garden plants. He trained as a chemist and received his Doctorate from Johns Hopkins University. In 1900 he became Professor of Chemistry at Hamilton College in Clinton, New York, and continued in this profession until he retired in 1939. A passionate gardener, he worked with peonies until his death in 1953.

At the beginning of the twentieth century there was a very limited range of peonies available in the U.S.A. These included a few forms of *Paeonia officinalis*, such as the Memorial Day peony ('Rubra Plena') and a large number of cultivars of the Chinese peony, *P. lactiflora*. While many of the latter were sweetly scented the colour range was restricted to white, pink and shades of magenta-red. Saunders' first attempt at growing peonies took place in 1905 when he raised some tree peonies from seed. After this he turned his hand to raising new cultivars of *P. lactiflora*.

Saunders was keen to extend the flowering period of peonies and to introduce plants with bright new colours. As a result of his breeding work he discovered many interesting facts about the inter-relationships of the different species and after thirty-seven years of work created some of the world's most stunning garden plants. One of the main problems he faced was that peonies take a long time to reach flowering size when they have been grown from seed, in some cases six to seven years. Matters were further complicated by the fact that many of the interspecific hybrids he created were completely sterile for the first two or three years after they had bloomed, and even when they were mature they often set only one or two viable seeds.

He set about creating a collection of species peonies, which were obtained from various botanic gardens and nurseries. In 1916 he started hybridizing the peonies, keeping detailed records of all the crosses in a series of twenty-three notebooks. He attempted to cross all of the available species with one another and achieved varying results. Like many other people he tried to cross Japanese tree peonies (*Paeonia ×suffruticosa*) with their herbaceous cousins, but failed. However he had more success when he attempted to cross *P. delavayi* and *P. lutea* with *P. ×suffruticosa*. This was not the first time that this had been attempted, because the French breeder Victor Lemoine had produced several hybrid tree peonies with *P. lutea* a couple of decades earlier. However, while Lemoine's 'Souvenir de Maxine Cornu' and 'Chromatella' were commercially successful they suffer from having very heavy flowers, which hang down among the foliage. To prevent this from happening Saunders used Japanese tree peonies with single and semi-double flowers to produce hybrids with similar blooms. Not all of the seedlings were satisfactory but a large number were considered good enough to be offered for sale. These small shrubs have dramatic flowers in shades of deep red, yellow and lilac.

Saunders appears to have had a major problem in trying to obtain truly wild specimens that were genetically pure, rather than hybrids. All of the forms of *Paeonia officinalis* he used were of garden origin and many of the other species were not collected directly from the wild but were at least two generations removed. *Paeonia lactiflora* was by far the most important parent and in most cases it was used as the seed parent because it flowered after the other species. However, on at least one occasion he collected pollen from plants of *P. lactiflora* growing in the southern part of the U.S.A., where the peonies were flowering several weeks earlier than in Clinton, and used this to pollinate other species, which became the seed parent. The majority of the plants he raised had single or semi-double flowers, but Saunders recommended future breeders should try using 'James Kelway' and 'Lady Alexandra Duff', which had shown promise in producing double blooms.

As a result of his experiments he found that one peony in particular had considerable potential for breeding. *Paeonia lobata* is now considered to be a synonym of *P. peregrina*, but in the early twentieth century it was widely sold in the nursery trade under the earlier name. Stern (1946) says that it is "a charming plant of smaller growth than the type, with a cup-shaped flower of a more salmon-red colour". Possibly the most important form of "*lobata*" was 'Otto Froebel', which has brilliant vermilion-red flowers and is still widely available today. Saunders was surprised to find that *P. lobata* was extremely compatible with *P. lactiflora* and produced a large amount of fertile seed. This union produced the popular hybrids 'Cytherea', 'Lovely Rose' and 'Red Red Rose'.

Saunders found one of his plants, which had vermilion flowers, produced seedlings with pale salmon, coral pink and cherry pink flowers, while another, which had crimson flowers, only produced descendants with crimson blooms.

At one time there seems to have been far greater variation among wild populations of *Paeonia peregrina* than can be found now. Peter Barr, the famous London nurseryman, seems to have specialized in obtaining these wild peonies and offered a wide range in his 1899 catalogue. Many of the plants were collected from the vicinity of Smyrna, in western Turkey. The nursery closed down after the Second World War and the site is now covered with houses.

In 1918 Saunders started making crosses between the Chinese peony (*Paeonia lactiflora*) and the coarse-leaved peony (*P. macrophylla*). He had little success in growing *P. wittmanniana* in Clinton, but *P. macrophylla* seemed to grow well. The union between these species was highly successful and he ultimately raised a thousand plants. The majority of these plants are substantial and imposing, with large, rather rounded, deep green leaves, but occasionally Saunders said the seedlings were dwarf with flowers measuring little more than 2.5 CM (1 IN.) across. Most of these F1 hybrids were sterile, but a few produced seed and their descendants were fertile. By backcrossing one of these F2 hybrids with another *P. lactiflora* cultivar he produced 'Requiem'. The *P. lactiflora* × *P. macrophylla* hybrids are very large plants with dark green, nicely rounded leaves and have been used as breeding stock by several modern peony breeders, such as Chris Laning. Saunders also crossed an F2 *lactiflora* × *macrophylla* hybrid called 'Albi' with *P. peregrina* 'Otto Froebel' and in doing so produced the blush pink 'Mid May'.

Because of his scientific background it was second nature for Arthur Saunders to keep detailed records of his breeding work and, according to his last notebook, he raised a total of 17,224 different peonies (Wister, 1995). However, of the thousands of plants he raised, only 165 were considered good enough to be named and propagated for sale.

Saunders achieved a quantum leap in the development of peonies as garden flowers. Modern breeders still benefit from the large gene pool he created and many of his hybrids are used to produce new plants. By crossing all of the available species he succeeded in producing some unusual and extremely beautiful hybrids, which would not have been achieved by a less ambitious person. Perhaps the most beautiful of all his creations is 'Lavender', a stunning lavender-flowered hybrid, which was produced by crossing *P. coriacea* with *P. lactiflora*. Unfortunately 'Lavender' is highly infertile and rarely produces viable seed, however, as Saunders indicated, it has the potential to create a new line of exotic hybrids with lavender-coloured flowers.

For all his success in breeding peonies one species remained his Holy Grail. He had always admired the yellow-flowered *Paeonia mlokosewitschii* and dreamt of producing a series of herbaceous peonies with bright yellow flowers. Unfortunately, however hard he tried he could not get this species to cross with *P. lactiflora*. The latter occasionally set a few seed after pollination, but the seedlings had none of the characteristics of *P. mlokosewitschii* and were presumably the result of self-pollination. Saunders tried to pollinate other species, but only succeeded with *P. macrophylla* and *P. tenuifolia*. (See table, opposite.)

During his research Saunders found that *Paeonia lactiflora* could be crossed successfully with any of the tetraploid species of peony, but very few of the diploid species set fertile seed when they were similarly crossed. He also discovered that many of the F1 hybrids were intermediate between the parents. Saunders felt strongly that because some species were inter-fertile they must be closely related to one another. However, species that evolve close to one another and are not separated by a geographical barrier often develop chemical incompatibility, which prevents them from pollinating one another. This process ensures that the two species retain their separate identity. After spending so many years studying peonies Saunders was ideally placed to write a summary of the genus, which was published in the *Manual of the American Peony Society*. While the taxonomy in this document is now rather out of date, it lists many of the older cultivars and selected forms of species that are no longer in cultivation.

Because of the time scale required to breed peonies it is extremely important that steps should be taken to conserve the Saunders' hybrid peonies. Another factor is the

Sources of Saunders propagation material.

Arthur Saunders obtained his plants from a wide range of sources, many of which have since gone out of business. Number refers to the generations the plant was removed from a wild specimen.

Name	Source	Material	Number
P. anomala	Highland Park, Rochester, New York, U.S.A.	Root	?
P. beresowskii	Glasnevin Botanic Garden, Dublin, Ireland, and Leningrad Botanic Garden, Russia	Root Seed	1–2
P. broteroi	Barr & Sons, London, England	Root	2–5
P. coriacea	Central Experimental Farm, Ottawa, Canada	Root	?
P. delavayi	C. G. Van Tubergen, Haarlem, Holland	Plant	2–3
	Vilmorin et Cie, Paris, France	Plant	?
P. emodi	Glasnevin Botanic Garden, Dublin, Ireland	Root	2–6
	Hyde Park, London, England	Seed	
P. lactiflora cultivars	Various		∞
P. lutea	Lemoine, France	?	?
P. macrophylla	C. G. Van Tubergen, Haarlem, Holland	Root	3–5
P. mascula subsp. *mascula*	Vilmorin et Cie, Paris, France	Root	∞
P. mlokosewitschii	C. G. Van Tubergen, Haarlem, Holland	Root & seed	2–3
P. obovata	Sakata & Co., Yokohama, Japan	Seed	1–2
P. obovata var. *willmottiae*	J. C. Allgrave, Langley, England	Root	1
P. officinalis 'Rubra Plena'	Various	Root	∞
P. officinalis single red	Own	Seed	∞
P. peregrina 'Otto Froebel'	Barr & Sons, London, England	Root	∞
P. ×suffruticosa	Various		∞
P. tenuifolia	Private garden	Root	?
P. mascula subsp. *triternata*	Barr & Sons, London, England	Root	?
P. veitchii	Vilmorin et Cie, Paris, France	Root	1–2
P. wittmanniana	C. G. Van Tubergen, Haarlem, Holland	Root	3–4

Compiled from Kessenich (1979), Saunders, A. P. and Stebbins, G. L. (1937) and Wister, J.C. (1995).

availability of the plants that Saunders originally used in his work. Some of his best pure red hybrids, such as 'Legion of Honor', were made using *Paeonia officinalis* 'The Sultan', which is now almost unobtainable. As new, improved cultivars are introduced there is a tendency for the earlier plants to fall from favour. In some cases it may be impossible to repeat the experiments that Arthur Saunders undertook in the early twentieth century, because the original parents are no longer available.

Chapter 13
Question Time

People regularly ask a number of questions about the culture of peonies, and I have included some of the most common ones below, together with the answers.

Q: Why aren't my peonies flowering?

A: Cultivars of *Paeonia lactiflora* must be planted so that their crown is approximately 5 CM (2 IN.) below the surface of the soil (or half this figure in southern parts of the U.S.A.). If this does not work, trying adding fertilizer or mulching with well-rotted manure in the spring, taking care to avoid the area immediately around the crown of the plant. If your affected peonies are in a shady position, they should be moved to a sunnier situation in your garden.

Q: Is it true that peonies do not like to be moved?

A: This is by far the most common misconception about peonies. On the whole, mature plants can be moved to another location without causing too much disruption to their flowering process. This should be done in the autumn, so plants can produce new feeding roots, and to help the plants recover quickly they should be given some fertilizer in the spring.

However, when peonies are divided it may take up to three years for plants to recover fully from this rather traumatic process. Very small divisions may not flower during the first summer after planting, but larger divisions with four or five buds are likely to produce one or two flowers. Wherever possible try to purchase your peonies from a specialist nursery, which will sell better quality and larger divisions. If you buy your peonies on price alone, you have to accept that there is a pay off and your plants may take several years to become established.

Q: Why has my tree peony only produced one straggly stem?

A: Japanese tree peonies are usually propagated by grafting a section of stem onto a piece of root from an herbaceous peony. If it is planted correctly the tree peony will produce its own roots and several stems, however in some cases this does not happen and the tree peony continues to grow with a single leafless stem. To ensure several stems are produced it is very important to plant the peony so that the graft union is approximately 15 CM (6 IN.) below the surface of the soil. This will enable the scion (the tree peony part) to produce its own roots and should result in it generating new shoots. Occasionally a tree peony will still fail to produce any more stems, even though it has been planted correctly. If this happens you should cut the plant back to ground level in autumn. All being well it will produce several new shoots in the spring, which will grow to form a nice bushy shrub.

Q: Why is my Japanese tree peony producing shiny purplish red suckers at the base?

A: These suckers are produced by the old *lactiflora* rootstock, which the tree peony was grafted onto when it was propagated. The suckers will not cause any damage as long as they are removed when they appear. However, if you leave them in place and allow them to develop leaves, the rootstock may eventually reject the scion, which will then die. The best solution is to remove the old rootstock when the tree peony has produced its own roots. Dig up the peony in autumn and inspect the roots. The tree peony has yellowish brown roots, which can be seen emanating from the bottom of the stem, while the old *lactiflora* rootstock is dark brown and can be removed with a sharp knife as long as the tree peony has developed its own roots. A word of caution: if the scion has not produced its own roots the tree peony will die when separated from the rootstock.

Q: Why have the flowers of my tree peony turned dark brown and become covered by a "fur"?

A: Your peony has been infected by peony blight (*Botrytis paeoniae*). This is a common disease of peonies in spring during damp weather. If only a few plants are affected the disease can be usually be controlled by removing the infected material and either burning it or burying it in a deep hole in the garden. If the infection is more serious, all of your peonies should be sprayed with a systemic fungicide or Bordeaux mixture, a traditional copper fungicide. The disease overwinters on infected leaves so it is very important to clear up and dispose of the dead foliage in the autumn.

Q: One of my peonies is looking rather sick and when I dug it up I found that the feeding roots were covered with small yellow nodules. What is causing this?

A: Your peony sounds as though it is infected with nematodes, or eelworms. There is no chemical treatment available to amateur gardeners so you only have one option. Dig up the peony and destroy it by burning and then remove any infected soil and dispose of it safely in bags in the refuse bin. If you have been bitten by the peony bug and are building up a large collection of plants, it is very good idea to quarantine new acquisitions for at least a month before they are planted out in your garden.

Q: The stamens in my hybrid peony flowers have turned black. Why has this happened?

A: Experience has shown that the flowers of hybrid peonies with *Paeonia wittmanniana* or *P. macrophylla* in their ancestry, such as 'Requiem' or 'Archangel', can be damaged by late frosts. Realistically, there is little you can do to prevent this, other than protecting the developing buds with horticultural or spun fleece.

Appendix A

Synonyms

The taxonomy of the genus *Paeonia* has been the subject of heated debate for many years and several people have described new species, only to have them treated as synonyms a few years later. Synonyms are names other than those that are generally accepted. Synonyms often arise because a botanist working in one part of the world has described a plant as a new species, not realizing that someone else had already collected it. The error may only appear when botanists are able to inspect herbarium specimens from both parties, in which case the first valid name will take precedence.

Until recently it was quite common for a well-accepted species to have its name changed because a taxonomist had discovered that it had not been correctly described (which is described by botanists as "*nomen nudum*"). However in recent years the *International Code of Botanical Nomenclature* has ensured that well-known names are conserved and if a botanist wants to rename a species the matter may be referred to a panel of experts.

Occasionally a botanist will give the same plant two names, not realizing that they have already described it. Pallas originally called the Chinese peony *Paeonia lactiflora*, but a few years later found another specimen, which he named *P. albiflora*. The Chinese peony was well known in the nursery trade as *P. albiflora* and there was uproar when it was decided that it should be renamed *P. lactiflora*. Several nurserymen refused to accept the "new name" and continued to list the plant in their catalogues as *P. albiflora*.

Another major cause of synonymy occurs when botanists have a different understanding of the term species. Peonies are so variable that it can sometimes be difficult to decide when a subspecies should be raised to the status of an independent species and vice versa. Botanists are forever arguing about what constitutes a species, but what really matters is that there should be a morphological difference between the different plants. Some characters, such as the presence of tomentose carpels, may appear to be a very good diagnostic feature, but it is useless if plants with tomentose and glabrous carpels occur in the same population and the morphological difference is not linked to a genetic one. Recent advances in DNA analysis have gone a long way to revealing the inter-relationships between different species and in the next few years it should be possible to decide whether *Paeonia wittmanniana* should be divided into two species; namely *P. steveniana* and *P. tomentosa*.

In the meantime I hope that the following list should bring some sense to the plethora of peony names.

P. abchasica Mischenko ex Grossheim (1930) = *P. wittmanniana.*

P. albiflora Pallas (1788) = *P. lactiflora.*

P. arborea Donn (1804) = *P. ×suffruticosa.*

P. banatica Rochel (1828) = *P. officinalis* subsp. *banatica.*

P. beresowskii Komarov (1921) = *P. veitchii* var. *beresowskii.*

P. biebersteiniana Ruprecht (1869) = *P. tenuifolia.*

P. brownii var. *californica* (Nutt. ex Torrey & Gray) Lynch (1890) = *P. californica.*

P. byzantina Clusius (1601) = *P. peregrina.*

P. carthalinica Ketzchoveli (1959) = *P. tenuifolia.*

P. chinensis Hort. ex Vilmorin (1870) = *P. lactiflora.*

P. corallina Retzius (1783) = *P. mascula* subsp. *mascula.*

P. corallina var. *triternata* (Pallas) Boissier (1867) = *P. mascula* subsp. *triternata.*

P. corsica Sieber ex Trausch (1828) = *P. mascula* subsp. *russoi* var. *leiocarpa.*

P. corsica Halda and Waddick (2004) = *P. cambessedesii.*

P. cretica Tausch (1828) = *P. clusii.*

P. daurica Andrews (1807) = *P. mascula* subsp. *triternata.*

P. decora Anderson (1818) = *P. peregrina.*

P. delavayi var. *angustiloba* Rehder & Wilson (1913) = *P. potaninii.*

P. delavayi var. *lutea* (Franch.) Finet & Gagnepain (1904) = *P. lutea.*

P. edulis Salisbury (1805) = *P. lactiflora.*

P. emodi subsp. *sterniana* J. J. Halda (1997) = *P. sterniana.*

P. foemina Miller (1768) = *P. officinalis.*

P. forresti trollioides Saunders = *P. potaninii* var. *trollioides.*

P. fragrans (Sabine) Redouté (1827) = *P. lactiflora.*

P. fructicosa Dumont de Courset (1811) = *P. ×suffruticosa.*

P. fulgida Sabine ex Salm-Dyck (1834) = *P. officinalis.*

P. humilis Retzius (1783) = *P. officinalis* subsp. *humilis.*

P. hybrida Lynch = Probably a hybrid of *P. anomala* and *P. tenuifolia.*

P. mascula subsp. *icarica* Tzanoudakis (1977) = *P. mascula* subsp. *hellenica.*

P. intermedia C. Meyer ex Ledebour (1830) = *P. anomala* var. *intermedia.*

P. jishanensis Hong Tao & W. Z. Zhao (1992) = *P. spontanea.*

P. kurdistanica Zohary (1942) = *P. kavachensis.*

P. laciniata Siev. (1795) = *P. anomala.*

P. lagodechiana Kemularia-Nathadze (1961) = possibly a hybrid between
   P. mlokosewitschii and *P. caucasica.*

P. lithophila Kotov (1956) = *P. tenuifolia?*

P. lobata Sweet (1824) = *P. peregrina.*

P. lutea var. *ludlowii* F. C. Stern and G. Taylor = *P. ludlowii.*

P. lusitanica Miller (1768) (species *non satis notae*) = *P. broteroi.*

P. majko Ketzchoveli (1959) = *P. tenuifolia* × *P. caucasica*.

P. makaschvilii Kaheladze = *P.* ×*chamaeleon*.

P. mascula subsp. *arietina* = *P. arietina*.

P. microcarpa Salm-Dyck (1834) = *P. officinalis* subsp. *villosa*.

P. microcarpa Boissier & Reuter (1852) = *P. officinalis* subsp. *humilis*.

P. modesta Jord. (1903) = *P. officinalis*.

P. moutan Sims (1808) = *P.* ×*suffruticosa*.

P. multifida Salm-Dyck (1834) = *P. peregrina*.

P. officinalis subsp. *microcarpa* = *P. officinalis* subsp. *humilis*.

P. oreogeton Moore (1879) = *P. wittmanniana*.

P. orientalis = *P. arietina*.

P. oxypetala Handel-Mazzetti (1920) = *P. mairei*.

P. papaveracea Andrews (1807) = *P.* ×*suffruticosa* 'Papaveracea'.

P. paradoxa Sabine (1817) = *P. officinalis* subsp. *humilis*.

P. peregrina Bornm. non Miller = *P. arietina*.

P. peregrina var. *romanica* = *P. peregrina*.

P. pubens Sims (1821) = *P. mollis*.

P. reevesiana (Paxt.) Loud. (1850) = *P. lactiflora*.

P. ruprechtiana Kemularia-Nathadze (1961) = ?

P. romanica Brandza (1881) = *P. peregrina*.

P. russi Bivona (1816) = *P. mascula* subsp. *russoi*.

P. sinensis Hort. ex Steud. (1841) = *P. lactiflora*.

P. steveniana (1848) = *P. wittmanniana* var. *nudicarpa*.

P. subternata Salm-Dyck (1834) = *P. officinalis*.

P. suffruticosa subsp. *rockii* Haw & Lauener (1990) = *P. rockii*.

P. szechuanica Fang (1958) = *P. decomposita*.

P. tenuifolia subsp. *biebersteiniana* (Rupr.) Takhtadzjan (1966) = *P. tenuifolia*.

P. triternata Pallas (1795) = *P. mascula* subsp. *triternata*.

P. troitsky = *P.* ×*chamaeleon*.

P. trollioides Stapf ex Stern = *P. potaninii* var. *trollioides*.

P. tomentosa (Lomak.) Busch ex Grossh.(1930) = *P. wittmanniana*.

P. vernalis Mandl. (1921) = *P. obovata*.

P. whitleyi (1889) = *P. lactiflora* 'Whitleyi'.

P. willmottiae Stapf (1916) = *P. obovata* var. *willmottiae*.

P. woodwardii Stapf & Cox (1930) = *P. veitchii* var. *woodwardii*.

P. yui Fang 1958 = *P. lactiflora* var. *trichocarpa*.

P. yunnanensis Fang 1958 = *P.* ×*suffruticosa*.

Appendix B

Peonies awarded a Gold Medal
by The American Peony Society

1923	'Mrs A. M. Brand'	1985	'Burma Ruby'
1933	'A. B. Franklin'	1986	'Coral Charm'
1934	'Harry F. Little'	1987	'Norma Volz'
1941	'Nick Shaylor'	1988	'Paula Fay'
1943	'Elsa Sass'	1989	'High Noon' (Tree peony)
1946	'Golden Glow'	1990	'Sea Shell'
1948	'Mrs F. D. Roosevelt'	1991	'White Cap'
1949	'Doris Cooper'	1992	'America'
1956	'Red Charm'	1993	'Mother's Choice'
1956	'Miss America'	1994	'Pillow Talk'
1957	'Kansas'	1994	'Shintenchi' (Tree peony)
1959	'Moonstone'	1995	'Sparkling Star'
1971	'Miss America'	1996	'Garden Treasure'
1972	'Nick Shaylor'		(Intersectional Hybrid)
1973	'Age of Gold' (Tree peony)	1997	'Old Faithful'
1974	'Walter Mains'	1998	'Myra Macrae'
1975	'Bu Te'	1999	'Ludovica'
1980	'Cytherea'	2000	'Pink Hawaiian Coral'
1981	'Bowl of Cream'	2001	'Early Scout'
1982	'Westerner'	2002	'Etched Salmon'
1983	'Chinese Dragon' (Tree peony)	2003	'Coral Sunset'
1984	'Dolorodell'	2004	'Do Tell'

Appendix C

Peony Conservation

There is little doubt that peonies are among the most beautiful of all flowering plants—but this beauty threatens their very survival. Peonies often hybridize when they are grown together and as a consequence most plants that have originated from open-pollinated flowers in gardens will be hybrid in nature. These hybrids make perfectly good garden plants, but most collectors will want to grow peonies that have been grown from wild-collected seed. Peonies are particularly vulnerable to over collection because it takes several years for a young seedling to grow to flowering size. The collection of seed from wild peonies does not *per se* cause serious damage as long as the collector leaves sufficient for the colony to be self-sustaining. However, if all of the seeds are removed the long-term survival of the colony is threatened, particularly if the peonies are damaged by botrytis or destroyed by people. If you should come across a single peony plant on holiday it is acceptable to remove a few seeds, but you must leave the majority *in situ*. Under no circumstances should you dig up a wild peony; the plant is almost certainly protected by that country's conservation legislation.

Peonies are rarely cultivated for use as medicinal plants and large quantities are still collected from the wild. This is clearly unsustainable and will eventually lead to the extinction of these plants unless urgent action is taken to prevent their unlicensed collection. One possible solution to the problem of over collection is to persuade endemic people to cultivate peonies for use as medicinal plants. This has been achieved in Turkey with snowdrops and there is no reason why it should not also work with peonies. Cultivated material should command higher prices and if sufficient peonies could be produced there would be no market for wild plants.

The International Union for the Conservation of Nature (IUCN) last reviewed the conservation status of peonies in 1997 and it is likely that several of the species listed in the table are now endangered, rather than vulnerable. According to the report 36 percent of peony species are threatened in their native habitat.

Endangered Peony Species

The *1997 IUCN Red List of Threatened Plants* (Walter, K. S. and Gillett, H. J., 1998) lists the status of peony species as follows.

Species	Endangered in	IUCN status
P. cambessedesii	Balearic Islands	Rare
P. clusii	Greece (Crete)	Vulnerable
P. delavayi var. *lutea*	China (Sichuan, Xiang Zizhiqu and Yunnan)	Vulnerable
P. kavachensis	Russian Federation (Caucasus)	Rare
P. macrophylla	Georgia	Indeterminate
P. mascula subsp. *hellenica*	Greece (Peloponnisos, West Aegean, Cyclades)	Rare
P. mascula subsp. *russoi*	France (Corsica), Italy (Sardinia)	Vulnerable
P. mlokosewitschi	Russia (North Caucasus)	Indeterminate
P. parnassica	Greece	Vulnerable
P. steveniana	Russia (North Caucasus) and Georgia	Indeterminate
P. decomposita (*P. szechuanica*)	China (Sichuan)	Endangered
P. ×suffruticosa var. *spontanea*	China (Shaanxi, Shanxi)	Endangered
P. ×suffruticosa var. *papaveracea* [this is presumably *P. rockii*]	China (Gansu, Henan, Shaanxi)	Vulnerable

A number of species, namely *Paeonia cambessedesii*, *P. rhodia*, *P. officinalis* subsp. *banatica*, *P. parnassica* and *P. tenuifolia*, are protected in Europe under the Bern Convention (Convention on the Conservation of European Wildlife and Natural Habitats). This requires national governments to introduce legislation to protect their natural and semi-natural habitats and their associated flora and fauna.

At the time of writing there were no species of peony that were sufficiently endangered for them to receive protection under CITES (Convention on International Trade in Endangered Species of Wild Fauna and Flora).

Glossary

Acuminate Gradually tapering to a point.

Adpressed This term usually refers to hairs that lie flat against the surface of a leaf, carpel or another part of the plant.

Adventitious This term means something that appears from an unexpected place, such as roots developing on a stem.

Androecium The male part of the flower, the stamens.

Anemone The third stage of flower doubling. The stamens are all converted into narrow petaloids and no sign of the anthers remains. Easily mistaken for Japanese-form flowers.

Anther The part of the stamen that produces pollen, supported by a filament.

Biternate The leaves are divided twice.

Bomb-shaped A double flower, with erect petaloids, often surrounded by a collar of differently coloured guard petals.

Carpel A single unit of a compound ovary, in peonies this is called a follicle.

Carpelodes These petals are derived from carpels, they are often pale green at the base and marked with splashes of red or deep magenta.

Caudate Tapers abruptly and then gradually to a point.

Circinate Curled in a circle like the unfurling leaves of a fern.

Colchicine An alkaloid chemical extracted from the meadow saffron (*Colchicum autumnale*), it prevents the chromosomes from dividing during mitosis and induces polyploidy. It is very poisonous.

Corolla The petals of a flower.

Crown-shaped A flower where the inner petals form a large raised mound, surrounded by enlarged guard petals.

Cuneate Inversely triangular.

Decurrent Where the base of the leaf or another organ continues down the stem or petiole.

Dehiscing The process of opening in a seed capsule.

Disc The staminoidal disc is a conspicuous feature in many peonies. It is often brightly coloured and situated at the base of the stamens and carpels.

Double Generally in horticulture double flowers have a large number of petals, but in peonies the term is more specific. Semi-double peonies have stamens converted into petals, while in fully double peonies both the stamens and carpels are converted into petals.

Emarginate A term used to describe petals or leaves which have a shallow notched apex. *Paeonia peregrina* has distinctive emarginate leaf tips.

Endemic A plant that is restricted to a specific geographical location, such as *P. clusii*, which is only found on the islands of Crete and Karpathos.

Eyes Another name for buds.

Filament The thread-like part of a stamen that supports the anther.

Flares Dark blotches of colour at the base of the petals. They are dark purple and well defined in *P. rockii* and diffuse in *P. ostii*.

Flower within a flower In some peonies the floral structure is duplicated, so that a tuft of petals emerges from the centre of the carpels. Close inspection may reveal a further set of stamens and carpels within the petals.

Foliaceous Leaf like.

Follicle A dry fruit derived from a single carpel, which dehisces along a single opening and has one or more seeds.

Fully double A flower where both the stamens and carpels are converted into petaloid segments and indistinguishable from the normal petals.

Fusiform Spindle shaped, broader in the middle than at the extremities.

Glabrous Smooth and hairless.

Glaucous A thin waxy layer, which gives leaves and stems a slightly bluish colour.

Guard petals Large, well rounded and often brightly coloured petals that surround the flower.

Gynoecium The female part of the flower, the carpel, stigma and styles; also called the pistil. At the bottom of the gynoecium is the ovary, which encloses the ovules.

Hirsute Covered with coarse hairs.

Intersectional hybrid A hybrid between two botanical sections, for example between *Moutan* and *Paeon*.

Interspecific hybrid A hybrid between two species, for example between *P. officinalis* and *P. lactiflora*.

Involucre A whorl of bracts beneath the corolla. *P. delavayi* is the only species of peony to have an obvious involucre.

ITS Internal transcribed spacers in ribosomal DNA are widely used in phylogenetic analysis to determine the inter-relationships of different species.

Japanese The second stage of doubling in a peony flower. The stamens are converted into masses of petal-like staminodes and are surrounded by brightly coloured guard petals. Japanese-type flowers are usually fertile with intact carpels and are sometimes referred to as "Imperial Peonies".

Maquis A plant community of small evergreen trees and dwarf shrubs, characteristic of the Mediterranean region. In most cases it has developed after the removal of the natural forest cover.

matK The matK gene is widely used for determining plant inter-relationships below the level of the family. It is found in plant cell chloroplasts.

Mudan The Chinese name for tree peonies, often spelt "moutan" in older books. In Japan they are called "Botan".

Multi-carpelled More than the usual number of carpels; usually a multiple of 5, so a multi-carpelled flower could have 10 or 15 carpels.

NCCPG The British National Council for the Conservation of Plants and Gardens has been instrumental in establishing many national plant collections in the United Kingdom. There are several collections of herbaceous peonies, but at the present time no collection of tree peonies.

Nomen illegitimum The name does not adhere to the accepted rules of nomenclature.

Nomen nodum To be recognised as a valid scientific name an organism must have been described in Latin and published in a recognised journal. If there is no such description the name is *nomen nudum*, and consequently invalid.

Nucleotide substitution DNA and RNA are made up of long chains of nucleotides. The more closely related two species are, the smaller the number of nucleotide substitutions.

Ovule The female part of the flower, which gives rise to a seed when it has been fertilized. Unfertilized ovules are often bright, almost fluorescent pink in herbaceous peonies.

Patent Spreading.

Pentamerous The floral structure is in multiples of 5; i.e. there are 5 sepals, 5 petals and 5 carpels. Some hybrid peonies are multi-carpelled, so that there are 10 or 15 carpels.

Petaloid Petal-like structures that are either derived from stamens (staminodes) or carpels (carpelodes).

Petiole The stalk of a leaf.

Petiolule The stalk of a leaflet in a compound leaf.

Pilose Covered with a layer of soft slender hairs.

Pistil The reproductive parts of the flower, which is composed of an ovary, style and stigma. Compound flowers have several pistils. The term is often used in older books.

Polymorphic This term is used to describe the variation in a morphological feature from one plant to another. One population may have ovate leaves, while another may have lanceolate; however both belong to the same species.

Recurved Curved back on itself.

Rhizome An underground stem. In many species of herbaceous peony the young roots are rhizomatous in character, but become tuberous storage organs as they become older.

Rose-shaped See fully double.

Semi-double The fourth stage of petal doubling. Carpels are usually functional, but the stamens are often partially converted into petal-like structures with narrow filaments. In some herbaceous peonies, the staminodes alternate with rings of functional stamens.

Sensu lato In the broadest sense.

Sensu stricto In the strict sense.

Sericeous Covered with adpressed, silky hairs.

Sessile Stalkless or without a petiole.

Sheath A thin envelope that covers the carpels of a tree peony. Often brightly coloured, it usually splits as the carpels develop and is often rudimentary in intersectional hybrid peonies. The sheath is actually an extension of the staminoidal disc and some authors refer to it as "the disc".

Silvered A common term in nursery catalogues, which describes the way that peony petals become bleached in bright sunlight.

Single A flower that has a single set of 5–10 petals and a large number of stamens.

Stamens The male part of the flower. A stamen consists of an anther, which contains the pollen, and a filament, which supports it.

Staminodes These petal-like structures are derived from stamens and are often coloured at the base. This pigment is derived from the original colour of the stamen filaments. In semi-double peonies the staminodes may not be completely converted to petals and are partially functional.

Stigma The tip of the pistil which receives pollen (plural stigmata).

Style The elongated part of the pistil between the stigma and the ovule.

Subsessile Almost sessile, with a very short stalk.

Taxon A taxonomic unit of any rank, for example order, genus, species, variety (plural taxa).

Tomentose A layer of dense short hairs.

Tomentum A tomentose covering.

Triternate Divided three times.

Tuber A swollen root, which acts as a storage organ.

Type The typical form of the species.

Type specimen These dried herbarium specimens are used as a reference when a plant is first described. Holotypes are those designated by the person who first described a new species, while an isotype is a duplicate of the holotype.

Villous Covered with shaggy hairs.

Bibliography

Andrews, H. (1804). *Paeonia suffruticosa. Botanical Repository*, 6: t.373.

Anderson, G. (1818). An Account of seven double Herbaceous Paeonies, now cultivated in England. *Transactions of the Horticultural Society of London*. 2: 273–281.

Armitage, A. A., and J. M. Laushman. (2003). *Speciality Cut Flowers*. Second edition. Timber Press, Portland, Oregon. 437–446.

Austin, C. (2001). *Iris: the classic bearded varieties*. Quadrille Publishing Ltd.

BCPP (1998). *Executive summary of BCPP CAMP on Selected Medicinal Plants of Northern, Northeastern and Central India* (www.cbsg.org/reports).

Boyd, J. (1928). *Peonies: The Manual of the American Peony Society*. Harrisburg, Pennsylvania.

Cox, E. (1943). Robert Fortune. *Journal of the Royal Horticultural Society* 68: 161–171.

Culpeper, N. (1653). *Complet Herbal and English Physician Enlarged*. London.

Davis, P. H., and W. T. Stearn. (1984). *Peonies of Greece*. The Goulandris Natural History Museum, Kifissia, Greece.

Fang, Wen-Pei. (1958). Notes on Chinese Peonies. *Acta Phytotaxonomica Sinica* 7(4): 297–323.

Farrer, R. J. (1917). *On the Eaves of the World*. Arnold. 1: 110–113.

Fishbein, M., C. Hibsch-Jetter, D. E. Soltis and L. Hufford. (2001). Phylogeny of Saxifragales (Angiosperms, Eudicots): Analysis of a Rapid, Ancient Radiation. *Systematic Biology* 50(6): 817–847.

Gast, K. (1998). *Production and Postharvest Evaluations of Fresh-Cut Peonies*. Kansas State University Agricultural Experiment Station and Cooperative Extension Service.

Good, W. (1997). Nassos Daphnis: A life for art and peonies. *Bulletin of The American Peony Society* 302: 23–35.

Habib, A., and D. Donnelly. (2001). Micropropagation of Herbaceous Peony. *Bulletin of The American Peony Society* 319: 19–24.

Halda, J. J. (1997). Systematic Treatment of the Genus *Paeonia* L. with some Nomenclatoric Changes. *Acta Musei Richnoviensis* 4(2): 25–32.

Halda, J. J., and J. W. Waddick. (2004). *The Genus Paeonia*. Timber Press, Portland, Oregon.

Hansen, C., L. Stephens and H. Zhang. (1995). In vitro propagation of fern-leaf peony *Bulletin of the American Peony Society* 296: 7–10.

Harding, A. (1993). *The Peony*. Introduced and updated by R. G. Klehm. B. T. Batsford Ltd., London.

Harris, R. A., and S. H. Mantell. (1991). Effects of Stage II subculture durations on the multiplication rate and rooting capacity of micropropagated shoots of tree paeony (*Paeonia suffruticosa* Andr.). *Journal of Horticultural Society* 66(1): 95–102.

Hashida, R. (2002). Tree peony breeding in Japan. *Bulletin of the American Peony Society* 321: 32–34.

——. (1990). *A Book of Tree and Herbaceous Peonies in Modern Japan*. Tatebayashi City, Japan: Japan Botany Society.

Haw, S. G., and N. E. Lauener. (1990). A review of the intraspecific taxa of *Paeonia suffruticosa* Andrews. *Edinburgh Journal of Botany* 47(3): 273–281.

Haw, S. G. (2001). Tree Peonies: A review of their History and Taxonomy. *The New Plantsman* 8(3): 156–171.

Hilu, K. W., T. Borsch, K. Müller, D. E. Soltis, P. S. Soltis, V. Savolainen, M. W. Chase, M. P. Powell, L. A. Alice, R. Evans, H. Sauquet, C. Neinhuis, T. A. B. Slotta, J. G. Rohwer, C. S. Campbell and L. W. Chatrou. (2003). Angiosperm phylogeny based on matK sequence information. *American Journal of Botany* 90(12): 1758–1776.

Hobhouse, P. (1992). *Plants in Garden History*. Pavilion Books Ltd., London.

Hong, D. Y. (1997). *Paeonia* (Paeoniaceae) in Xizang (Tibet). *Novon* 7(2): 156–161.

——. (1997). Notes on *Paeonia decomposita* Hand.-Mazz. *Kew Bulletin* 52(4): 957–963.

——. (1998). Taxonomical history and revision of *Paeonia* sect. Moutan (Paeoniaceae). *Acta Phytotax. Sin.* 36(6): 542.

Hong, D. Y., P. Kaiyu and N. J. Turland. (2001). *Flora of China* 6: 127–133.

Hong, D. Y. and K. Y. Pan. (2004). A taxonomic revision of the *Paeonia anomala* complex (*Paeoniacae*). *Annals of the Missouri Botanical Garden* 91: 87–98.

Hong, T., J. X. Zhang, J. J. Li, W. Z. Zhao and M. R. Li. (1992). Study on the Chinese Wild Woody Peonies I. New Taxa of *Paeonia* L. Sect. Moutan D.C. *Bulletin of Botanical Research* (Harbin) 12(3): 223–234.

Hong T., and G. L. Osti. (1994). Study on the Chinese Wild Woody Peonies (II) New Taxa of *Paeonia* L. Sect. Moutan D.C. *Bulletin of Botanical Research* (Harbin) 14(3): 237–240.

Hsüeh, Fêng-Hsiang. (1610). *Mu-Tan Pa Shu (Eight Epistles on the Tree Peony)*.

Ingram, C. (1963). Propagation of Tree Peonies. *Journal of The Royal Horticultural Society* 88: 449–450.

International Code of Botanical Nomenclature (St Louis Code). (2000). Regnum Vegetabile 138. Koeltz Scientific Books, Königstein.

Jalas, J., and J. Suominem. (1991). *Atlas Florae Europaeae: Paeoniaceae to Capparaceae.* 9: 13–21.

Kaempfer, E. (1712). *Amoenitates exoticae.* 862.

Kai-Yu, D., and L. Ming-Yuan. (1991). Taxonomic studies on the so-called *Paeonia obovata* Maxim. From Northeast China. *Bulletin of Botanical Research* 4: 85–90.

Kelway, J. (1954). *Garden Paeonies.* Eyre & Spottiswoode, London.

Kemularia-Nathadze, L. M. (1961). Caucasian Representatives of the Genus *Paeonia* L. Translated by N. Kravchuk and V. Kuznetsov. *Transactions of the Tbilisi Botanical Institute* 21: 51p.

Komarov, V. L. (1937). *Flora URSS.* Ranales and Rhoeadales. Izdatel "stvo Akademii" Nauk SSSR. Moskva-Leningrad. 7: 21–29.

Krekler, B. (2002). Bill Krekler Selects. *Bulletin of the American Peony Society.* 322: 10–11.

Kumazawa, M. (1935). The Structure and Affinities of *Paeonia. The Botanical Magazine* (Tokyo) 49: 306.

Langhammer, J. (1997). "Oriental Gold" may be an ancient peony! *Bulletin of the American Peony Society* 304: 8–10.

——. (2004). Toichi Itoh's Four Original Intersectional Hybrid Peonies. *Bulletin of the American Peony Society* 329: 26–29.

Léveillé, A. A. H. (1915). *Paeonia mairei. Bulletin de l'Academie Internat. Géographe Botanique* (Le Mans). 25: 42.

Lianying, W. *et al.* (1998). *Chinese Tree Peony.* The Peony Association of China, China Forestry Publishing House.

Linnaeus, C. (1753). *Species Plantarum.* 1: 530.

Lupo, G. L. (1999). *The Book of Tree Peonies.* Umberto Allemandi & C., Turin.

Lynch, R. I. (1890). A new classification of the genus *Paeonia. Journal of the Royal Horticultural Society* 12: 428–445.

Mabberley, D. J. (1997). *The Plant Book.* Second edition. Cambridge University Press.

Magallón-Puebla, S., P. S. Herendeen and P. R. Crane. (1999). *Annals of the Missouri Botanical Garden* 86: 297–372.

Makino, T. (1898). Contributions to the study of the flora of Japan, VII. *The Botanical Magazine* (Tokyo) 12: 302.

Melville, R. (1983). The Affinity of *Paeonia* and a Second Genus of Paeoniaceae. *Kew Bulletin* 38: 87–105.

Miller, P. (1768). *The Gardener's Dictionary.* Eighth edition. 1.

Miyabe, K., and H. Takeda. (1910). *Gardener's Chronicle* (Series 3) 48: 366, fig. 153.

Musacchio, A., L. Pellegrino, L. Bernardo, N. G. Passalacqua and G. Cesca. (2000). On the taxonomy and distribution of *Paeonia mascula* s.l. in Italy based on rDNA ITS1 sequences. *Plant Biosystems* 134(1): 61–66.

Needham, J., L. Gwei-Djen and H. Hsing-Tsung. (1986). *Science and Civilisation in China*. Volume 6, Biology and Biological Technology, Part I: Botany. Cambridge University Press. 394–409.

Ouyang Xiu. (*c.* 1034). *Luoyang Mudan Ji*. Reprinted in: DU Weimo and Chen Xin (eds.) (1982). Ouyang Xiu Wen Xuan. Beijing, Renmin Wenxue Chunbanshe. 43–56.

Özhatay, N., M. Page and M. Sinnott. (2000). *Paeonia turcica. Curtis's Botanical Magazine* t.390: 92–97.

Page, M. (1997). *The Gardener's Guide to Growing Peonies*. David and Charles, Newton Abbot.

Page, M., and M. Sinnott. (2001). *Paeonia japonica. Curtis's Botanical Magazine* t.413: 79–84.

Pallas, P. (1776). *Reise durch verschiedene Provinzen des russischen Reiches* (Leningrad) 3: 286.

Pallas, P. (1788). *Flora Rossica*, 1(2): 92, t.84.

Pan, K. Y. (1993). Paeoniaceae. In W. T. Wang and S. G. Wu, eds. *Vascular Plants of the Hengduan Mountains*. Science Press, Beijing. 545–546.

Paul, G. (1890). Herbaceous Paeonies. *Journal of the Royal Horticultural Society* 12: 422–428.

Pei, Y. L., and D. Y. Hong. (1995). *Paeonia qiui:* A new woody species of *Paeonia* from Hubei, China. *Acta Phytotaxonomica Sinica* 33(1): 91–93.

Peyton, G (1943). Outstanding Peonies. *American Peony Society Bulletin* 51.

Rehder, A. (1920). New species, varieties and combinations from Herbarium and the collections of the Arnold Arboretum. *Journal of the Arnold Arboretum* 1: 193–194.

Reidl, H. (1969). *Flora Iranica*. Paeoniaceae: 1–6.

Rogers, A. (1995). *Peonies*. Timber Press. Portland, Oregon.

Sabine, J. (1826). On the *Paeonia* Moutan or Tree Peony, and its varieties. *Transactions of the Horticultural Society of London* 6: 465–492.

Sang, T. (1995). *Phylogeny and Biogeography of Paeonia* (Paeoniaceae). Unpublished Ph.D. Thesis. Ohio State University, 1995.

Sang, T., D. J. Crawford, and T. F. Stuessy. (1997). Chloroplast DNA Phylogeny, Reticulate Evolution and Biogeography of *Paeonia* (Paeoniaceae). *American Journal of Botany* 84: 1120–1136.

Sawada, M. (1970). Floral Vascularization of *Paeonia japonica* with Some Consideration on Systematic Position of the Paeoniaceae. *The Botanical Magazine* (Tokyo) 84: 51–60.

Smith, D. R. (2002). Color Streaking Effects in Intersectional Hybrid Flowers. *Paeonia* 32: 2.

Soltis, D. E., and P. S. Soltis. (1997). Phylogenetic relationships in Saxifragaceae sensu lato: a comparison of topologies based on 18S rDNA and rbcL sequences. *American Journal of Botany* 84: 504–522.

Stebbins, G. L. (1938). The American species of *Paeonia*. *Madrono* 4: 252.

Stern, F. C. (1939). The Moutan Tree Peony. *Journal of the Royal Horticultural Society* 64: 550–552.

——. (1946). *A Study of the Genus Paeonia*. Royal Horticultural Society. London.

Thomas, G. S. (1976). *Perennial Garden Plants or The Modern Florilegium*. J. M. Dent & Sons, London.

Thunberg, C. P. (1784). *Flora Japonica*.

Tzanoudakis, D. M. (1977). *Cytotaxonomic Study of the Genus Paeonia in Greece*. Patras. 1–32.

Vera, F. (2000). *Grazing Ecology and Forest History*. CABI.

Walter, K.S., and H. J. Gillett, eds. (1998). *1997 IUCN Red List of Threatened Plants*. IUCN, The World Conservation Union, Gland, Switzerland and Cambridge, U.K.

Wang, W. T. (1979). *Fl. Reipubl. Popularis. Sin.* 27: 37–59.

Wister *et al.* (1995). *The Peonies*. Second reprint. The American Peony Society.

Worsdell, W. C. (1908). The affinities of *Paeonia*. *Journal of Botany* 46: 114.

Where to see Peonies

Canada

Devonian Botanic Garden, University of Alberta, Edmonton, Alberta, T6G 2E1.
Tel. +1 780 987–3054, Fax. +1 780 987–4141. (www.discoveredmonton.com/devonian/)

Peony garden at Van Dusen Botanical Garden, 5251 Oak Street (37th and Oak St.), Vancouver, British Columbia, V6M 4H1.
Tel. +1 604 878–927.
(www.vandusengarden.org)

Royal Botanical Gardens, P.O. Box 399, Hamilton, Ontario L8N 3H8.
Tel. +1 905 527–1158. (www.rbg.ca)
Tree peonies.

China

For further information about Chinese tree peonies please see *Chinese Tree Peony* (Wang Lianying *et al.*, 1980).

Luoyang, Henan Province

Henan boasts several large peony gardens, and includes those in Wang Cheng Park (20,000 tree peonies), the Peony Park (4000), Guose Peony Garden (200,000), Xiyuan Park (6000) and Luoyang (100,000). The scale of these gardens dwarfs those in the West.

Heze, Shandong Province

Heze is one of China's major centres of tree peony production and hosts an international tree peony fair every year on 20–28 April. Tree peonies can be found in the Zhao Lou, Li Ji and He Lou Peony gardens and the Caozhou Hundred-Flower Garden. The latter has 60,000 tree peonies in over 400 cultivars.

Gujin Peony Garden, Wangli Village, Heze, Shandong Province

Beijing

Beijing Botanical Garden is divided into two parts; the northern is in Sleeping Buddha Temple Road, in the Western Suburbs, while the southern is at 20, Nanzincun, Xianshan. The garden has 230 cultivars of tree peony and 200 of herbaceous peony.

Jing Shan Park, Beijing. One of the older tree peony gardens with many old plants.

Others

Peace Garden, Gansu Province.
This is China's main centre for the production of Gansu hybrid tree peonies and has a collection of 130,000 tree peonies.

Mount Danjingshan, Sichuan Province.
This ancient town has several peony gardens, including Peony Ground, Heavenly Fragrance Garden, Red Sun Glow Garden, Eternal Peace Yard and Steles Forest Garden.

Mount Wanhua Peony Garden, Shaanxi Province.
An ancient garden with 30,000 tree peonies.

Lake Tian-jing Park, Tongling, Anhui Province.
A collection of 10,000 tree peonies in 140 cultivars.

Shanghai Botanical Garden, Longwu Road, Shanghai.
A massive garden with over 7,000 tree peonies.

Dry Twig Peony Garden, Yancheng, Jiangsu Province.
This ancient garden was established in the thirteenth century and includes ten of the original tree peonies that were planted during the time of the Song dynasty. One of these trees is 1.8 m (6 ft.) high and bears almost 200 flowers.

Twin Pagoda Temple Garden, Taiyuan, Shanxi Province.

France

Villa Noailles, 59, Avenue Guy-de-Maupassant, Grasse 01630 France.
This famous Riviera garden has a large collection of tree peonies in a terraced garden, which is surrounded by a clipped yew hedge. Group visits only, by written appointment.

Germany

Arboretum Baumpark Ellerhoop-Thiensen, 25373 Ellerhoop, Thiensen 17, Schleswig-Holstein.

Tel. 04120/218; fax. 909981.

Established in 1960, this garden has 1,300 tree peonies including a large number of *P. rockii* (Gansu) hybrids and American hybrids from Arthur Saunders and Nassos Daphnis.

Japan

Mobara Peony Garden, 210, Yamazaki, Mobara-shi, Chiba-ken, 297–0016.

Tel. 0475–22–4224.

Opening times 8.00 AM-6.00 PM, from the last ten days of April, until the first ten days of May. Started in 1979, it is 0.5 HA (1.24 acres) in extent with 2,500 tree peonies in 250 cultivars and 500 herbaceous in 130 cultivars.

The Sugakawa Peony Garden, Sugakawa Peony Garden Society, 80–1, Peony Garden, Sugakawa-shi, Fukusima-ken.

Tel. 0248–73–2422; fax. 0248–72–5335.

It includes collections of peonies from 1766; 7,000 plants in 290 cultivars; 10 hectare garden (25 acres).

Tsukuba Peony Garden, 500, Wakaguri, Tsukuba-shi, Ibaragi-ken.

Tel. 0298–76–3660.

Around 9000 plants in 430 cultivars; 5 HA (12.36 acres).

Yuushi-en, 1260–2, Hanyu, Yatuka-cho, Yatuka-gun, Shimane-ken.

Tel. 0852–76–2255; fax. 0852–76–2508. E-mail: yuusien@daikonshima.or.jp

This is a beautiful Japanese garden, which is at its best from the last ten days of April until the first ten days of May and during January and February. Around 7,000 plants flowering in the spring and 150 during the winter.

Switzerland

Ingenieurschule Wädenswil (ISW) Strasse Postfach 335 PLZ / Ort 8820 Wädenswil.

A large botanic garden with over 250 cultivars and species, planted according to the geographic origin (China, Europe, Japan and the United States of America); 600 SQ M (0.15 acres) in extent.

United Kingdom

Cambridge University Botanic Garden, Bateman Street, Cambridge CB2 1JF.
Tel. +44 01223 336265. (www.botanic.cam.ac.uk)
When I first visited this famous botanic garden the labels were rather out of date, but this has been rectified and they now adhere more closely to modern peony taxonomy. The collection consists mainly of herbaceous peonies and there are good specimens of *P. mascula* subsp. *mascula* and *P. emodi* on the Limestone Rock Garden.

Hatfield House, Hatfield, Hertfordshire AL9 5NQ.
Tel. +44 01707 262823; fax. 01707 275719. (www.hatfield-house.co.uk)
Hatfield House is famous as the childhood home of Queen Elizabeth I. The Marchioness of Salisbury is one of Britain's most influential gardeners; her collection includes herbaceous peonies, species peonies and several of Saunders' hybrid tree peonies—all of which are labelled. The garden is completely organic.

The Royal Botanic Gardens, Kew, Richmond, Surrey TW9 3AB.
Tel. +44 020 8332 5655. (www.rbgkew.org.uk)
Kew has a particularly large collection of peonies, mainly planted in the order beds and the rock garden. The collection includes a wide range of species peonies, mainly collected from the wild. A new peony garden, in memory of Michael Haworth-Booth, was established in May 1999, close to the Cambridge Gate.

The Royal Horticultural Society's Garden, Wisley, Woking, Surrey.
Tel. +44 01483 224234 (www.rhs.org.uk)
While Wisley is not a botanic garden it has a large number of species peonies, which can be found on the rock garden and among the trees in the wild garden. There are mature lactifloras, mainly originated by the Kelway family, several mature tree peonies and a couple of large specimens of *P. rockii* 'Rock's Variety'.

Kelways Ltd, Barrymore Farm, Langport, Somerset TA10 9EZ.
Tel. +44 01458 250521. (www.kelways.co.uk)
Kelways is one of the most famous names in British horticulture. The company is home to a National Plant Collection of *Paeonia lactiflora*, which includes the majority of the cultivars that were raised by three generations of the Kelway family.

Highdown Gardens, Goring-by-Sea, near Worthing, West Sussex BN12 6NY.
Tel. +44 01903 239999
Highdown House was formerly the home of Sir Frederick Stern, the author of the landmark monograph, *The Genus Paeonia*. The garden has suffered during the last few years and many of the plants have lost their labels. However, sufficient plants remain to justify a visit and there are some very rare tree peonies on display. The garden has one of the largest specimens of *P. rockii* in the United Kingdom.

United States of America

Nichols Arboretum, University of Michigan, 1610 Washington Heights, Ann Arbor, Michigan.

Tel. +1 48104–1700. (www.umich.edu/~wwwarb/index.html)

Aubrey Tealdi, the garden's first Director, established the arboretum's Peony Garden in 1927. It has over 700 plants including 260 old cultivars of herbaceous peonies, introduced between 1807 and 1948.

Portland Classical Chinese Garden, NW 3RD and Everett, Portland, OR 97208.

Tel. + 1 503–228–8131. (www.portlandchinesegarden.org)

This is an authentic Suzhou-style Chinese garden with serpentine walkways, a bridged lake and open colonnades. The garden was designed by Chinese architects and built with the help of Chinese artisans. It has a collection of Chinese tree peonies.

Arnold Arboretum of Harvard University, The Arborway, Jamaica Plains MA 02130.

Tel. +1 617–524–1718. (www.arboretum.harvard.edu)

There is a large number of tree peonies including unusual cultivars such as 'Satin Rouge'.

The Grant Garden, Hamilton, New York 13323.

(www.hamilton.edu)

The Grant Garden was established in the late nineteenth century and renovated in 1996 to provide a display garden for Arthur Saunders' tree peonies. Arthur Saunders was Professor of Chemistry at Hamilton College and it is working hard to collect all of his hybrid tree peonies. It currently has forty-four cultivars and welcomes donations of the ones that are missing.

Linwood Garden, c/o 1912 York Road, Pavilion NY 14525.

This unique collection includes all of the tree peonies bred by Arthur Saunders, Nassos Daphnis and Bill Gratwick. The garden is open to the public for a few days during the summer and by appointment only.

Missouri Botanical Garden, P.O. Box 299, St. Louis, Missouri 63166–0299.

(www.mobot.org)

The Margaret Grigg Nanjing Friendship Garden is considered to be the most authentic-looking Chinese garden in the U.S.A. It was designed by the Chinese-born architect Yong Pan and is modelled on a Chinese "scholar's garden".

Staten Island Botanic Garden, 1000 Richmond Terrace, Staten Island, New York 10301.

(www.sibg.org)

The New York Chinese Scholar's Garden is an authentic Chinese-style garden, built by Chinese artisans in 1998. It took six months to build and is planted with a large number of Chinese tree peonies.

New York Botanical Garden, 200th Street and Southern Boulevard, Bronx, New York 10458.
Tel. +1 718 817 8700. (www.nybg.org)
Around 200 cultivars of Chinese tree peony.

Cricket Hill Garden, 670 Walnut Hill Road, Thomaston, CT 06787.
Tel. +1 860 283 1042. (www.treepeony.com)
Kasha and David Furman have one of the most extensive collections of Chinese tree peonies outside China, planted in a beautiful woodland setting. Over the years they have assessed several hundred cultivars, many of which are still grown in the garden. Cricket Hill supplied the majority of the tree peonies in the New York Botanic Garden.

Sarah P. Duke Gardens, 426 Anderson Street, Box 90341, Duke University, Durham, North Carolina 27708–0341.
Tel. +1 919–684–3698. (www.hr.duke.edu)
Chinese tree peonies.

Scott Arboretum, Swarthmore College, Swarthmore, PA 19081.
Tel. +1 610 328 8025. (www.scottarboretum.org)
Mainly Japanese tree peonies, but also have a few Chinese.

List of Suppliers

The following list is not comprehensive and includes those companies that I have had personal dealings with. They range from small nurseries with a few dozen cultivars to larger concerns with many hundreds. All of these people share a passion for peonies and you should receive good service.

France
Pivoines Rivières, La Plaine, 26400 Crest.
Tel. +4 75 25 44 85; fax. +4 75 76 77 38. (www.pivoinesriviere.com)
Established in 1849, France's pre-eminent peony nursery is now managed by Jean-Luc Rivière. The company has a wide range of herbaceous and tree peonies, including many plants bred by Sir Peter Smithers and Jean-Luc's ancestors. The nursery is situated in the South of France and as a consequence their tree peonies start to flower at the beginning of April and their lactifloras have usually finished by the end of May. They have a good collection of American hybrid tree peonies and French tree peonies from the early twentieth century.

Italy
Vivai delle Commande, Tenuta delle Commande
Frazione Tuninetti, 10022 Carmagnola (Torino).
Tel. & fax. ++39 011 9430623 or ++39 011 9795046; e-mail: mail@vivaicommande.com

New Zealand
Craigmore Peonies Partnership, Kathryn Hill, Craigmore, RD2, Timaru.
Tel. & fax. +64 3 612 9802; e-mail: peonies@craigmore.com.
This wholesale nursery is operated by Sir Peter and Lady Fiona Elworthy. Retail sales are restricted to New Zealand residents.

Marsal Paeonies, Old South Road, RD, Dunsandel.

Tel.: +64 (0) 3 325 4003; fax: +64 (0) 325 4222.

The Peony Gardens, 3 RD, Lumsden.

Tel. +64 (03) 248 7468; e-mail: theHamiltons@thepeonygardens.co.nz, or theRudds@thepeonygardens.co.nz.

Simmons Peonies, 389 Buchanans Road, RD6, Christchurch 8004.

Tel. +64 3 342 1160; fax. +64 3 342 1162; e-mail: p.e.simmons@clear.net.nz

This nursery sells a large selection of herbaceous and intersectional hybrid peonies.

United Kingdom

Claire Austin Hardy Plants, The Stone House, Coppice Green Lane, Cramp Pool, Shifnal, Shropshire TF11 8PE.

Tel. +44 (1952) 463700; fax. +44 (1952) 463111; e-mail: enquiries@claireaustin-hardyplants.co.uk.

Claire Austin has one of the widest selections of peonies in the United Kingdom and an extensive range of herbaceous perennials. The majority of peonies are shipped with bare roots in autumn, but a limited selection can be purchased from the nursery throughout the year. Claire also owns an NCCPG National Plant Collection of herbaceous hybrid peonies, which can be viewed at her nursery.

Kelways Ltd, Barrymore Farm, Langport, TA10 9EZ.

Tel. +44 (1458) 250521; fax. +44 (1458) 253351; e-mail: sales@kelways.co.uk.

Kelways Nursery has been growing peonies for over 140 years and has over 500 cultivars of *Paeonia lactiflora*. The company has won many awards at the Royal Horticultural Society's flower shows and sells a wide range of tree peonies. Peonies are sold with bare roots in autumn, or a limited range can be purchased direct from the nursery. The company has an NCCPG National Plant Collection of *Paeonia lactiflora*, which are grown in the famous Peony Valley.

Paul Christian Rare Plants, PO Box 468, Wrexham LL13 9XR.

Tel. +44 (1978) 366399; fax. +44 (1978) 266466.

Paul Christian has an excellent list of species peonies. Sales are by mail order only.

Will McLewin, Phedar Nursery, Bunker Hill, Romiley, Stockport, SK6 3DS.

Tel. & fax. +44 (1614) 303772.

Will McLewin is best known for his interest in hellebores, but he also has one of the largest collections of species peonies in the world. Will prides himself on the authenticity of his peonies and the great majority have been raised from wild-collected seed. He produces an extensive seed list.

United States

Adelman Peony Gardens, 5690 Brooklake Road NE, PO BOX 9193, Salem, Oregon 97305.
Tel. +1 (503) 393–6185.
Jim and Carol Adelman sell a wide range of herbaceous and intersectional peonies, including a wide range of Saunders' herbaceous hybrids.

A. & D. Peony and Perennial Farm, 6808 180th St. SE Snohomish, WA 98296-8340.
Tel. +1 (206) 485–2487 or +1 (360) 668–9690; fax. +1 (360) 668–6031;
e-mail:adpeonies@earthlink.net.

Brothers Herbs & Peonies, Richard W. Rogers, PO BOX 1370 Sherwood, Oregon 97140.
Tel. +1 (503) 625–7548; fax. +1 (503) 625–1667; e-mail:rick@treony.com.
Rick Rogers' nursery is situated a short distance from Portland, Oregon. He specializes in tree peonies and offers a range of Daphnis and Saunders tree peonies, and a wide range of Chinese tree peonies. He also sells authentic specimens of *Paeonia rockii* and *P. ostii*.

Callies Beaux Jardin, 10875 Old Hwy, 169 Blvd, Belle Plaine, Minnesota 56011–9272.
This nursery originally belonged to Roger Anderson, the well-known breeder of intersectional hybrid peonies. Roger sold the business to Tim Kornder in 2004, so that he could concentrate on breeding peonies.

Caprice Farm Nursery, 10944 Mill Creek Road SE, Aumsville, Oregon 97325.
Tel. +1 (503) 749–1397; fax. +1 (503) 749–4097; e-mail: cyndicap@wvi.com.

Countryman Peony Farm, 818 Winch Hill Road, Northfield, Vermont 05663.
Tel. +1 (802) 485-8421; fax. +1 (802) 485-9421.
The Countryman family nursery is situated in the beautiful Green Mountains of Vermont. Bill Countryman has approximately 1500 different cultivars of herbaceous peony, making it the largest collection in the U.S.A.; it includes 200 cultivars from Kelway's. Their flowering season is quite late because the nursery is situated so far north and the best time to visit the nursery is between 15 and 21 June. It is open to visitors throughout June from 10.00 AM to dusk.

Cricket Hill Garden, 670, Walnut Hill Road, Thomaston, Connecticut 06787.
Tel. +1 (860) 283–1042; fax. +1 (860) 283–5508; e-mail:kasha@treepeony.com.
David and Kasha Furman's nursery is situated in a beautiful woodland location in New England. They were among the first to import Chinese tree peonies into the West and have established a large display garden, which is full of mature tree peonies. Bare-root plants are shipped between September and November or can be purchased from the nursery in large root control bags. They also sell Chinese umbrellas, which can be used to protect tree peony flowers from rain and bright sunshine. They produce a very informative video about tree peonies.

Galen Burrell, PO BOX 754, 818 Sunset Lane, Ridgefield, Washington 98642.
Galen Burrell is the best source for authentic species peonies in the U.S.A.

Gilbert H. Wild & Son Inc., Sarcoxie, Missouri 64862.
Tel. +1 (417) 548–3514; fax. +1 (417) 548–6831; e-mail:wilds@socket.net.
This is an old, established company, which specializes in supplying cultivars of *Paeonia lactiflora*. They have a good display garden, where plants can be selected for autumn delivery.

Don & Lavon Hollingsworth, Hollingsworth Nursery, RR3, Box 27 Maryville, Missouri 64468.
Tel. +1 (660) 562–3010; fax. +1 (660) 582–8688; e-mail:hpeonies@asde.com.
Don Hollingsworth is one of the leading peony breeders in the U.S.A. and has an extensive collection of herbaceous peonies. He has produced some wonderful hybrid peonies, many of which are only available from his nursery. The nursery only sells bare-root plants, which are shipped in autumn.

Klehm's Song Sparrow Perennial Farm, 13101, East Rye Road, Avalon, Wisconsin 53505.
Tel. +1 (800) 553–3715; fax. +1 (608) 883–2257; e-mail:info@songsparrow.com.
The Klehm family have been breeding peonies for over one hundred years. Song Sparrow Perennial Farm is one of the largest exporters of perennial plants in the world and was established by Roy Klehm and his family in 1996. It has an extensive catalogue. The nursery sells a wide range of herbaceous peonies, including modern cultivars of *Paeonia lactiflora* and hybrids. It also has the widest range of American hybrid tree peonies (*P. delavayi* × *P.* ×*suffruticosa*) for sale in the United States. Mail order only.

Reath's Nursery, Country Road 577, Box 247 Vulcan, Michigan 49892.
Tel. & Fax. +1 (906) 563–9777, e-mail:reathnur@up.net.
Situated in the extreme north of the country, this nursery was originally established by David Reath in 1961. The nursery has one of the largest collections of Saunders and Daphnis hybrid tree peonies in the U.S.A. and is operated by David's son, Scott.

Smirnow's Son's Peonies, 168, Maple Hill Road, Huntington, New York 11743.
Tel. +1 (631) 421–0836; fax. +1 (631) 421–0818.

White Flower Farm, PO BOX 50, Litchfield, Connecticut 06759–0050.
Tel. +1 (800) 503–9624. Mail order only.

Micropropagated peonies

Planteck Biotechnologies Inc., 801, Route 344, PO 3158, L'Assomption, Quebec J5W 4M9 Canada.

Tel. +1 (450) 589–6162; fax. +1 (450) 589–1440; e-mail: info@planteck.com.

Until recently it was thought that it would be impossible to micropropagate peonies. Planteck has concentrated on propagating high value plants such as intersectional hybrids and tree peonies. However, while these plants represent good value they are considerably smaller than normal divisions and it will be several years before they reach an equivalent size.

Peony Societies

The American Peony Society, c/o 713, White Oak Lane, Gladstone, Missouri 64116-4607, U.S.A.

(www.americanpeonysociety.org.)

The American Peony Society was established in 1904 and is the international registrar for the genus *Paeonia*. New registrations are listed in their quarterly bulletin and it produces several extremely useful books and registers.

The Canadian Peony Society, c/o The Royal Botanic Gardens, Box 399, Hamilton, Ontario L8N 3H8, Canada.

The Heartland Peony Society, 15738 Horton Lane, Overland Park Kansas 66223, U.S.A..

The Pacific Northwest Peony Society, c/o 5465, SE Prosperity Park Road, Tualatin, Oregon 97062, U.S.A.

Tel. +1 503 638 5445.

The Peony Society, c/o Peening Farmhouse, Wittersham, Kent TN30 7NP, United Kingdom.
(www.peonysociety.org)

Originally called the British Peony Society, this society has changed its name to reflect its international membership. Many of its members are interested in species peonies. It produces a quarterly newsletter and organizes symposia.

The New Zealand Peony Society, BOX 29312, Christchurch, New Zealand.

Index